Marriage in Past, Present and Future Tense

Marriage in Past, Present and Future Tense

Edited by

Janet Carsten, Hsiao-Chiao Chiu, Siobhan Magee,
Eirini Papadaki and Koreen M. Reece

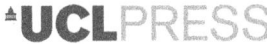

First published in 2021 by
UCL Press
University College London
Gower Street
London WC1E 6BT

Available to download free: www.uclpress.co.uk

Collection © Editors, 2021
Text © Contributors, 2021
Images © Contributors and copyright holders named in captions, 2021

The authors have asserted their rights under the Copyright, Designs and Patents Act 1988 to be identified as the authors of this work.

A CIP catalogue record for this book is available from The British Library.

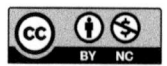

Any third-party material in this book is not covered by the book's Creative Commons licence. Details of the copyright ownership and permitted use of third-party material is given in the image (or extract) credit lines. If you would like to reuse any third-party material not covered by the book's Creative Commons licence, you will need to obtain permission directly from the copyright owner.

This book is published under a Creative Commons Attribution-Non-Commercial 4.0 International licence (CC BY-NC 4.0), https://creativecommons.org/licenses/by-nc/4.0/. This licence allows you to share and adapt the work for non-commercial use providing attribution is made to the author and publisher (but not in any way that suggests that they endorse you or your use of the work) and any changes are indicated. Attribution should include the following information:

Carsten, J., Chiu, H-C., Magee, S., Papadaki, E. and Reece, K.M. (eds). 2021. *Marriage in Past, Present and Future Tense*. London: UCL Press. https://doi.org/10.14324/111.9781800080386

Further details about Creative Commons licences are available at http://creativecommons.org/licenses/

ISBN: 978-1-80008-040-9 (Hbk.)
ISBN: 978-1-80008-039-3 (Pbk.)
ISBN: 978-1-80008-038-6 (PDF)
ISBN: 978-1-80008-041-6 (epub)
ISBN: 978-1-80008-042-3 (mobi)
DOI: https://doi.org/10.14324/111.9781800080386

Contents

List of figures	vii
List of contributors	ix
Acknowledgements	xi

	Introduction: marriage in past, present and future tense Janet Carsten, Hsiao-Chiao Chiu, Siobhan Magee, Eirini Papadaki and Koreen M. Reece	1
1	*Go fiwa molao*/giving the law: marriage, law and social change in Botswana Koreen M. Reece	34
2	'You can learn to do it right, or you can learn to do it wrong': marriage counselling, togetherness and creative conservatism in Lynchburg, Virginia Siobhan Magee	54
3	Marriage, time, affect and the politics of compromise in Athens Eirini Papadaki	76
4	Getting married as a trial: deferring marriage in Jinmen, Taiwan Hsiao-Chiao Chiu	95
5	(Un)certain futures: rhythms and assemblages of transnational Sri Lankan Tamil marriages Sidharthan Maunaguru	118
6	Marriage and self-fashioning in Penang, Malaysia: transformations of the intimate and the political Janet Carsten	140

Index	160

List of figures

1.1 *Go fiwa molao*: Batswana women 'give the law' to the new bride, covered in blankets. © Koreen M. Reece.   35
4.1 Steady rise in the age at first marriage for both sexes. Department of Household Registration, Ministry of the Interior, Taiwan (https://www.ris.gov.tw/app/portal/674).   97
4.2 Declining marriage rates in Jinmen and throughout Taiwan. Department of Household Registration, Ministry of the Interior, Taiwan (https://www.ris.gov.tw/app/portal/674).   98
6.1 Some of the antique objects collected and stored by Anna at her business premises. © Janet Carsten.   151

List of contributors

Janet Carsten is Professor of Social and Cultural Anthropology at the University of Edinburgh. Her research focuses on the anthropology of kinship and relatedness. She is the author of *The Heat of the Hearth: Kinship and community in a Malay fishing village* and *After Kinship*. Her edited volumes include *Cultures of Relatedness: New approaches to the study of kinship* and *Ghosts of Memory: Essays on remembrance and relatedness*. *Blood Work: Life and laboratories in Penang* was published in 2019.

Hsiao-Chiao Chiu is ERC Postdoctoral Research Fellow with the Global Anthropology of Transforming Marriage project at the University of Edinburgh. She has conducted research on kinship and social change in post-Cold War Jinmen, Taiwan.

Siobhan Magee is Lecturer in Social Anthropology at the University of Edinburgh. As a Research Fellow working on the Global Anthropology of Transforming Marriage project, she has carried out ethnographic research on the political, legal and religious contestations surrounding marriage in Virginia, USA. Her monograph, *Material Culture and Kinship in Poland: An ethnography of fur and society*, was published in 2019.

Sidharthan Maunaguru is Associate Professor in Comparative South Asian Studies at the National University of Singapore. His work focuses on the anthropology of marriage, migration and political violence, the anthropology of politics, religion, ethics and conscience. His monograph, *Marrying for a Future*, was published in 2019.

Eirini Papadaki is ERC Postdoctoral Research Fellow with the Global Anthropology of Transforming Marriage project at the University of Edinburgh. She has published articles on kinship, marriage, adoption, gender and parenthood in contemporary Greece.

Koreen M. Reece was ERC Postdoctoral Research Fellow with the Global Anthropology of Transforming Marriage project at the University of Edinburgh and is currently Assistant Professor in Anthropology at the University of Bayreuth. She conducts research on kinship and intervention in Botswana's time of Aids and is the author of several articles. Her monograph, *Pandemic Kinship: Families, intervention and social change in Botswana's time of AIDS*, is forthcoming with Cambridge University Press.

Acknowledgements

The research on which the introduction and chapters 1–4 and 6 in this volume are based and the editing of this work were funded by a European Research Council (ERC) Advanced Grant under the European Union's Horizon 2020 Research and Innovation programme, grant agreement no. 695285 AGATM ERC-2015-AdG, held at the University of Edinburgh, which we gratefully acknowledge here. The members of the advisory committee of the Global Anthropology of Transforming Marriage (AGATM) project – Ammara Maqsood, Sidharthan Maunaguru, John McInnes, Susan McKinnon, Perveez Mody and David Sabean – generously gave their support and comments on our work at different stages. We thank them all.

We are grateful to all the participants at a workshop on 'Marriage in Past, Present and Future Tense: Biography, Intimacy and Transformation', held at the University of Edinburgh in September 2019, for their insightful and constructive comments on earlier versions of these chapters. Thanks are due to Sarah Walker for help with collecting bibliographic materials, and to Chris Penfold at UCL Press for guiding us smoothly through the publication of this book. We are extremely grateful to two anonymous reviewers and to Jonathan Spencer for their very helpful comments.

Introduction: marriage in past, present and future tense

Janet Carsten, Hsiao-Chiao Chiu, Siobhan Magee, Eirini Papadaki and Koreen M. Reece

In March 2020, as the coronavirus pandemic swept Spain and sent its citizens into lockdown, a couple in the north-western city of A Coruña stood in their window to celebrate a special occasion. Alba Díaz and Daniel Camino had been planning a large-scale wedding for months, and had even transformed a warehouse for the purpose. But their preparations came to grief in the face of a government ban on social gatherings, and on all movement except for trips to acquire essential items. Undaunted, they asked guests to send photos of themselves dressed up for the wedding, recruited a next-door neighbour to lead the ceremony from his window and found another to act as witness. The bride wore her wedding gown. The event was reported by the *Guardian*:

> A bouquet was crafted out of a few boxes of flowers that hadn't been used at the venue . . . As they began – 'on this special day, two friends are getting married', their neighbour called out, his voice filling the empty street – others, stuck in their homes by the same lockdown orders, began poking their heads out. Soon dozens were cheering them on, calling for the couple to kiss as Díaz threw her bouquet into the apartment of a friend who lives across from her. 'In the end it felt our wedding [sic],' said Díaz. 'It was unique, special and very personal,' added Camino. (Kassam 2020)

Innovation in marriage has not been confined to the personal efforts of couples or individuals, of course. In May 2015, Ireland stunned the world with a decisive 'yes' vote to approve same-sex marriage ('Ireland becomes first country to approve same-sex marriage by popular vote', *Irish Times*, 23 May 2015). With an exceptional turnout, and a result of 62 per cent in favour to 38 per cent against, the predominantly Catholic nation set a striking new standard for promulgating progressive marriage law. The Minister for Children, James Reilly, was reported as saying that 'a lot of voters have been thinking about their grandchildren and giving them the same opportunities in life, should they be gay' (Ó Caollaí and Hilliard 2015). In the *Guardian* report on these events from the same day, Taoiseach Enda Kenny was quoted as saying,

> In the privacy of the ballot box, the people made a public statement. With today's vote we have disclosed who we are. We are a generous, compassionate, bold and joyful people who say yes to inclusion, yes to generosity, yes to love, yes to gay marriage. (McDonald 2015)

It wasn't until five years later that a Belfast couple celebrated the first same-sex marriage across the border in Northern Ireland. The couple, Robyn Peoples, 26, and Sharni Edwards, 27, 'made history at a ceremony in a hotel in Carrickfergus, County Antrim, on Tuesday afternoon'.

> Edwards, a waitress from Brighton who did not know the law was different in Northern Ireland until she moved from England to Belfast, said: 'We feel humbled that our wedding is a landmark movement for equal rights in Northern Ireland. We didn't set out to make history – we just fell in love.
> 'We are so grateful to the thousands of people who marched for our freedoms, to the Love Equality campaign who led the way, and the politicians who voted to change the law. Without you, our wedding wouldn't have been possible. We will be forever thankful.' (PA Media 2020)

What do these media stories tell us about weddings, and about marriage? Weddings are celebrations, and as such, they are emotionally charged occasions – sources of hope and delight in dark times, the culmination of extensive planning and build-up, subject to the pressures and expectations of friends and family. They are also formal, public events, rituals undertaken as much for the guests as for the couple involved. Like other rituals, weddings involve recognisable symbolic objects dense with meaning: material markers, like the bride's dress and the bouquet, or symbolic acts like the kiss, which signify the relationship, situating it in family and community traditions and histories. Although weddings may be suffused with intimate resonances, 'unique, special and very personal' (Kassam 2020) – as Camino aptly put it, under conditions which threatened to stymie his own celebration – they require the presence of witnesses for both their symbolic and legal efficacy. One may get married from a window 'with the street as witness', but not behind closed doors, without people there to see. And the public enactment of marriage in weddings is also, as the vignettes from the Republic of Ireland and from Northern Ireland make especially clear, politically constituted and legally framed. Weddings may thus render personal and emotional occasions as political milestones, victories for human rights and equality with intense significance far beyond the couple who are marrying.

The scenarios depicted in these accounts might have seemed implausible some years – or even months – before they took place. While we may think of marriage as a stable social institution with considerable historic depth, bound by convention and tradition, these reports – like the detailed cases we examine across this volume – demonstrate that marriage retains a remarkable flexibility, and remains a source of innovation and surprise. And it is partly through bridging the intimate, private worlds of protagonists and the wider public one that marriage generates opportunities for historical change. As Sharni Edwards succinctly stated, 'We didn't set out to make history – we just fell in love' (PA Media 2020); but in her case, falling in love made history regardless. Our title, *Marriage in Past, Present and Future Tense*, captures this central paradox – that it is under the cloak of apparent conservatism that marriage may express or produce radical change. The Republic of Ireland seemed an unlikely nation to be at the vanguard of progressive marriage reform when its referendum on same-sex marriage was passed in 2015. And yet. This book explores that 'and yet': the imaginative space that marriage occupies, the element of surprise conveyed in these short depictions. What is it about marriage that creates flexibility and generativity? How can we account for the transformative potential of marriage? What are its implications?

As these and many other popular reports show, marriage is a topic of immense public interest and commentary. Apart from the excitement afforded by its romantic and aesthetic aspects, concerns about marriage are also expressed in more negative terms: in worries over excessive displays of consumption at weddings, its patriarchal overtones, or its apparently increasing instability and associated rising divorce rates. A decline in rates of marriage is often connected to a decline in fertility and a rise in solo-living arrangements, cast as problematic trends (Jamieson and Simpson 2013); strongly held opinions or doubts about same-sex marriage may reflect anxieties about the religious meaning of marriage, and the unpredictable ways it is changing. And many of these changes are taken as signs of broader social and moral breakdown – indicating that marriage is not only a potent subject for ethical reflection and debate, but is also widely understood to be central to socio-political life. Concerns about changing forms of marriage are woven through the cases we explore in the following chapters. Marriage remains a core institution and reference point cross-culturally (see, for example, Segalen 2003; Stacey 2011), in spite of fears for its demise, in part because it tracks, expresses and – we suggest – creates opportunities to produce social change.

Marriage is unusual as a social institution in bringing together so many apparently disparate social fields: family and state, religion and economy, the personal and the public, the affective and material, the intimate, political, ritual and legal are all implicated in marriage. In this sense, it can be construed as a total social fact in the Maussian sense. And this might be one reason why it has the capacity to evoke such deeply felt, widespread interest. Taking as our starting points this multifaceted nature of marriage, its changing contours in contemporary societies and the tensions and contestations that surround these, our volume explores marriage as a site and agent of transformation. We thus suspend the commonly held assumptions that the state is the main driver of changes to familial and intimate life, and that the family is a sphere of conservatism, and instead consider the possibility that intimate and familial realms may *produce* wider change – across a range of significantly different contexts.

Here we follow a lead from McKinnon and Cannell's (2013a) discussion of kinship in regimes of modernity. They argue that the notion that family life and kinship constitutes a separate zone from the state and politics is part of the ideology of modernity, rather than a reflection of its reality. They show how kinship is in fact deeply embedded in the politics and economics of modern states, which constitute themselves through domaining practices in which kinship – rendered as 'family' and as 'immodern' (Lambek 2013) – is ideologically separated from the political functioning of the state (see also Carsten 2004; McKinnon 2013; Thelen and Alber 2018). Relegated to a 'private' sphere to be controlled and regulated by the state, family is cast both as a realm of emotional and material support, a 'haven in a heartless world' (Lasch 1977), but also as a potential source of abuse and corruption, a zone of primordial ties and nefarious interest requiring intervention and control. In this volume, we set out to show that the 'excesses' of kinship (Lambek 2013, 255) – here, in marriage – not only disrupt this domaining project and blur separations between family and state, but also animate broader socio-political processes, and thereby drive social change.

Unusually, this volume is the outcome of an experiment in collaborative ethnography. We set out to look at marriage in very particular conditions: the HIV/Aids epidemic in Botswana; economic austerity in Greece; religious and political contestations over same-sex marriage in the US; complex geopolitical relations between Taiwan and China; the civil war in Sri Lanka; and rapid 'middle-classification' in Malaysia. Our studies were conceived, planned, undertaken and developed in conversation with each other. This has paid remarkable dividends. We have worked together as researchers to explore thematic resonances between our cases and to consider their divergences. And we have found unexpected congruences as well as differences as we have moved between the contexts of our work in Botswana, the US, Greece, Taiwan, Sri Lanka and Malaysia, and as our work evolved. The fact that our cases share backgrounds of colonialism, anti-colonial struggle and/or civil war has stimulated a line of enquiry that we had not anticipated, but which has proved fruitful for considering the temporal dimensions of marriage and its socio-political effects. The continued salience of concerns about marriage – its emotional hold and apparent resilience in the face of 'deinstitutionalisation' (see Cherlin 2004; Lewin 2004) – has further encouraged us to explore the themes of materiality and temporality in marriage. Our essays illuminate in different ways and contexts the centrality of the past, present and future tense in which the imaginative and relational possibilities of marriage are lived, and which are central to its ethical and political possibilities – its capacity for change. In the final section of this introduction, we turn to these transformative qualities of marriage to consider its simultaneously conservative and innovative potential, and the uncertainties and ambiguities that they produce.

In what follows, we suggest that marriage is itself a comparative ethical project. It begins with assessing the relative merits of different partners, or considering different ideas about what marriage is and ought to be. In imagining or planning a future marriage, narrating a present one or assessing a marriage's history, explicit and implicit comparisons are made to other marriages – often of parents, grandparents and other relatives. Lives before and after marriage are compared; marital histories are set alongside the imagined path-not-taken. These comparisons invoke evaluative assessments, and offer morally inflected benchmarks of success or failure. And those apparently personal assessments and judgements about marriage through time have a political dimension and potential. As the Irish Minister for Children observed, the results of the 2015 referendum on same-sex marriage came from voters imagining the opportunities that might one day be available – or not – to their grandchildren, and comparing those opportunities to their own. We place our cases side by side, much as our informants placed marriages side by side, to illuminate the changing contemporary meanings of marriage – the creative, transformative and expansive possibilities of its ideals and practice.

Marriage work

Perhaps the most obvious and important feature of marriage to nineteenth-century anthropologists, legal scholars, historians and political commentators was that it brought together matters of property, law, economics and family – it was, in short, a political institution. From their widely varying viewpoints, the works of Henry Maine (1861, 1873), Lewis H. Morgan (1871, 1877), John Stuart Mill (1869) and Friedrich Engels (1972 [1884]) – to take some prominent examples – had this perception at their core; and these authors cast the changing nature of marriage in evolutionary terms. Their (sometimes polemical) discussions were part of a broad canvas of public understandings of the role of marriage in the societies where these scholars lived. The so-called 'marriage question' in late Victorian Britain, for example, was actually a set of debates concerned with women's rights, property and divorce that was seen to have implications beyond individuals, for society more broadly. While they distanced themselves from their predecessors, mid-twentieth-century anthropologists continued to consider marriage as a pivotal social institution largely in terms of its political and economic significance (see, for example, Evans-Pritchard 1951; Fortes 1949; Lévi-Strauss 1969 [1949]; Radcliffe-Brown and Forde 1950). What we might term the 'fantasy' of modern marriage (Osella 2012, 253) – that it is a broadly egalitarian relationship, contracted through choice between individuals, and fundamentally about love, intimacy and companionship – has been propounded more by sociologists of modernity than by anthropologists (see, for example, Bauman 2003; Giddens 1992). Anthropology in the mid-twentieth century continued to concern itself with questions raised by the study of social cohesion and political organisation in non-Western societies, and undertook the study of marriage in those terms. While the disciplinary focus had shifted to include Western societies too by late century, the relative paucity of research by anthropologists on Western marriage suggested a lingering supposition that it was a less important matter in modern, politically organised states.

How do people in any given place manage to live alongside people whom they consider to be different from themselves? Claude Lévi-Strauss can be considered in some ways typical of anthropologists of the mid-twentieth century, and his framing of the question of marriage proved especially influential. In Brazil, he reported, 'small nomadic bands' (1969 [1949], 67) keep peace with each other through exchange. The longer-term upshot was that

> Two bands which have come to establish lasting cordial relations can decide in a deliberate manner to join by instituting between the male members of the two respective bands the artificial kinship relationship of brothers-in-law. Given the marriage system of the Nambikwara, the immediate consequence of this innovation is that all the children of one group become the potential spouses of the children of the other group and vice versa. Thus a continuous transition exists from war to exchange, and from exchange to intermarriage, and the exchange of brides is merely the conclusion to an interrupted process of reciprocal gifts, which effects the transition from hostility to alliance, from anxiety to confidence, and from fear to friendship. (Lévi-Strauss 1969 [1949], 67–8)

These observations about marriage and exchange among the Nambikwara are literally and figuratively 'of another time'; they come with considerable gendered and evolutionist baggage (see, for example, McKinnon 2013, 46–8; Rubin 1975). But Lévi-Strauss's insights foreshadow possibilities that we take up in this volume. Marriage, in his account, is not only about spouses, but also about groups and societies, and about creating change in their political relationships. And time matters: marriage weaves groups together generation after generation, effecting historical change. Our essays show that these dynamics are not limited to 'small-scale' societies in Brazil, but characterise contemporary experiences of marriage in 'modern' societies around the world.

What has been called the 'new kinship studies' – emerging from the 1980s onwards – addressed glaring gaps in earlier analyses by drawing on feminist scholarship and focusing attention on gender as a topic of enquiry, as well as attending to the everyday practices, processes, lived experience and symbolic work of kinship. Much of this work has privileged the study of birth and reproduction over marriage, situating 'nature', 'biology', 'blood' and indeed 'kinship' itself as ethnographic questions rather than universally applicable analytic categories. In order to defamiliarise anthropological understandings of these terms, the new kinship studies have focused predominantly on non-normative kin relationships, especially in the West: on situations in which people make kinship 'against the odds', creatively and often in the face of exclusion (see, for example, Goodfellow 2015; Hayden 1995; Lewin 1998; Weston 1991). Some of these studies illuminate how 'innovative' ways of making kinship can reveal surprisingly 'traditional' or 'normative' ideas about gender, sexuality, parenthood and reproduction. Topics such as LGBTQ kinship, reproductive technologies and transnational adoption have enabled the denaturalisation of anthropological assumptions about kinship, and also illuminated how naturalisation works as a social process (see, for example, Franklin 1997, 2014; Thompson 2007; Weston 1995; Yanagisako and Delaney 1995). The denaturalisation of gender and heteronormativity, and new understandings of power and inequality in kin relationships, have important implications for the study of marriage – which we pursue further in the following section.

Marriage, however, has often been beyond the purview of these studies, perhaps partly because of assumptions about its normativity – the way it hides in plain sight as an institution. John Borneman writes of 'the normative trinity of birth, marriage, and death' (1997, 582), for example, in part to suggest that these categories have led anthropologists to overlook important 'processes of voluntary affiliation: processes of caring and being cared for' (1997, 574). But as Evelyn Blackwood (2005) notes, 'the normative' is a discursive construction in academic literature as much as our field sites. Close ethnographic examination is required to determine 'whether marriage constitutes the focal relationship or not' (Blackwood 2005, 15), and what sort of relationship it might be. Perhaps what the new kinship studies are able to offer to the anthropology of marriage is a reminder that we need to denaturalise marriage too – as well as an ethnographic and comparative lens that resists binaries, such as tradition/innovation, precisely by exploring how they are constructed or resisted in lived experience. Expanding our remit to include 'care', as suggested by Borneman, or 'meaningful relationships', as suggested by Blackwood, allows us to include both affective connection and material support or collaboration, and it prioritises the ways in which people describe and experience these relationships themselves. As Perveez Mody has observed in a review of anthropological literature on marriage, early work on the subject took 'little consideration of how people actually experienced the processes of marrying and making kin' (2015, 599). These insights encourage us to pay attention to how people describe, construct and reflect on marriage themselves, in comparison and conjunction with other relationships.

Part of Borneman's original concern was with the relationship between anthropology and law, and specifically the overlaps between assumptions that anthropology makes about kinship and assumptions states and legal systems make. As we have seen, states monitor, condone or condemn certain types of relationship. Recent scholarship shows how, under specific local and historical conditions, versions of 'modern marriage' have been created as a political enterprise of the state. Contemporary struggles with state control have focused on rights for same-sex couples, but their history runs much deeper, to the legacy of colonial administrations in ordering intimate and family life (see, for example, Hughes 2021; Kholoussy 2010; Majumdar 2009). Mody's (2008) study of 'love-marriage couples' in 1990s Delhi unfolds against a backdrop of civil marriage laws instituted in the nineteenth century, which require such couples to undertake careful 'strategies' in order to pursue a life together legally. In Mody's work, marriage is not only a topic of the broadest societal interest and contestation, drawing in ideas of class, caste and religion, but also a site of active tension and innovation. The state retains power in legitimating and authenticating marriage, but also requires and opens opportunities for creativity in doing so.

Pursuing a similar lead, a significant branch of anthropological work approaches marriage and kinship through the entanglements of intimacy with the state (Andrikopoulos and Duyvendak 2020; Charsley 2012; Constable 2005; Davis and Friedman 2014; Hirsch and Wardlow 2006; Padilla et al. 2007). The question of how to manage intimacy in both affective and geographical terms emerges in recent studies of marriage and migration (see Brettell 2017), including in the idiom of transnational marriage (Constable 2015; Hannaford 2017). What 'transnational marriage' means varies widely, and has captured cinematic and literary imaginations, while generating sometimes alarmist or stereotyped political subjectivities. Through accounts of 'mail-order brides' (Constable 2003; Heywood 2009; Patico 2009), 'arranged marriages' (Charsley 2005; Charsley and Shaw 2006), 'marriages of convenience' (Andrikopoulos 2021; Mody 2013; Maskens 2015; Wray 2006), and perceived 'shortages' of marriageable-age men or women (see Kaur 2016), a picture emerges of the ways in which demographic shifts or even 'trends' in marriage respond to political and economic change – including wars – and to various state policies regarding family reunification. Work on globalisation and intimacy, however, sometimes omits to scrutinise the place of kinship *within* ideologies and practices of modernity (McKinnon and Cannell 2013a; *pace* Foucault 1980).

Kin networks across borders and continents are key to enabling such transnational matches, but equally important is a highly responsive class of professionals – from marriage brokers to wedding photographers (Maunaguru 2019, and in this volume) – whose work is both keyed to and enables evasion of the expectations of the state. Photographs, clothing and ritual items are part of the material culture of weddings and marriage to which we return below, but marriages are also bureaucratic events that require and produce sometimes life-changing paperwork, including marriage contracts (Hughes 2015). Efforts to obtain marriage visas or please immigration officials reify a state's ideals regarding marital intimacy and the kinds of affective, temporal, economic and kin-based bonds that must be performed and observed in order to authenticate a relationship. Further, the availability of, and pressure to use, communication technologies can make women, in particular, subject to control and suspicion from their husbands (Hannaford 2015).

Situated at the intersection of power, economy and social reproduction, marriage is also about class, and how class is made. Anthropological engagement with these question traces back to the question: 'who should marry whom?' Isabelle Clark-Decès's (2014) study of preferential marriage in Tamil Nadu explores relations between kin and also between those who almost married – the fabled 'ones who got away', who recur, tellingly, in different ethnographies of marriage. But her work also bridges older ideas about prescriptive marriage 'systems' in kinship studies (in this case, the world of Dravidian kinship) and more recent discussions of the affective dimensions of marriage. Clark-Decès's work overlaps with other relatively recent literature in which 'compatibility' and 'marriageability' take on new meanings for those who fear genetic illness as a result of marrying (and having children with) kin (Shaw and Raz 2020; Kilshaw, Al Raisi and Alshaban 2015).

Marriage provides a window onto gendered and generational ideas about how elites are created and naturalised. Monarchies, political dynasties and prosperous family businesses use marriages to reproduce themselves over time, demonstrating a dialectical relationship between marriage and capitalism (see Marcus 1992; Oppong 2009 [1974]; Yanagisako 2002). By the same token, in some settings, people without a certain degree of personal or familial prosperity or other sorts of capital are stigmatised as 'unmarriageable'. Pierre Bourdieu puts it plainly:

> [I]t is difficult to characterize an individual without including all the properties (and property) which are brought to each of the spouses, and not only the wife, through the other – a name . . .

goods, an income, 'connections', a social status . . . (Bourdieu 1984 [1979], 108–9)

Bourdieu's perspective emphasises that neither couples nor spouses are autonomous; relative class positions define both the relationship and the characterisations of individuals within it. At the same time, marriage can enable mobility. Bourdieu's reflection on what marriage may do for an individual's class position evokes other depictions of marriage and weddings as emblematic of the ascendancy of a relatively new global middle class, from South Africa (James 2017) to India (Fuller and Narasimhan 2008; Donner 2016) to Russia (Luehrmann 2004). If weddings and homes are both sites of class-making consumption and taste, and thought to express materially 'who a couple are', they may also stand at odds with one another, as couples navigate individual preferences and broader kin-based obligations to decide whether to spend money on lavish weddings or on keeping a home (Solway 2016).

Related questions of choice, autonomy and self-fashioning have also occupied the anthropological imagination as more women have joined the labour market worldwide. In many places, marriage has become less important to economic survival and the achievement of adult personhood, especially on the part of women, than it once was (see Mayblin 2010; Carsten, this volume). As we noted above, some scholars have proposed the apparent pervasiveness of 'companionate marriage' as a key paradigm for understanding 'modern' spousal relationships (Giddens 1992; Hirsch and Wardlow 2006). In this literature, love, romance and compatibility are more important means of making individuals into spouses, and adults, than considerations of material or economic advantage (Bauman 2003; Cole and Thomas 2009). These analyses reflect changing norms of gender and class, and changing expectations around the kinds of support and affection spouses anticipate from one another. They highlight too an increasing emphasis on the individual pursuit of personal desires, and on the relevance of biography and personal history to social change.

Rather than necessarily connoting the values of equality and companionate marriage, however, an expansion of the space of personal desires may itself be an expression of wider politico-economic contradictions and double binds, as suggested by Lauren Berlant's evocative phrase 'cruel optimism' (2011). Several of our chapters speak to these themes while keeping in view their connections to wider histories (see Holland and Lave 2001), and also to marriage's part in the purported 'middle-classification' (Edwards, Evans and Smith 2012) of many societies, expressed in the gloss of consumption and self-fashioning.

Rather than straightforwardly supporting any particular thesis about secularisation, these ideas are linked in complex ways to discourses about both 'religious revivals' and piety, and to the adoption by some religions of therapeutic 'self-help' talk in reference to marriage (see, for example, Maqsood 2017; van Dijk 2013).

Religious concerns, care and love are key dimensions of the 'ethical work' of marriage, which we discuss in later sections of this introduction and in the chapters of this volume. But this ethical work runs both in concert and in competition with aspirations for paid work, relationships with friends and natal family, and children. Riché J. Daniel Barnes's (2016) work with Black middle-class married mothers in Atlanta shows how women 'juggle' obligations to husbands, children, other kin and wider communities with work both inside and outside of the home. For these women, achieving a position of apparent personal happiness and professional 'success' may create more significant demands and pressures.

These accounts of marriage have spanned the globe, but comparisons have been mainly regional in focus. Important recent work on changing forms of marriage and intimacy *within* particular geographic locations and regional or religious cultures has demonstrated the considerable variation in local trajectories of marital transformation (see, for example, Basu and Ramberg 2015; Cole and Thomas 2009; Constable 2005; Charsley 2005; Davis and Friedman 2014; Miles, Mody and Probert 2015; Pauli and van Dijk 2016; Rebhun 1999; Shaw 2006; Shaw and Charsley 2006). The implication that there is a radical break between 'traditional' and 'modern' marriage, and that marriage is everywhere changing from a relation primarily about property arrangements to one of egalitarian intimacy, is countered or tempered by studies that remain attentive to wider contexts of familial relations and norms of filial duty (Ikels 2004; Yan 2003, 2005).

The idea that marriage signifies 'tradition' seems to haunt both public discourse and anthropology alike. Concerns expressed in public discourse about instability and change often coalesce around marriage, as both a bellwether and an antidote. These anxieties may be articulated in the form of stark dichotomies, for example between marriage 'by arrangement' and by 'choice'. But recent studies of middle-class marriage in India and Sri Lanka, among others, show clearly that while the language in which marriages are described may have changed, actual practices may have altered less than might appear. Thus a parental generation may speak of how their marriages were 'arranged', while having had considerable latitude to exercise their own preferences; and while their adult children describe their own marriages as 'modern', their parents remain heavily invested and involved (see Abeyasekera 2021;

Donner 2016; Fuller and Narasimhan 2008; Osella 2012; *pace* Giddens 1992). By pursuing a broader comparative perspective, this volume seeks to link up the insights developed in regional contexts, and to examine and unsettle their implicit assumptions about global trends.

Chapters, contexts and themes

The simultaneous resilience, flexibility and creativity of marriage, as well as the fact that it straddles several domains, make it an apt arena for investigating socio-political change. The case studies in this volume consider different aspects of contemporary marriage in six very different cultural contexts: Botswana, the United States, Greece, Taiwan, Sri Lanka and Malaysia. Each takes a different entry point, building on the trajectories outlined above while charting new paths, and in this sense the order in which we have placed our chapters is to some extent arbitrary. Opening the theme of the transformations produced by marriage, Koreen Reece investigates how, in Botswana, passing on customary law in wedding ceremonies creates opportunities to change gendered and generational relationships and to make selves, but also to constitute and distinguish state, polity and family in the context of the apparent 'crisis' of the HIV/Aids epidemic. Developing further the theme of advice-giving in Reece's chapter, Siobhan Magee depicts how pre-marital counselling in the state of Virginia in the US provides a set of discourses for understanding the precepts on which marriage should be founded. Counselling illuminates tensions between an ideal in which two individuals – heterosexual and opposite-sex, in accordance with dominant conservative Christian discourses and ideologies – come together and merge their interests, and one in which the individual is deemed to have primacy above other bonds. Tensions between politics, family and the self are palpable in the southern US, and are explored further by Eirini Papadaki in her chapter on marriage in Greece. Under conditions of economic austerity in Athens, these tensions are manifested in an evolving notion of what it means to 'compromise', in political and relational and affective terms, through different generations of twentieth- and twenty-first-century families. Hsiao-Chiao Chiu pursues a different tack by considering the apparent difficulty of getting married in contemporary Taiwan, and a trend towards delayed marriage. These trends – which are partly associated with women's increased education and participation in the workforce – are matched only by the difficulties of *not* marrying. Getting married becomes a 'trial' in multiple senses of the word. The

Sri Lankan Tamil case explored by Sidharthan Maunaguru concerns a much more extreme case of difficulty in marrying: transnational marriages contracted in the aftermath of prolonged war and disruption. Marriage is crucial here to envisaging a future that can transform the losses of warfare and upheaval – but must be performed in particular ways to satisfy the requirements of international immigration controls. Finally, the life stories of two women in Penang, Malaysia, described by Janet Carsten, call the place of marriage in upward class mobility into question. Rather than providing the linchpin for a successful life, marriage here is one of many avenues in already-advancing trajectories of self-fashioning – raising questions about what marriage obscures as well as what it enables.

Hierarchies of marriage

Hierarchy is deeply embedded in marriage, and takes multiple forms. Perhaps the most apparent of these is the hierarchy of gender. Koreen Reece's chapter on 'giving the law' in Botswana begins with a vivid depiction of *patlo*, a part of the wedding ceremonies in which a bride is given instruction on the proper way to behave as a wife according to the precepts of customary law. Suggestively, the instruction is both public – in that it takes place in front of a crowd of women – and simultaneously secret, in that the bride is hidden under a blanket, and much of it is delivered in whispers that are inaudible to those assembled. As Reece emphasises, however, the ceremony of *patlo*, giving the law to a new bride, is not simply one in which Tswana law (*molao*) is imparted as age-old tradition. Rather, there is scope for creativity and innovation – perhaps all the more so since witnesses cannot always be sure what instructions have been issued. Thus her argument is not so much about the inculcation of hierarchy, but a more subtle one about how marriage may also disrupt it, and provides a means by which the law is actually produced and changed.

The performative aspects of such instruction should give us pause, since there can be no doubt that, by the time she becomes a bride, a young Tswana woman will already have had ample opportunity to observe and understand the customary ways that women and men should behave towards each other. These may be silently conveyed and remain unarticulated as household members go about their everyday tasks (Bourdieu 1977), but are also reflected upon explicitly in the everyday negotiation of interpersonal conflict (Reece 2019).

The pre-marital instruction that couples in Lynchburg, Virginia receive from pastors or others (the subject of Siobhan Magee's chapter) – which inculcates the virtues of, for example, not getting angry at one's spouse for the trifling irritations of marital life – has a similar element of performance, and also builds on subtler forms of socialisation at home and in religious practice, including at church. Whether it is the importance of wives staying away from mobile phones in Botswana, or the question of how to deal with a husband who 'leaves his undershorts on the floor' in Virginia, instruction and counselling set explicit standards, which reflect on and seek to shape the practical hierarchies of everyday life. But we should attend carefully to the gendered nature of this instruction as we take up Reece's suggestion that, under the guise of imparting well-known rules for proper married life, instruction provides an opportunity for adjusting such rules and producing new ones.

Eirini Papadaki's chapter on Greece and Hsiao-Chiao Chiu's on Taiwan make clear how the hierarchical conventions on which marriage is based may shift more or less dramatically in just a few generations. In the Greek case, the gendered hierarchy of marriage in a strongly patriarchal context emerged clearly in ethnographies of village life in the mid-twentieth century (see Loizos and Papataxiarchis 1991 for an overview). But as Papadaki shows, contemporary middle-class Athenians, particularly women, voice concerns about the compromises married life imposes in terms of a loss of self, rather than in terms of their subjugation as women. This discourse is one that registers the affective gains and losses of marriage; it is articulated in ways that acknowledge but also bypass feminist understandings of marital relations. Part of the story of the resilience of marriage in the Greek context has to do with the social recognition that it affords women in particular, and the difficulty of achieving that recognition outside marriage. In the Taiwanese case, the early to mid-twentieth-century expectation that marriage involved the thoroughgoing incorporation of a wife into her husband's natal household and patrilineage has been mitigated, as women are increasingly able to delay marriage, work independently and continue to reside with their parents, while apparently contemplating having children on their own. The persistence of patrilineal and patriarchal values alongside the possibility of remaining unmarried, and now of same-sex marriage in Taiwan (instituted in 2019), suggests substantial changes and ambiguities in gender relations. A shift in gender hierarchies here intersects with changes in intergenerational ones, as adult children follow their own wishes in marriage and are less subject to parental control, but still maintain relations of respect and values of filial piety.

As we discuss further in the next section, the hierarchical ordering of marital relations is entwined with other hierarchies, including between state and family, or of class. Here we build on the insights of feminist scholarship over several decades, which has illuminated how kinship and gender are mutually constituted (Collier and Yanagisako 1987), and how the domaining of kinship, politics and economics into separate spheres is constructed in part through the naturalisation of gendered hierarchies (Carsten 2004; MacCormack and Strathern 1980; McKinnon and Cannell 2013b; Yanagisako 2002; Yanagisako and Delaney 1995). Marriage, as central to the reproduction of the family, and simultaneously legally constituted by the state, has a critical role in the intersection of these domains and in both the institution and reproduction of these hierarchies (McKinnon 2019a; 2019b). In Magee's and Reece's chapters, we see how in both the southern US and in Botswana – as in many other contemporary cultures – proper relations between husband and wife are part of what is taught to couples prior to marriage. This formal 'teaching' is not only an ethical matter, but also a political undertaking. As well as being publicly or semi-publicly imparted, the precepts of gendered hierarchy in marriage also implicitly reference and underpin other forms of hierarchy – including that between family and state.

In Lynchburg, Virginia, and in Athens, tensions of different kinds emerge between understandings of marriage as a relationship and corporate project, and of spouses as two individuals. The ideology of marriage implies that the former should take precedence over the latter: for a marriage to succeed, the larger and more social entity of the family must take priority over the desires and whims of individuals. But this prioritisation presents problems in a context where individualism is a strongly held political value, as it is in the US. If the limits to self-expression and individuality imposed by marriage are experienced or articulated more keenly by women than men, this too is an expression of linked gender hierarchies in marriage. In the Greek case, and others, these limitations may be expressed in the register of sacrifice, connoting religious sacrifice (Dubisch 1995; Iossifides 1991; Mayblin 2014; Paxson 2004). The expansive space occupied by discourses of love and emotion evident in the US and Greek cases may overlap or merge with those of individuality, and with overtly religious discourses. But forms of self-expression suggest that these are all historically situated terms. That they manifest themselves differently at different historical junctures is clear from Papadaki's analysis. In the two generations she considers, the resonance of 'compromise' in marriage has shifted from an association with defeat for the older generation that emerged from the military junta in the 1970s and 1980s, to a more personalised feeling of affective loss for couples who are now in their forties. This loss is understood by the latter to be the concomitant of gains in the form of stability, security, children and family life. A reading of twentieth-century Greek history suggests that, for an even earlier generation, which endured the German occupation and civil war in the 1940s and 1950s, 'compromise' carried powerful connotations of political and familial betrayal – especially in the form of forced public recantations (see Mazower 2000). In these shifts, we can detect reorganisations of the relationships between individual, family and state, as well as in gendered relations, unfolding against a turbulent political landscape.

All of these instances illuminate how the hierarchy of relations within marriage resonates with and animates more explicitly political relations. Marriage incorporates, produces and reproduces further hierarchies, including those of economy and class. Most of the case studies in our volume concern middle-class marriage, often in the context of considerable class mobility. Here changing patterns of consumption, reflecting increasingly middle-class tastes and preferences (Bourdieu 1984 [1979]), are expressed at weddings. In parts of southern Africa, a region long associated with protracted bridewealth payments and a processual understanding of marriage, the expense of increasingly lavish weddings means that marriage seems to have become an elite practice, raising questions about whether this may be relevant for Botswana (see James 2017; Pauli 2019; Pauli and van Dijk 2016). In Taiwan, patterns of delayed marriage discussed in the chapter by Chiu are associated with education and employment opportunities that are available to some, but not all. Here too, the emergence of different, class-based forms of marriage informs marital choice. And these new forms may be linked to migration. The scholarly literature on migration describes lower-class women migrating in order to marry into better-off families and/or more prosperous locations (see, for example, Brettell 2017; Charsley 2012; Constable 2005, 2014); Chiu's own contribution references marriage migration between mainland China and Taiwan, with similar aims (see Chao 2008; Lu 2005, 2012; Friedman 2015). Hierarchical class distinctions can thus be reproduced and entrenched as different marital forms are enacted over generations, but they can also be masked or mitigated through marriage in contexts of social mobility.

Separations, erasures and comparisons

In our introductory section, we highlighted the multifaceted nature of marriage – the way that it draws together different fields of social life, including family, politics, law, religion, economics and the nation. The received wisdom of liberal modernity (McKinnon and Cannell 2013a) arranges these in a hierarchy of scales so that, for example, intimate and affective realms of experience can appear to be encompassed by the state and its legal enactments. But as our opening vignettes reflect, it is far from straightforward to pick apart the entanglements between these domains. Mody's (2008) work on love marriage and the law in India shows how, at some moments, law and intimacy emerge clearly as separable fields and, at others, they seem to blur into each other. Marriage, particularly in class-based contexts of modernity, is conceived and experienced as an individual project as well as one that is undertaken under the auspices of the state. However, as Michael Lambek puts it, 'Despite its encapsulation within the order of the state, kinship always threatens to be something more' (Lambek 2013, 255). Whether the 'something more' alluded to by Lambek is the overwhelming emotions associated with love and marriage, or their unexpected ability to evade and even redirect the power of the state to legitimate marriage (as in our opening account of a wedding in Northern Ireland), it unsettles assumptions about encapsulation, encompassment and even separation between these domains.

Rather than understanding the realms of social life condensed in marriage as contained and organised in some prefigured order of encompassment, we instead explore these separations as *effects* of ideologies of modernity, which have the capacity to make such hierarchies appear self-evident (McKinnon and Cannell 2013a; Lambek 2013). It is through the active separation of spheres of the family and the state, the intimate and the political, that this hierarchy is embedded, internalised and naturalised. This domaining process emerges in several of the essays in this volume. Maunaguru's exploration of transnational Sri Lankan Tamil marriages in the aftermath of war vividly demonstrates how wedding photographers and protagonists 'stage' rituals in ways that they hope will later be legible to Canadian immigration officials. Moments of performed intimacy crystallise here, and are absorbed into the way weddings are celebrated. They have the purpose of rendering the rituals as 'authentic' rather than fake – not for the bride and groom or their family and friends, but for the Canadian state. In this moment of photographic visualisation, the separations and hierarchies of different domains are made unusually evident.

By contrast, in the Botswana case, we see how the parallel systems of civil and customary law merge and are embedded in marriage, as much as their separation is produced by marriage, in what Reece suggests is a kind of 'ordinary ethics' (see Lambek 2010). Law, as she argues, is a way of making distinctions – of legal forms, of gender, generation, kinship and politics. But here it seems that what the law does is enact distinctions that are otherwise obscure, and in so doing, produce them. The allusion to 'ordinary ethics' is apt because, as several of our essays show, marriage is inevitably a process that requires comparative assessments and judgements, which are crucial to the ways that hierarchies, distinctions, separations and exclusions are produced and reproduced. This dynamic is made explicit in the pre-marital counselling in Virginia examined by Magee, where the kinds of marriages advocated by conservative Christians are actively discussed in religious and simultaneously personal terms. Behaviour that does not conform to these ideals – expressing anger over seemingly trivial matters, for example – is discouraged. As we have seen, such advice implicitly incorporates and inculcates gendered models of behaviour, and it either implicitly or explicitly excludes certain forms of marriage. As Magee indicates, there is a powerful history in play here. Until the Supreme Court judgement on *Loving v. Virginia* in 1967, marriage across 'racial' lines was illegal in Virginia. This 1967 ruling was drawn on as a precedent in the subsequent Supreme Court judgement making it illegal to ban same-sex marriage in 2015. Certain forms of marriage are thus not only beyond the purview of conservative Christian counselling, they have historically also been outside the law. In the US, the law delineates normative marriage and places non-normative forms outside the law (see Borneman 1996; McKinnon 2017, 2019a, 2019b). In this sense, it forecloses some possibilities even as it expands others. And this is one reason that historians of the US have seen marriage as a central institution and metaphor of the nation (Cott 2000).

The work of 'ordinary ethics' in marriage does not necessarily need to be the subject of explicit instruction, although this may occur. Our essays also show how marriage inevitably enfolds everyday ethical judgements and comparisons as it is envisaged, planned, described and narrated. Carsten's rendering of the life stories of two upwardly mobile women of different generations and ethnic backgrounds in Penang, Malaysia, traces how the comparisons of their own marriages with those of others, especially of close family members, is woven through their narratives. The narratives illuminate how the 'everyday' or 'ordinary' is suffused with ethics (Das 2018). Marriage provides an expansive ground for making ethical assessments, and these come to constitute life stories. Such comparative judgements evaluate relations in both positive and negative terms, with or without reference to religious precepts or discourses about love. This tendency reminds us that kinship and relatedness might be the most obvious realm of everyday life through which ethics are imaginatively and practically lived (see Carsten 2019; Faubion 2001; McKinley 2001).

Far from providing a teleological story of the rise of autonomous individuals and the progressive marginalisation of kinship in institutions of modernity, then, the essays in this volume collectively show how marriage, and kinship more broadly, may make innovation possible. The chapters by Papadaki and Chiu exemplify how marriage provides the ground for, and is enacted through, ethical comparison. In the case of Athenian middle-class women, suggestively, such assessments pertain to the self, and the imaginative consideration of lives not lived – roads not taken. But the manner in which such imaginary paths are balanced against the actuality of family life with children is suggestive of the ways that love and care (even when they are not directly spoken of) are part of the 'everyday ethics' of marriage.

In Taiwan, Chiu's discussion of the 'trials' endured by young people who delay marriage makes clear that the alternatives of marrying and not marrying must be understood beside other generational shifts in forms of marriage and in gender relations. A delayed marriage, among other things, means that single women continue to live with and support their parents. This choice may occasion conflict, negotiation, accommodation and compromise between generations – incorporating other forms of economic and affective care in turn. Here, as in Penang, Lynchburg or Athens, we sense divergent models for marriage embedded in different versions of gender and generational hierarchy, and cross-cut by changing educational and employment opportunities for women.

What is moot in our accounts is what happens when contested models of marriage conflict with each other – for example, when Taiwanese women reject the patriarchal and patrilineal tenets on which 'traditional' marriage is based. Rather than see these tensions in terms of direct competition, it might be more plausible to look for measured adjustments – the 'compromises' articulated by couples in Athens, for instance. Such scenarios and their accommodations are suggestive too of the 'cruel optimism' (Berlant 2011) that attention to personal desire may connote. At the limits, individual marriages may break down, as is the case in one of the narratives from Penang. The recently instituted possibility of same-sex marriage in Taiwan suggests that everyday gossip and judgements about unmarried people's behaviour, which Chiu's chapter documents for Jinmen, must, over time, incorporate subtle shifts in the valuation of norms and conventional behaviour. These, as Carsten argues in her contribution, flow and ricochet between individuals, families and communities. They have profound implications for transformations in marriage, and for the further transformations these produce, which we explore further in the final section of this introduction.

Marital histories, material histories

As we have suggested above, the fact that marriage may come to 'stand for' the nation, and that its forms are crucially linked to and framed by legal and religious enactments, should not lead us to assume that the state thereby exercises full control of marriage and its changing practice. Because of the intimate, relational and everyday dimensions of its lived experience, kinship always exceeds or evades state attempts at regulation. State and other institutionalised attempts to shape marriage, and the evasions and innovations that emerge in spite and because of them, thus provide complementary perspectives on national, familial and personal histories. The reform of Greek family law enacted in 1983 and referred to in Papadaki's chapter, for example, was an attempt to institutionalise gender equality in terms of marital property, relations and familial authority. But it is not at all clear whether, in enacting this far-reaching reform, the Greek government was attempting to drive social change forward, or was catching up with wider changes in attitudes and practices that were already manifest by the time of the fall of the junta in 1974. To take another example from this volume, one could suggest that the US Supreme Court judgements of 1967 and 2015 – respectively making it illegal for states to ban 'interracial' and same-sex marriage – were *responding* to widespread shifts in attitudes, rather than simply prescribing new ways of doing marriage. These interpretive possibilities raise wider questions about the transformations marriage undergoes and produces, how they occur, and their implications for historicising social analysis.

One striking aspect of the cases in our volume, as we observed above, is that they share historical backgrounds of colonialism, anti-colonial struggle and/or civil war. In the case of Botswana, the sustained if unsuccessful attempt by British colonial authorities to prevent the marriage of the white English woman, Ruth Williams, to Seretse Khama – heir to the Bangwato paramount chiefship – powerfully symbolised the last throes of Britain's imperial influence across Africa. It highlighted the ugly legacies and dependencies colonialism had created in and on apartheid South Africa, and became a focal point for imagining Botswana's independence (Williams 2007). Having failed to block his marriage, the British government went to great lengths to displace Khama, including by keeping him in exile. When he finally renounced his chiefship, however, Khama was freed to lead the movement for independence – and ultimately became the new nation's first president. In Virginia, the shadow of the American Civil War stretches from a rather distant past when compared to the war in Sri Lanka, which forms the immediate backdrop to the marriages depicted by Maunaguru. But the prominence of Civil War monuments in Lynchburg, including the Confederate section of its historic cemetery – a picturesque wedding site – belies this distance. Nearby, in the university town of Charlottesville, as elsewhere in the American South, such monuments are heavily contested. The history of this war remains a contemporary concern. In Jinmen, situated at the literal front line of civil war in China and the ensuing, prolonged Cold War, military sites and museums across the island are pervasive commemorative markers on the landscape. As Papadaki's and Carsten's chapters show, even where such history is less physically memorialised, as in the Greek and Malaysian cases – condensed instead in the interstices, gaps and silences of state monuments – it can nevertheless be traced in family histories and narratives.

The prominence of commemorative sites and monuments draws our attention to the role of material sites and artefacts in connecting memories of personal and familial loss in warfare with the nation (see Kwon 2006, 2013; Winter 1995). Histories of marriage are generally less visible than those of warfare in the stories nations tell about themselves. But the power of objects and places to evoke affective qualities and past experience is equally crucial in marriage, and has some similar qualities. Our opening report, suggestively, highlighted a wedding bouquet and the bride's dress in the severely pared-down version of a wedding in Spain during the Covid-19 pandemic. And many accounts of communal solidarity during lockdown mentioned 'the balcony' and 'the street' as sites where sociality could be enacted in emotionally powerful ways, despite social distancing measures.

It is not accidental that venues, costumes, jewellery, food, photographs and other material items should feature prominently in the planning and descriptions of weddings (see Charsley 1992; https://anthropology-of-weddings.org.uk). All have the capacity to condense and evoke the affective qualities associated with marriage. Maunaguru's depiction of Sri Lankan Tamil weddings celebrated out of place in India, by uprooted couples who hope eventually to settle in Canada, conveys how temporary sites in India may be actively remade to summon up a lost Sri Lankan home. Food and commensality are a central feature of such evocations of a 'village-like' atmosphere. But his chapter also draws attention to two highly unusual features of these celebrations – which are also occasions for the reparation of loss. One is the figure of the tree that should be planted as part of the wedding rites, to mark the 'emplacement' of marriage in a local house site, and the growth and fertility that marriages signify. But here the trees that are planted are in a transient spot that is left behind once the rituals are completed. The other extraordinary element of these marriages 'on the move' is the insertion of images of deceased relatives into wedding photographs, as if to mark their absent presence.

What is the import of such striking implantations into the material iconography of weddings? It seems that the inclusion of the figures of a tree planted only to be left behind, or relatives whose death is conspicuous in their photographic presence, bridge the breaks in continuity of place and people occasioned by war. They allow the reconstruction of chains of transmission from the past and into the future – which is part of the work of marriage. In this respect, the possibility of celebrating a wedding in a Confederate cemetery in Lynchburg might perhaps seem less incongruous. As Maunaguru's essay illuminates, the rituals of marriage evoke the past, but they look towards, and make possible, a new future. This evocation happens in everyday registers, as well as ritual ones: in Carsten's chapter, the recuperation or collection of objects that recall a lost childhood can materialise a vision of continuity in a life and marriage that have been disrupted by upward mobility and achievement.

In these and other ways, our essays illustrate the importance of material objects and referents to place in the transmission of the past into the present and future. Here we refer to work by Thomas B. Trautmann, Gillian Feeley-Harnik and John C. Mitani (2011), which considers the 'mnemonic properties of artefacts deliberately intended to bind relations over time and space' (2011, 185). Their argument about the 'deep history' of kinship focuses on houses and food as evoking memories and emotional responses through their association with patterns laid down in childhood. But it also includes other items: jewellery, pots, clothing, kinship terminologies and genealogies, which, as they suggestively argue, are part of 'the heavy memory work' that operates through kinship (2011, 186). We note here that such objects, whether as gifts or trousseaux, are often an important focus of betrothal and wedding rituals. The bridal bouquet and wedding gown, the seemingly banal items mentioned in our opening vignette, may thus be passed on or lovingly preserved, carrying their condensed meanings 'to bind relations over time and space', and to history.

Temporalities of marriage

Andrew Shryock has suggested that we should think of kinship as 'a special mode of travel, a way to engineer secure social landscapes and reliable histories' (2013, 278). This formulation seems particularly apt for the dislocations and uncertainties documented in Maunaguru's chapter; it also underlines the centrality of imaginative 'time travel' to the capacities of marriage and of kinship. The 'entangled temporalities' explored by Maunaguru resonate with Laura Bear's (2014) discussion of the heterochrony or multiplicity of modern time. Such multiplicity in the context of wedding rituals is perhaps unsurprising given the inherently processual nature of marriage, which commentators have noted in different contexts (Carsten 1997; Comaroff and Roberts 1977). The condensed signification that operates for the kinds of objects discussed in the previous section evokes the 'heterochronicity' (the simultaneous co-existence of different temporal registers) proposed by Nikolai Ssorin-Chaikov (2006) for Soviet displays of birthday gifts to Stalin in 1949. Photographs of a celebration of marriage into which deceased relatives have been inserted could be considered as exemplary cases of 'objects and images . . . whose time does not appear to be "our" time' (Pinney 2005, 262–3, punctuation omitted).

Rather than focus on the exceptional qualities of time under modernity, we connect such temporal entanglements to our earlier assertion that marriage affords opportunities for, and encompasses, ethical judgements about relations. We could see these assessments as part of a kind of 'comparative time travel' within and between generations. As Danilyn Rutherford notes, 'kinship is about time' (2015, 241). Time travel is silently enabled through the deployment of material forms with strong affective and ethical resonances – as in the wedding celebrations depicted by Maunaguru and Reece. But the ethical evaluations of affection, care and individual expression in the counselling described by Magee, and the assessments of everyday life discussed by Carsten, Chiu and Papadaki, are also explicitly or implicitly comparative, and occur in multiple tenses. In figuring out how best to do marriage in the present, prospective spouses, as well as those who narrate a conjugal life retrospectively, look forward and backward in time.

While, as Shryock suggests, we should think of time travel as an important quality of kinship more generally, there are moments in planning and enacting a marriage when ethical evaluations and their inherent timescapes become especially palpable. Betrothal, marital dispute or divorce mark such moments of high tension – when marriages come into being, or risk being torn apart. Notably, betrothal often takes a heavily ritualised form in which doing things in the prescribed manner, as handed down by tradition over generations, matters. Betrothal, one might say, is an imaginary time travel into the future that is built on – or pretends – a recapitulation of the past. In divorce, as Carsten's chapter suggests, it is not only for economic reasons that items of marital property with their heavy symbolic and emotional freight are the focus of contention. Divorce is a rupture in the present that risks becoming entrenched; it requires the unpicking of the past to enable participants to move forward. Many divorcing couples might wish they could unravel time.

Time is central to Tom Boellstorff's (2007) discussion of contestations over the implications of same-sex marriage in the US, using the lens of queer theory. Boellstorff argues that 'straight time', with its linear assumptions of biography in terms of progression, imposes a heteronormative understanding of marriage as necessarily reproducing patriarchy (see also Dinshaw et al. 2007; Freeman 2010). In this reading, same-sex marriage appears as an inherently conservative or regressive innovation, consolidating and legitimising the role of the state and heteronormativity. Boellstorff proposes instead to 'destabilize straight time – to queer it, in fact' (2007, 240). Bringing to bear alternative regimes of temporality, he suggests, such as Javanese or Balinese ideas of time, which emphasise the coincidence of different cyclical rhythms (Dreyfuss 1985; Geertz 1973), 'might make possible contingent, ironic, and above all imbricated stances toward structures of domination' (Boellstorff 2007, 240). A switch to 'coincidental time' thus disrupts the assumptions of straight time, 'making it possible to imagine two entities in the same temporality', and to realise 'the potential of a coeval relationship between same-sex marriage and opposite-sex marriage' (Boellstorff 2007, 243), and thus to arrive at an alternative political understanding of same-sex marriage.

In this analysis, temporality is central to how marriage works. Drawing on Boellstorff's discussion, we suggest that, rather than understanding same-sex marriage to encapsulate some singular quality, distinct from all other marriage, *all* marriages have the capacity to take place in 'coincidental time' or 'queer time'. While opposite-sex marriage, as we have outlined, undoubtedly participates in and reproduces state institutions and normative framings, it also carries with it the possibility of being reimagined, and enacted in new ways. This reformulation occurs through the simultaneous imagining, comparison and evocation of other and alternative scenarios in past, present, and future. Such creative potentiality is an intrinsic capacity of kinship. In this way, we argue, it is not only through 'denaturalizing straight time' (Boellstorff 2007, 241) that we can understand the potentialities of marriage, but through denaturalising marriage itself.

Conjugal transformations

In recounting the 2015 referendum on same-sex marriage in the Republic of Ireland, and a same-sex wedding in Northern Ireland in 2020, our opening reports refer to perhaps the most profound change that marriage has undergone in recent times (in some places, at least). Whether in Ireland or Taiwan, Costa Rica or the US, such developments would not have been foreseen just a few decades ago. They raise the questions: how do transformations in marital forms occur? And how do they propel further social change? Our essays provide instances of other shifts in gender relations and marital forms evident in contemporary marriage. And they indicate too the tensions that emerge around new ways of doing marriage. As Carsten's, Chiu's and Papadaki's chapters illuminate, changes to how marriage is judged and imagined may occur incrementally through the ways people consider and talk about themselves and others. Change may be welcomed in some quarters, and resisted in others. The US Supreme Court judgements on 'interracial' and same-sex marriage referred to by Magee were the outcome of considerable political struggle, and are still heavily contested zones, rather than an indication of the inexorable and inevitable march of liberal reform.

All of the chapters in this book illustrate how the institution of marriage and the content of conjugal relations may display striking degrees of ambiguity and uncertainty. This ambiguity connects to the difficulty that an earlier generation of anthropologists had in ascribing a universal definition to marriage (Leach 1955; Needham 1971). Marriage as an institution is extraordinarily hard to pin down. But another way of depicting this elusiveness would be to say that it is an unusually flexible and expansive institution – it can take many forms, sometimes simultaneously (see, for example, Basu and Ramberg 2015). This might provide one (counter-intuitive) response to Berlant's question: 'What does it mean about love that its expressions tend to be so *conventional*, so bound up in institutions like marriage and family, property relations, and stock phrases and plots?' (Berlant 2012, 7, original italics). Rather than only normalising and domesticating desire, as Berlant (2011) suggests, our project shows how marriage also has the potential to resist or enlarge what constitutes the normal. The flexibility and expansiveness of marriage thus casts a different light on the supposed linear shift from arranged marriage to marriage by choice as an effect of modernity which, as we noted above and discussed in Maunaguru's chapter, has been called into question particularly in ethnographies of South Asia (see Abeyasekera 2021; Donner 2016; Fuller and Narasimhan 2008; Osella 2012; Parry 2020, chapter 11). The entanglements of 'arrangement' and 'choice' with class and/or caste and other factors that are documented in these studies suggest considerably less stable temporalities than implied in models of linear progress.

The ethnography in our volume reveals small 'slices' of much larger worlds of marriage in each of the contexts studied. But anything like a 'complete' picture, covering all its forms and aspects, would be impossible to achieve. Instead, by placing these cases side by side, we have been able to reflect on the resonances between them, and to use insights from one to draw out inferences in others. Collectively, our essays describe the simultaneous conservatism and innovation that marriage instantiates and allows. We suggest that it is partly through its apparent cloak of conformity that innovation is made possible. And this may help to explain the intense attention paid to the conventional enactment of ritual at betrothals and weddings. Whether in the 'secret' advice given to brides in Botswana, in the implicit comparisons made between marriages over several generations of one family in Malaysia, or the gossip and rumours circulating about unmarried single people in Jinmen, Taiwan, understandings about the proper way to behave in relationships circulate and are the subject of moral judgements and comparative evaluation. These judgements have the capacity gradually to become part of a wider field of accepted and acceptable behaviour. Seen in this light, same-sex marriage can appear as both an inherently conservative move and a radical innovation (Boellstorff 2007; Butler 2002). The legal right to gay marriage provides, as we have seen, a rare instance when the simultaneity of these aspects becomes strikingly apparent. Marriage is broad, flexible and accommodating in its capacities as well as in its ambiguities.

We have suggested that it is partly through the work of 'ordinary ethics' – everyday comparisons, evaluations and judgements – that transformations occur in and through marriage. We see marriages, in other words, as both 'imaginative projections and arrangements of power' (Rose 2020 [1983], 16). Here we push back against understandings of the state as the overriding driver of change. While marriage is undoubtedly a political institution, subject to controls exerted by the modern state, its power derives from the fact that it is also an expression of familial, individual and affective lives that exceed those controls. Making marriages involves families, couples and individuals creatively planning for a future, often one they hope to make different from the past – but, paradoxically, also similar. Inescapably, they draw on and sometimes adjust rituals that have been passed down through generations, or have the appearance of having done so. Spouses adopt and remake ways of celebrating a wedding, and they also consider their own conjugal relationship in the light of others – especially those of their parents, close family members and consociates. Given the commemorative and imaginative possibilities in play, and the evaluations and investments entailed, it is not surprising that marriages are fraught with the potential for considerable family tension. It is in this broad sense that we understand marriage, transforming and transformative at once, to occur in past, present and future tense.

In seeing marriage as a comparative endeavour that takes place simultaneously in past, present and future, we also return it as subject matter to an anthropology that has comparison at its core. The cloak of conformity that marriage wears so persuasively has perhaps diverted anthropologists from attending to its elastic, shape-shifting and transformative potential, concentrating instead on other aspects of kinship that seem more obviously new. The work of our volume has much in common with the kinds of comparative everyday ethics we document in our chapters. As in the narratives of participants in Penang, Athens, Jinmen or elsewhere, evaluations take conversational forms, alluding to one another and to shared references, invoking resonances, similarities and contrasts. This work of comparison, which we have suggested is a defining feature of marriage, enabling its transformative possibilities, is also at the heart of anthropology's radical potential.

References

Abeyasekera, Asha. 2021. *Making the Right Choice: Narratives of marriage in Sri Lanka.* New Brunswick, NJ: Rutgers University Press.

Andrikopoulos, Apostolos. 2021. 'Love, money and papers in the affective circuits of cross-border marriages: Beyond the "sham"/"genuine" dichotomy', *Journal of Ethnic and Migration Studies* 47 (2): 343–60.

Andrikopoulos, Apostolos, and Jan Willem Duyvendak (eds). 2020. 'Special issue: Transnational migration and kinship dynamics', *Ethnography* 21 (3).

Barnes, Riché J. Daniel. 2016. *Raising the Race: Black career women redefine marriage, motherhood and community.* New Brunswick, NJ: Rutgers University Press.

Basu, Srimati, and Lucinda Ramberg (eds). 2015. *Conjugality Unbound: Sexual economies, state regulation and the marital form in India.* New Delhi: Women Unlimited.

Bauman, Zygmunt. 2003. *Liquid Love: On the frailty of human bonds.* Cambridge: Polity.

Bear, Laura. 2014. 'Doubt, conflict and mediation: An anthropology of modern time', *Journal of the Royal Anthropological Institute* 20 (S1): 3–30.

Berlant, Lauren. 2011. *Cruel Optimism.* Durham, NC: Duke University Press.

Berlant, Lauren. 2012. *Desire/Love*. New York: Punctum.
Blackwood, Evelyn. 2005. 'Wedding bell blues: Marriage, missing men, and matrifocal follies', *American Ethnologist* 32: 3–191.
Boellstorff, Tom. 2007. 'When marriage falls: Queer coincidences in straight time', *GLQ: A Journal of Lesbian and Gay Studies* 13: 227–48.
Borneman, John. 1996. 'Until death do us part: Marriage/death in anthropological discourse', *American Ethnologist* 23: 215–35.
Borneman, John. 1997. 'Caring and being cared for: Displacing marriage, kinship, gender and sexuality', *International Social Science Journal* 49: 573–84.
Bourdieu, Pierre. 1977. *Outline of a Theory of Practice*. Cambridge: Cambridge University Press.
Bourdieu, Pierre. 1984 [1979]. *Distinction: A social critique of the judgement of taste*. Cambridge, MA: Harvard University Press.
Brettell, Caroline. 2017. 'Marriage and migration', *Annual Review of Anthropology* 46: 81–97.
Butler, Judith. 2002. 'Is kinship always already heterosexual?', *Differences: A Journal of Feminist Cultural Studies* 13: 14–44.
Carsten, Janet. 1997. *The Heat of the Hearth: The process of kinship in a Malay fishing community*. Oxford: Clarendon Press.
Carsten, Janet. 2004. *After Kinship*. Cambridge: Cambridge University Press.
Carsten, Janet. 2019. 'The stuff of kinship'. In *The Cambridge Handbook for the Anthropology of Kinship*, edited by Sandra Bamford, 133–50. Cambridge: Cambridge University Press.
Chao, Yen-Ning. 2008. 'Rethinking nationalism through intimate relationships: Conflicts in cross-strait marriages', *Taiwanese Sociology* 16: 97–148.
Charsley, Katherine. 2005. 'Unhappy husbands: Masculinity and migration in transnational Pakistani marriages', *Journal of the Royal Anthropological Institute* 11: 85–105.
Charsley, Katherine (ed.). 2012. *Transnational Marriage*. Abingdon: Routledge.
Charsley, Katharine, and Alison Shaw 2006. 'South Asian transnational marriages in comparative perspective', *Global Networks* 6: 331–44.
Charsley, Simon. 1992. *Wedding Cakes and Cultural History*. London: Routledge.
Cherlin, A. 2004. 'The deinstitutionalization of American marriage', *Journal of Marriage and Family* 66: 848–61.
Clark-Decès, Isabelle. 2014. *The Right Spouse: Preferential marriages in Tamil Nadu*. Stanford, CA: Stanford University Press.
Cole, Jennifer, and Lynn M. Thomas (eds). 2009. *Love in Africa*. Chicago: University of Chicago Press.
Collier, Jane F., and Sylvia J. Yanagisako (eds). 1987. *Gender and Kinship: Essays towards a unified analysis*. Stanford, CA: Stanford University Press.
Comaroff, John L., and Simon Roberts. 1977. 'Marriage and extra-marriage sexuality: The dialectics of legal change among the Kgatla', *Journal of African Law* 21: 97–123.
Constable, Nicole. 2003. *Romance on a Global Stage: Pen pals, virtual ethnography, and 'mail-order' marriages*. Berkeley: University of California Press.
Constable, Nicole (ed.). 2005. *Cross-Border Marriage in Asia*. Philadelphia: University of Pennsylvania Press.
Constable, Nicole. 2014. *Born Out of Place: Migrant mothers and the politics of international labor*. Berkeley: University of California Press.
Constable, Nicole. 2015. 'Migrant motherhood, "failed migration", and the gendered risks of precarious labour', *TRaNS. Trans-Regional and National Studies of Southeast Asia* 3:135–51.
Cott, Nancy F. 2000. *Public Vows: A history of marriage and the nation*. Cambridge, MA: Harvard University Press.
Das, Veena. 2018. 'Ethics, self-knowledge, and life taken as a whole', *HAU: Journal of Ethnographic Theory* 8: 537–49.
Davis, Deborah S., and Sara L. Friedman (eds). 2014. *Wives, Husbands, and Lovers: Marriage and sexuality in Hong Kong, Taiwan, and urban China*. Stanford, CA: Stanford University Press.
Dinshaw, Carolyn, Lee Edelman, Roderick A. Ferguson, Carla Freccero, Elizabeth Freeman, Judith Halberstam, Annamarie Jagose, Christopher S. Nealon and Nguyen Tan Hoang. 2007. 'Theorizing queer temporalities: A roundtable discussion', *GLQ: A Journal of Lesbian and Gay Studies* 13: 177–95.
Donner, Henrike. 2016. 'Doing it our way: Love and marriage in Kolkata middle-class families', *Modern Asian Studies* 50: 1147–89.

Dreyfuss, Jeff. 1985. 'A coincidence of metaphors: Notes on two modes of text building in the Indonesian novel Surabaya', *Journal of Asian Studies* 44: 755–63.

Dubisch, Jill. 1995. *In a Different Place: Pilgrimage, gender, and politics at a Greek island shrine*. Princeton, NJ: Princeton University Press.

Edwards, Jeanette, Gillian Evans and Katherine Smith. 2012. 'The middle class-ification of Britain', *Focaal* 62: 3–16.

Engels, Frederick. 1972 [1884]. *The Origin of the Family, Private Property and the State*. London: Lawrence and Wishart.

Evans-Pritchard, Edward E. 1951. *Kinship and Marriage among the Nuer*. Oxford: Oxford University Press.

Faubion, James (ed.). 2001. *The Ethics of Kinship: Ethnographic enquiries*. Lanham, MD: Rowman & Littlefield.

Fortes, Meyer. 1949. *The Web of Kinship among the Tallensi: The second part of an analysis of the social structure of a Trans-Volta tribe*. London: Oxford University Press.

Foucault, Michel. 1980. *The History of Sexuality*, vol. 1. New York: Vintage.

Franklin, Sarah. 1997. *Embodied Progress: A cultural account of assisted conception*. London: Routledge.

Franklin, Sarah. 2014. *Biological Relatives: IVF, stem cells, and the future of kinship*. Durham, NC: Duke University Press.

Freeman, Elizabeth. 2010. *Time Binds: Queer temporalities, queer histories*. Durham, NC: Duke University Press.

Friedman, Sara. *Exceptional States: Chinese immigrants and Taiwanese sovereignty*. Oakland: University of California Press, 2015.

Fuller, Chris, and Haripriya Narasimhan. 2008. 'Companionate marriage in India', *Journal of the Royal Anthropological Institute* 14: 736–54.

Geertz, Clifford. 1973. 'Person, time and conduct in Bali'. In *The Interpretation of Cultures*, 360–411. New York: Basic Books.

Giddens, Anthony. 1992. *The Transformation of Intimacy: Sexuality, love and eroticism in modern societies*. Cambridge: Polity Press.

Goodfellow, Aaron. 2015. *Gay Fathers, Their Children, and the Making of Kinship*. New York: Fordham University Press.

Hannaford, Dinah. 2015. 'Technologies of the spouse: Intimate surveillance in Senegalese transnational marriages', *Global Networks* 15: 43–59.

Hannaford, Dinah. 2017. *Marriage Without Borders: Transnational spouses in neoliberal Senegal*. Philadelphia: Pennsylvania University Press.

Hayden, Corinne P. 1995. 'Gender, genetics, and generation: Reformulating biology in lesbian kinship', *Cultural Anthropology* 10: 41–63.

Heywood, Paolo. 2009. 'Topographies of love: Two discourses on the Russian mail-order bride industry', *Cambridge Anthropology* 29: 26–45.

Hirsch, Jennifer S., and Holly Wardlow (eds) 2006. *Modern Loves: The anthropology of romantic courtship and companionate marriage*. Ann Arbor: University of Michigan Press.

Holland, Dorothy, and Jean Lave (eds) 2001. *History in Person: Enduring struggles, contentious practice, intimate identities*. Santa Fe, NM: SAR Press.

Hughes, Geoffrey. 2015. 'Infrastructures of legitimacy: The political lives of marriage contracts in Jordan', *American Ethnologist* 42: 279–94.

Hughes, Geoffrey. 2021. *Kinship, Islam, and the Politics of Marriage in Jordan*. Bloomington: Indiana University Press.

Ikels, Charlotte (ed.). 2004. *Filial Piety: Practice and discourse in contemporary East Asia*. Stanford, CA: Stanford University Press.

Iossifides, Marina A. 1991. 'Sisters in Christ: Metaphors of kinship among Greek nuns'. In *Contested Identities: Gender and kinship in modern Greece*, edited by Peter Loizos and Evthymios Papataxiarchis, 135–55. Princeton, NJ: Princeton University Press.

James, Deborah. 2017. 'Not marrying in South Africa: Consumption, aspiration and the new middle class', *Anthropology Southern Africa* 40: 1–14.

Jamieson, Lynn, and Roona Simpson. 2013. *Living Alone: Globalization, identity and belonging*. Basingstoke: Palgrave Macmillan.

Kassam, Ashifa. 2020. 'Spanish couple hold wedding from their window to beat coronavirus lockdown'. *Guardian*, 20 March. https://www.theguardian.com/world/2020/mar/20/love-coronavirus-spanish-couple-balcony-wedding.

Kaur, Ravinder (ed.). 2016. *Too Many Men, Too Few Women: Social consequences of gender imbalance in India and China*. Hyderabad: Orient Blackswan.

Kholoussy, Hanan. 2010. *For Better, For Worse: The marriage crisis that made modern Egypt*. Stanford, CA: Stanford University Press.

Kilshaw, Susie, Tasneem Al Raisi and Fouad Alshaban. 2015. 'Arranging marriage; negotiating risk: Genetics and society in Qatar', *Anthropology and Medicine* 22: 98–113.

Kwon, Heonik. 2006. *After the Massacre: Commemoration and consolation in Ha My and My Lai*. Berkeley: University of California Press.

Kwon, Heonik. 2013. *Ghosts of War in Vietnam*. Cambridge: Cambridge University Press.

Lambek, Michael (ed.). 2010. *Ordinary Ethics: Anthropology, language, and action*. New York: Fordham University Press.

Lambek, Michael. 2013. 'Kinship, modernity, and the immodern'. In *Vital Relations: Modernity and the persistent life of kinship*, edited by Susan McKinnon and Fenella Cannell, 241–60. Santa Fe, NM: SAR Press.

Lasch, Christopher. 1977. *Haven in a Heartless World: The family besieged*. New York: Basic Books.

Leach, Edmund R. 1955. 'Polyandry, inheritance and the definition of marriage', *Man* 55: 182–6.

Lévi-Strauss, Claude. 1969 [1949]. *The Elementary Structures of Kinship*, revised edition, translated by James Harle Bell, John Richard von Sturmer and Rodney Needham. Boston, MA: Beacon Press.

Lewin, Ellen. 1998. *Recognizing Ourselves: Lesbian and gay ceremonies of commitment*. New York: Columbia University Press.

Lewin, Ellen. 2004. 'Does marriage have a future?', *Journal of Marriage and Family* 66: 1000–6.

Loizos, Peter, and Evthymios Papataxiarchis. 1991. 'Introduction: Gender and kinship in marriage and alternative contexts'. In *Contested Identities: Gender and kinship in modern Greece*, edited by Peter Loizos and Evthymios Papataxiarchis, 3–25. Princeton, NJ: Princeton University Press.

Lu, Melody Chia-wen. 2005. 'Commercially arranged marriage migration: Case studies of cross-border marriages in Taiwan', *Indian Journal of Gender Studies* 12: 275–303.

Lu, Melody Chia-wen. 2012. 'Transnational marriages as a strategy of care exchange: Veteran soldiers and their mainland Chinese spouses in Taiwan', *Global Networks* 12: 233–51.

Luehrmann, Sonja. 2004. 'Mediated marriage: Internet matchmaking in provincial Russia', *Europe-Asia Studies* 56: 857–75.

MacCormack, Carol, and Marilyn Strathern (eds). 1980. *Nature, Culture and Gender: A critique*. Cambridge: Cambridge University Press.

Maine, Henry. 1861. *Ancient Law: Its connection with the early history of society, and its relation to modern ideas*. London: John Murray.

Maine, Henry S. 1873. *The Early History of the Property of Married Women*. Manchester: A. Ireland.

Majumdar, Rochona. 2009. *Marriage and Modernity: Family values in colonial Bengal*. Durham, NC: Duke University Press.

Maqsood, Ammara. 2017. *The New Pakistani Middle Class*. Cambridge, MA: Harvard University Press.

Marcus, George E. 1992 *Lives in Trust: The fortunes of dynastic families in late twentieth-century America*. Boulder, CO: Westview.

Maskens, Maïté. 2015. 'Bordering intimacy: The fight against marriages of convenience in Brussels', *Cambridge Anthropology* 33: 42–58.

Maunaguru, Sidharthan. 2019. *Marrying for a Future: Transnational Sri Lankan Tamil marriages in the shadow of war*. Seattle: University of Washington Press.

Mayblin, Maya. 2010. *Gender, Catholicism, and Morality in Brazil: Virtuous husbands, powerful wives*. New York: Palgrave Macmillan.

Mayblin, Maya. 2014. 'The sacrifice untold: The monotony and incompleteness of self-sacrifice in northeast Brazil', *Ethnos* 79: 342–64.

Mazower, Mark (ed.). 2000. *After the War Was Over: Reconstructing the family, nation, and state in Greece, 1943–60*. Princeton, NJ: Princeton University Press.

McDonald, Henry. 2015. 'Ireland becomes first country to legalise gay marriage by popular vote'. *Guardian*, 23 May. https://www.theguardian.com/world/2015/may/23/gay-marriage-ireland-yes-vote.

McKinley, Robert. 2001. 'The philosophy of kinship: A reply to Schneider's *Critique of the Study of Kinship*'. In *The Cultural Analysis of Kinship: The legacy of David M. Schneider*, edited by Richard Feinberg and Martin Oppenheimer, 131–67. Urbana and Chicago: University of Illinois Press.

McKinnon, Susan. 2013. 'Kinship within and beyond the "movement of progressive societies"'. In *Vital Relations: Modernity and the persistent life of kinship*, edited by Susan McKinnon and Fenella Cannell, 39–62. Santa Fe: SAR Press.

McKinnon, Susan. 2017. 'Temperamental differences: The shifting political implications of cousin marriage in nineteenth-century America', *Social Analysis* 60: 31–46.

McKinnon, Susan. 2019a. 'Cousin marriage, hierarchy, and heredity: Contestations over domestic and national body politics in nineteenth-century America', *Journal of the British Academy* 7: 62–88.

McKinnon, Susan. 2019b. 'Reading the contested forms of nation through the contested forms of kinship and marriage'. In *The Cambridge Handbook of Kinship*, edited by Sandra Bamford, 605–28. Cambridge: Cambridge University Press.

McKinnon, Susan, and Fenella Cannell. 2013a. 'The difference kinship makes'. In *Vital Relations: Modernity and the persistent life of kinship*, edited by Susan McKinnon and Fenella Cannell, 3–38. Santa Fe: SAR Press.

McKinnon, Susan, and Fenella Cannell (eds). 2013b. *Vital Relations: Modernity and the persistent life of kinship*. Santa Fe: SAR Press.

Miles, Joanna, Perveez Mody and Rebecca Probert (eds). 2015. *Marriage Rites and Rights*. Oxford: Bloomsbury.

Mill, John Stuart. 1869. *The Subjection of Women*. London: Longman.

Mody, Perveez. 2008. *The Intimate State: Love-marriage and the law in Delhi*. New Delhi and Abingdon: Routledge.

Mody, Perveez. 2013. 'Marriages of convenience and capitulation: South Asian marriage, family and intimacy in the diaspora'. In *The Handbook of the South Asian Diaspora*, edited by Joya Chatterji and David Washbrook. London: Routledge.

Mody, Perveez. 2015. 'Marriage'. In *International Encyclopedia of the Social and Behavioural Sciences*, edited by James D. Wright, 599–604. Oxford: Elsevier.

Morgan, Lewis H. 1871. *Systems of Consanguinity and Affinity of the Human Family*. Washington, DC: Smithsonian Institution Press.

Morgan, Lewis H. 1877. *Ancient Society: Researches in the lines of human progress from savagery through barbarism to civilization*. New York: Holt.

Needham, Rodney. 1971. 'Remarks on the analysis of kinship and marriage'. In *Rethinking Kinship and Marriage*, edited by Rodney Needham. London: Tavistock.

Ó Callai, Éanna, and Mark Hilliard. 2015. 'Ireland becomes first country to approve same-sex marriage by popular vote'. *Irish Times*, 23 May. https://www.irishtimes.com/news/politics/ireland-becomes-first-country-to-approve-same-sex-marriage-by-popular-vote-1.2223646.

Oppong, Christine. 2009 [1974]. *Marriage among a Matrilineal Elite: A family study of Ghanaian senior civil servants*. Cambridge: Cambridge University Press.

Osella, Caroline. 2012. 'Desires under reform: Contemporary reconfigurations of family, marriage, love and gendering in a transnational South Indian matrilineal Muslim community', *Culture and Religion* 13: 241–64.

Padilla, Mark B., Jennifer S. Hirsch, Miguel Munoz-Laboy, Robert Sember and Richard G. Parker (eds). 2007. *Love and Globalization: Transformations of intimacy in the contemporary world*. Nashville, TN: Vanderbilt University Press.

PA Media. 2020. 'First same-sex marriage takes place in Northern Ireland'. *Guardian*, 11 February. https://www.theguardian.com/uk-news/2020/feb/11/first-same-sex-marriage-northern-ireland-belfast-robyn-peoples-sharni-edwards.

Parry, Jonathan. 2020. *Classes of Labour: Work and life in a central Indian steel town*. Abingdon: Routledge.

Patico, Jennifer. 2009. 'For love, money, or normalcy: Meanings of strategy and sentiment in the Russian-American matchmaking industry', *Ethnos* 74: 307–30.

Pauli, Julia. 2019. *The Decline of Marriage in Namibia: Kinship and social class in a rural community*. Bielefeld: Transcript.

Pauli, Julia, and Rijk van Dijk. 2016. 'Marriage as an end or the end of marriage? Change and continuity in southern African marriages', *Anthropology of Southern Africa* 39: 257–66.

Paxson, Heather. 2004. *Making Modern Mothers: Ethics and family planning in urban Greece*. Berkeley: University of California Press.

Pinney, Christopher. 2005. 'Things happen, or from which moment does that object come?' In *Materiality*, edited by Daniel Miller, 256–72. Durham, NC: Duke University Press.

Radcliffe-Brown, A.R., and Daryll Forde (eds). 1950. *African Systems of Kinship and Marriage*. London: Oxford University Press.

Rebhun, Linda-Anne. 1999. *The Heart is Unknown Country*. Stanford, CA: Stanford University Press.

Reece, Koreen M. 2019. '"We are seeing things": Recognition, risk, and reproducing kinship in Botswana's time of AIDS', *Africa* 89: 40–60.
Rose, Phyllis. 2020 [1983]. *Parallel Lives: Five Victorian marriages*. London: Daunt.
Rubin, Gayle. 1975. 'The traffic in women: Notes on the "political economy of sex"'. In *Toward an Anthropology of Women*, edited by Rayna Reiter, 157–210. New York: Monthly Review Press.
Rutherford, Danilyn. 2015. 'Introduction: about time', *Anthropological Quarterly* 88: 241–50.
Segalen, Martine. 2003. *Éloge du mariage*. France: Gallimard.
Shaw, Alison. 2006. 'The arranged transnational cousin marriages of British Pakistanis: Critique, dissent and cultural continuity', *Contemporary South Asia* 15: 209–20.
Shaw, Alison, and Katherine Charsley. 2006. '*Rishtas*: Adding emotion to strategy in understanding British Pakistani transnational marriages', *Global Networks* 6: 405–21.
Shaw, Alison, and Aviad Raz (eds). 2020. *Cousin Marriages: Between tradition, genetic risk and cultural change*. Oxford: Berghahn.
Shryock, Andrew. 2013. 'It's this, not that: How Marshall Sahlins solves kinship', *HAU: Journal of Ethnographic Theory* 3: 271–9.
Solway, Jacqueline. 2016. '"Slow marriage", "fast *bogadi*": Change and continuity in marriage in Botswana', *Anthropology Southern Africa* 39: 309–22.
Ssorin-Chaikov, Nikolai. 2006. 'On heterochrony: Birthday gifts to Stalin, 1949', *Journal of the Royal Anthropological Institute* 12: 355–75.
Stacey, Judith. 2011. *Unhitched: Love, marriage, and family values from West Hollywood to western China*. New York: NYU Press.
Thelen, Tatjana, and Erdmute Alber (eds). 2018. *Reconnecting State and Kinship*. Pittsburgh: University of Pennsylvania Press.
Thompson, Charis. 2007. *Making Parents: The ontological choreography of reproductive technologies*. Cambridge, MA: MIT Press.
Trautmann, Thomas, Gillian Feeley-Harnik and John C. Mitani. 2011. 'Deep kinship'. In *Deep History: The architecture of past and present*, edited by Andrew Shryock and Daniel Lord Smail, 160–88. Berkeley: University of California Press.
van Dijk, Rijk. 2013. 'Counselling and Pentecostal modalities of social engineering of relationships in Botswana', *Culture, Health and Sexuality* 15: 509–22.
Weston, Kath. 1991. *Families We Choose: Lesbians, gays, kinship*. New York: Columbia University Press.
Weston, Kath. 1995. 'Forever is a long time: Romancing the real in gay kinship ideologies'. In *Naturalizing Power: Essays in feminist cultural analysis*, edited by Sylvia Yanagisako and Carol Delaney, 87–110. New York: Routledge.
Williams, Susan. 2007. *Colour Bar: The triumph of Seretse Khama and his nation*. London: Penguin.
Winter, Jay. 1995. *Sites of Memory, Sites of Mourning: The Great War in European cultural history*. Cambridge: Cambridge University Press.
Wray, Helena. 2006. 'An ideal husband? Marriages of convenience, moral gate-keeping and immigration to the UK', *European Journal of Migration and Law* 8: 303–20.
Yan, Yunxiang. 2003. *Private Life under Socialism*. Stanford, CA: Stanford University Press.
Yan, Yunxiang. 2005. 'The individual and transformation of bridewealth in rural North China', *Journal of the Royal Anthropological Institute* 11: 637–58.
Yanagisako, Sylvia J. 2002. *Producing Culture and Capital: Family firms in Italy*. Princeton, NJ: Princeton University Press.
Yanagisako, Sylvia, and Carol Delaney (eds). 1995. *Naturalising Power: Essays in feminist cultural analysis*. New York and London: Routledge.

1
Go fiwa molao/giving the law: marriage, law and social change in Botswana

Koreen M. Reece

> Most of us, although we are Bechuana, do not know our laws and customs.
>
> (Customary court attendee, in Schapera 1938, viii)

'And stay away from phones! Phones destroy marriages!'

I could scarcely see her between the scarved heads of the women seated around me, but the woman speaking was projecting her voice loudly enough that everyone in the *lelwapa*, or courtyard, could hear. With her heavy, blue-checked blanket pinned round her shoulders, she was seated near the centre of the crowd, immediately behind the carefully concealed figure of the bride – to whom her remonstrations on the management of modern technology were directed.

The woman expanded on the threat posed by mobile phones in some detail. She advised the bride never to look at her husband's phone; simply to tell him when it was ringing, never to answer it or check who it was; but always to show him who was calling her, whom she was texting and what she was saying. The woman went on to explain that the bride would now have many obligations to attend family events, and that she should always tell her husband where she was going well in advance, and return promptly when the event was over. If her husband was inexplicably absent or late to return home, however, she must not question where he'd been. Her children, she was warned, would take her the way she took her husband; and so she must heed him, if she wanted to be heeded.

It was impossible to gauge how the bride was reacting. Braced on either side by her mother's brothers' wives, she was covered from head to

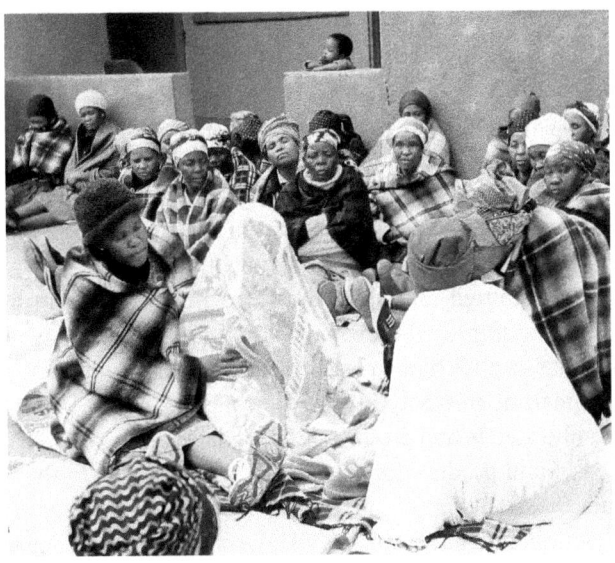

Figure 1.1 *Go fiwa molao*: Batswana women 'give the law' to the new bride, covered in blankets. © Koreen M. Reece.

toe in heavy blankets (see Figure 1.1). Across the *lelwapa*, women from the groom's family sat on carefully stitched-together sacks laid on the ground for them, their ranks of blanketed shoulders running three deep. Mirroring them from against the wall of the house, we too sat in rows with our legs stretched out in front of us, taking care not to dirty one another's skirts and blankets with the dusty soles of our shoes. Most of us remained silent, our heads bent to avoid the glare of the sun as it crept higher in the sky.

When the first woman finished, Mmapula[1] leaned in from the front row towards the bride, introducing herself and reminding the young woman how they were related, before beginning to offer her own input. Mmapula was the bride's *mmamalome* (her mother's brother's wife), and also the elderly matriarch of the family into which I had been absorbed years previously (see Reece in press). She had been involved in the wedding negotiations for months, and had asked me to drive her to the ceremony – called *patlo* – *go fiwa molao*, to give the law to the new bride. '*Patlo, le bogadi: ke lenyalo la Setswana*', she stressed; *patlo*, and bridewealth, make a Tswana marriage. 'But I'm not married – I won't be allowed in, will I?' I asked. 'Hm, we'll see', she'd responded, packing an extra blanket just in case. While she had successfully ensconced me in the event, I wouldn't hear the law Mmapula gave: she proceeded, at some length, in a whisper audible to no-one but the bride herself.

In this chapter, I ask: what does marriage tell us about law, what does law tell us about marriage, and what do both tell us about managing and producing social change in contemporary Botswana? Taking the lead of the mobile phone exhortations and whispered intervention above, I argue that marriage is not only a prominent subject of *molao*, or Tswana law, but a key means by which the law – both civil and customary – is produced, transmitted and changed. More than existing in a simply dialectic relationship – where changes in marital practice create new dilemmas that require new laws, with new laws opening new opportunities for marital creativity in turn (Strathern 2005) – I suggest that *molao* is embedded in and produced by marriage, as much as marriage is embedded in and produced by *molao*. Neither confined to the remit of courts and the discretion of judges, nor simply a matter of custom and culture (cf. Comaroff and Roberts 1981), *molao* on this reading emerges as a sort of 'ordinary ethics' (Lambek 2010) – a matter of everyday practice in ethical reflexivity and judgement, which permeates Botswana's parallel systems of customary and common law (Werbner 2014; see also Gluckman 1955). *Molao* is specifically oriented towards addressing disputes in ways that prioritise and protect opportunities for relational self-making (Alverson 1978; Reece 2019). But as we will see, it also emerges as a key means of making and navigating distinctions: by gender and generation, between legal forms, and between the domains of kinship and politics (McKinnon and Cannell 2013). To this extent, the practice of *molao* in weddings also shapes relations of power; but it does so in ways that are prone to disruption and reconfiguration, rather than simply enacting domination. And it is in this sense that the *molao* of marriage creates generative, if highly unpredictable, possibilities for social change.

Botswana provides a particularly apt context in which to consider these questions – not only for its rich veins of anthropological work on both law and marriage, stretching back to the colonial era, but because both have figured prominently in public imaginations of and reckonings with the rapid, vast changes the country has faced since it gained independence in 1966. Often called 'Africa's miracle', Botswana's postcolonial discovery of diamonds transformed the country from one of the poorest in the world to one of the wealthiest and most stable in southern Africa. But public anxiety about everything from Botswana's devastating Aids epidemic to its rampant rates of inequality is significant – and often condensed around concerns with the purported breakdown of families in general, and of marriage in particular. In public discourse, a 'crisis of care' feared to be destroying families since the onset of Aids has been echoed by a 'crisis of marriage', discerned in dwindling marriage rates and rising rates of cohabitation and divorce (Pauli and van Dijk 2016). And indeed, while it remains a highly valued goal, for over a generation marriage has proven increasingly rare and difficult to attain (compare Chiu in this volume on the difficulties both of marrying and of remaining single in Jinmen, Taiwan). Young people and their elders often blame one another for this impasse, decrying demands for increasingly showy, lavish celebrations, or expensive expectations of *bogadi* (bridewealth; see Solway 2019). This discourse of crisis is neither imported nor imposed, but part of a genre,[2] which offers a means of engaging and directing social change in meaningful, manageable terms. Community leaders, churches, NGOs and government alike have cast marriage as a potential panacea to the epidemic (van Dijk 2010), and to the full range of apparent social and moral failures to which Aids has drawn attention. Marriage, in other words, is broadly understood to be both a bellwether and a key mechanism of social change in Botswana.

This understanding of marriage has a long history in Botswana, dating at least as far back as the colonial era; and it has been bound up with the management of marriage in law throughout. Marriage became a site of notable jural innovation in Tswana customary law during and after the time of the British protectorate (Comaroff and Roberts 1977), as changing socio-economic realities – especially around labour migration (Gulbrandsen 1986) – generated new dilemmas and disputes between spouses and their families, creating imperatives and opportunities for new precepts to be introduced. Missionaries in all the major *merafe* (tribal polities; sing. *morafe*) of Botswana prioritised the eradication of polygamy and bridewealth as key to the Christianisation and 'civilisation' of the country, and were supported in their efforts by colonial administrators (Comaroff and Comaroff 1991). But that history has been beset by ambivalent results. While polygamy has long been illegal in Botswana's common law, it remains possible in principle under customary law, and a man could marry different wives under different legal regimes. Many argue that polygamy has simply shape-shifted into a widespread concubinage that particularly disadvantages women (see Comaroff and Roberts 1977; Solway 1990). And bridewealth remains a central feature of marriage, having become, by some accounts, more expensive and rigidly implemented in the process. A similar ambivalence characterises contemporary marriage interventions. While the rate of marriage appears to be picking up again in some parts of Botswana – with younger couples marrying more quickly than their forebears, at greater expense, sometimes with the assistance of churches and community-based initiatives – public concern has refocused on purportedly skyrocketing rates of divorce, raising persistent questions about what these modern marriages might mean.

I suggest that the ambivalent afterlives of attempts to create social change by changing marriage practice have to do, at least in part, with the relationship between Tswana marriage and Tswana law, or *molao* (pl. *melao*). Historically, Tswana marriage has been described as highly processual and ambiguous, unmarked by ritual events and stretched out over long periods of time (Comaroff and Roberts 1977). On this understanding, marriage was only definitively defined in dispute, when the intervention of the law was required – often in hindsight, at or after a relationship's termination. And indeed, these sorts of disputes form the major preoccupation not only of Tswana customary law, but also of the extensive anthropological literature on Tswana law (see, for example, Comaroff and Roberts 1977; Griffiths 1997; Schapera 1938). But, I suggest, switching focus to look at law from the perspective of marriage offers a very different picture of what the law is, and of how marriage – for our present purposes, weddings specifically – structures sociality through law. And this perspective gives us a new approach to long-standing debates around whether *mekgwa le melao ya Setswana*, Tswana laws and customs, are best understood as an undifferentiated, interchangeable repertoire of norms (Comaroff and Roberts 1977, 1981; Roberts 1979, 1985); a spectrum differentiable in terms of what is and isn't enacted, enforced or punished by the customary court, the *kgotla* (Schapera 1983); or something else altogether.

Tswana weddings are characterised by multiple events, among which couples and their families may choose more or less freely, depending on their values and priorities. Most include a formal notification, made in person by the potential groom's family to the potential bride's, that they are seeking a wife, followed by negotiations on the form of the wedding and the terms of *bogadi*, or bridewealth. Most also include mass ceremonies either at the *kgotla* or at the District Administrator's office; church ceremonies; the prestation of *bogadi*; *patlo*, or advice-giving ceremonies, held separately for the bride and groom; and feasts, one at the home of the bride, and a second at the home of the groom. These events may happen over a few days, or over weeks, months and even years. Each secures recognition of the union in specific spheres – in common law, customary law or the eyes of the church, for example – but none secures recognition in all spheres on its own (Reece 2019). In the next two sections, I explore the possibilities sketched above by comparing two of these wedding events: *patlo*, the ceremony introduced above; and a mass wedding conducted by a local non-governmental organisation (NGO). The first, as Mmapula pointed out, is a crucial dimension of Tswana customary marriage; the second a means of enabling and legitimating marriages under common law, and in the eyes of the state. In the first, I examine how *patlo* among the Balete *morafe* (polity) in south-eastern Botswana transmits, contests and changes *molao* in ways to which gender segregation and secrecy are key. In the second, I consider how civil weddings figure in the transmission and transformation of *molao* as well, and in producing distinctions between Botswana's parallel systems of customary and common law – as well as between the spheres of the domestic and the political.

Patlo: gender, secrecy and *molao*

'Ah! A o a apara Setswana jaanong?' ('Are you wearing Setswana then?').[3] Modiri and his brother Moagi greeted me with surprise as Mmapula and I arrived back in the yard, noting my tailored German-print skirt and white shirt with approbation. They sat near the fire, pouring out tea from an enamel kettle for our neighbour Rra Ditau. '*Akere* we are from *patlo*', I pointed out, knowing this would surprise them further. Laughing, they asked how I managed to get into *patlo* without being married. I indicated that Mmapula had sneaked me in. 'And I heard everything!' I added, provoking more laughter. 'Well, everything except what *Mma* said, she was whispering', I admitted. '*Ee*, because I didn't want you to hear!' Mmapula rejoined, making everyone laugh again. 'And are you going to explain our secrets to white people now?' Rra Ditau asked, giving me a mischievous look. 'Agh, what can they do with our secrets?' Mmapula wondered rhetorically, sitting down to her tea.

Patlo is not understood the same way everywhere in Botswana. Friends from other *merafe* (tribal polities) associated the term with the process of marriage negotiations, starting when the groom-to-be's family approached the bride-to-be's kin; and indeed much of the literature on marriage in Botswana understands the term the same way (e.g. Schapera 1940; Comaroff 1982). The noun *patlo* is derived from the verb *go batla*, to seek. But when I asked Balete friends about this interpretation, they were unequivocal: '*Patlo* is *patlo*', one said; 'Negotiations are different.' She described her husband's kin's visits to her family as *go itisa mafoko*, to bring word, or to make known/notify – implying a rather different understanding of negotiation as well.[4] Among the Balete, the ritual I describe here began with the bride-to-be's in-laws making a formal, collective and repeated request for the bride – *re kopa ngwetsi*, we ask for a daughter-in-law – but was conducted long after the negotiations had been concluded. For the Balete, the primary purpose of *patlo* was *go fiwa molao* (to give the law), also described as *go laya* – to instruct, exhort or advise (Matumo 1993, 187). The noun *molao* is derived from *go laya*, as is *taolo*, for authority or power, and *ditaolo*, for the lots used by diviners (Werbner 2015). *Go laya* appears in different forms in the wedding ceremonies of different *merafe*, but is common to most; and, as its etymology implies, it is distinguished from simple advice-giving by its relation to power. The meanings and practice of *patlo* seem likely to have followed different historical trajectories among different *merafe* – much as customary law itself has done.

For Balete, *patlo* is a singular, gender-segregated and (at least nominally) secret event. It is generally held early in the morning, usually the morning after the couple has been wed by the local District Administrator in a mass ceremony under the common law. And it usually precedes the payment of bridewealth on the part of the groom's kin, which in turn precedes the feast. While we sat in the *lelwapa* giving the new bride the law, the groom, men from his family and men from the bride's had convened elsewhere. Sometimes the men convened in a nearby *lelwapa*, but sometimes they preferred the *kgotla*, or customary court; and usually they came together earlier than the women, in order to finish before them. Any children or members of the opposite sex who stumbled upon either event were scolded for their impropriety and promptly chased off. And, as the brothers' and neighbours' teasing above suggests, anything said at *patlo* was subject to censorship.

The actual secrecy of *patlo* was, of course, somewhat partial. While unmarried women are not supposed to hear the *molao* given there, to which only married women ought to be privy, many of its precepts were subject to widespread rumour and speculation, and were already familiar to me. I recognised the saying 'A man is to be cooked for' immediately, an injunction that was both literal and a coded reminder that a husband was owed sex on demand; also 'A man is an axe, he is to be loaned around', meaning both that his labour should be made freely available to his kin and neighbours, and that his affections may also be borrowed by others, which a good wife must simply accept. But the principle of secrecy, more than its strict observation, meant that one could never be entirely certain what was being said in any given *patlo* ceremony. Even attendance was no guarantee of insight: whispering to the bride as Mmapula had done was not uncommon, such that the only one who could be sure of everything that was said was the bride herself.[5] Combined with the principle of segregation, this secrecy meant that one could never be sure what one's spouse was hearing, either. As one friend commented, anticipating her own forthcoming wedding:

> *Kana* the way they do *patlo*, you will never know what the men have told your husband, and he will never know what you have been told. We are not even supposed to tell each other, and anyway you could say anything you want! So how do you know if he's doing something he shouldn't?

Like other forms of customary law in the region, then, the *molao* given at *patlo* is scripted, but highly indeterminate, subject to discretion and interpretation (see also Gluckman 1955). The underlying message – that the bride ought to defer to her husband, respect and care for his family, and avoid questioning him or fomenting conflict with his kin – was consistent, but demonstrated by way of different, sometimes even contradictory examples (see Ellece 2011). In this sense, *patlo* might also be understood as a ritualized form of ordinary ethics (Lambek 2010). The law the bride is given is not so much a set of ordinances as a set of perspectives and practices, focused on 'everyday comportment and understanding', 'drawn into and drawn from the ordinary' (Lambek 2010, 3). It is a law of precedent, focused less on abstract values than on daily interactions, with specific implications for relations between the self and others – especially newly dangerous others, the bride's new kin. The fact that *molao* is given by the bride's natal kin as well as her new in-laws – who may come from different *merafe* with quite different *melao* – underscores both tacit agreement (Lambek 2010, 2) and the simultaneous likelihood of divergence and contestation.

Perhaps above all, *molao* is shaped less by the threat of sanction or punishment than by uncertainty and ambiguity, and the necessity of continuous consideration and assessment. As Richard Werbner (2015) has demonstrated in his ethnography of Tswapong wisdom divination, making the hidden seen is a key dimension of Tswana ethical practice; but equally, it is the things remaining unseen that require and enable interpretation and ethical reflexivity – and *molao* works to guide this reflexivity in part by keeping such things opaque. While the secrecy with which *patlo* is conducted conveys an air of acquiring arcane knowledge, it is more a knowing *how* than a knowing *that*; and it is partial at best, the first step in an ongoing process of skill acquisition (cf. Werbner 2009, 450; also Magee in this volume on the work of marriage and self-making). It is perhaps in this sense that, as the man quoted by the colonial-era administrator in the epigraph to this chapter claimed – at a *kgotla* no less, where laws and customs are weighed, debated and pronounced upon regularly – Batswana may not 'know' their laws and customs, and yet be continuously engaged in practising, challenging and refiguring them.

But the secrecy and gender segregation of *patlo* meant these powers of discretion, interpretation and innovation were lodged with unexpected figures. One day, as we were discussing weddings we'd been attending over the weekend, I asked a friend at the University of Botswana what she thought about the sort of advice given at *patlo*. Having married into a different but nearby *morafe*, she understood *patlo* the same way the Balete did, but had had slightly different experiences of it. 'We've changed the advice we give these days', she noted. 'We decided to stop saying some of those other things, about a man being an axe and so on. You can't advise people like that these days, not with Aids.' Surprised, I admitted I hadn't realised that *molao* was so easily revised – though it made sense of what I'd heard about mobile phones. 'Yes, we change it, we can adapt to the circumstances. And you know, some people just say what they want, quietly, so the others can't hear.' We laughed, and I admitted feeling overwhelmed by a sense of pressure just listening at *patlo*, in spite of being deeply sceptical of some of the pronouncements made. She chuckled, and looked reflective for a moment.

> I remember after mine, my mother was there in the house after they took me back in. And I was so scared and overwhelmed by everything they said! I was just thinking, this is not how I want my marriage to be. But my mother just said, 'Don't worry about them, they are just talking. You will figure things out for yourself.'

Giving the law at *patlo* anticipates future problems that may beset the marriage, their causes and effects, and how they might be avoided. As the problems themselves change – moving into the new medium of mobile phones, for example – they invite novel interpretations of causal logics and suitable responses. The question of how specific problems will be addressed should they arise, by whom, using what rationales, is left to be inferred, learned or invented in practice. While they are guided by shared precedent and experience, none of these things is fixed; they are characterised by ambiguity and doubt, and require continuous reflexivity and the exercise of judgement (the 'fulcrum of everyday ethics': Lambek 2010, 26; see also Papadaki in this volume on how spouses reflect on and assess change in selves and relationships). And both reflexivity and judgement must be cultivated and demonstrated over time, requiring creativity and innovation (Faubion 2010; Laidlaw 2002, 315). Rather than laying down a fixed law, *patlo* equips the bride for an ongoing, open-ended ethical engagement, in which her ability *go itirela*, to make-for-herself, is deeply implicated (on *go itirela*, see Alverson 1978, 133; also Reece 2019 on self-making and marriage).[6] She must, ultimately, figure things out for herself. 'In Botswana, the ethical temporality' – like the temporality of self-making – 'is the present continuous' (Livingston 2019, 126); and both tap into extensive, only partially known histories, and anticipate a wide range of possible futures, including the potential for shaping change.

Of course, just as not just anyone can attend *patlo*, not just anyone can give the law, and not just anyone can, or does, change it. For the bride, the task is preferentially undertaken by the wives of maternal uncles (the bride's, or her mother's), or by other elder women. The mother of the bride is often barred from the event – especially if she is unmarried (see Solway 2019 on the marginalisation of single people in Tswana weddings) – and generally remains inside the house. While any married women may attend, younger and more recently married women remain silent. The participation of divorced women is subject to conflicting opinion: while they have been given the law, the question of whether their experience of marital discord uniquely qualifies or disqualifies them from giving the law in turn is hotly debated. As one friend noted, there is a difference between *go tsa molao*, taking the law, and *go kgona molao*, being able to live or manage the law. While my friend from the university described novel adaptations, the exhortations we heard at the outset of this chapter echo long-standing expectations that above all, wives should defer to their husbands and their husbands' kin. As in the telling of the lots by wisdom diviners, in *patlo* 'patriarchy is elaborated as a fundamental moral order' (Werbner 2016, 85; see also Ellece 2011; Solway 2019). At the same time, 'this elaboration . . . is different from the world of everyday experience, where values of patriarchy are . . . argued over, contested, and sometimes marginalized' (Werbner 2016, 85). As my friend's observations demonstrate, those who do not give the law at one *patlo* may well be called upon to give it at another, may discuss what ought to be said with others, may adjust it based on insight from their own and others' experiences, and adapt it to changing socio-political circumstances. And ultimately, the everyday practice of *molao*, in the management of disputes at home, will rest with the bride and groom, and be shaped by their respective judgement and discretion and negotiations between them – as well as that of the kin who negotiated their marriage and might be called in to mediate their difficulties as well.

Molao, then, structures distinctions and hierarchies, by gender and generation; it shapes patterns of power (see Carsten in this volume on how marriage engenders ethical reflections that are simultaneously intimate and political). But it also asserts connections across these distinctions, destabilising those patterns. Thus, men and women both acquire and give *molao* separately, and the *molao* given to a woman specifies her responsibility to cede to her husband (see Ellece 2011 on the language of *patlo*). Only married people who have successfully overseen the negotiation of others' conflicts and major life events can give the law, generally to the children of their siblings (for men) or siblings-in-law (for women). But these structures prove somewhat fluid and inclusive. Internal contradictions in the advice given both to men and to women (Ellece 2011) create the room for, and necessity of, ongoing interpretation. A form of knowledge like a skill – acquired, practised and executed with greater or lesser success – *molao* must be exercised and refined over time, in a variety of contexts within and beyond the family. The opportunity to influence, reconfigure or change the law comes only after a great deal of experience in exercising it; but *molao* is, in principle, something enacted and adjudicated by everyone, and potentially subject to change by anyone – particularly once they are married.

In this sense, *patlo* is reminiscent of initiation, which is also gender-segregated, highly secretive, exclusively managed by those who have been initiated, and oriented towards the transmission of *molao*. When initiated men returned to Dithaba, they were greeted with the call, '*O tla nyala!*' – 'You will marry!' The connection underscores the fact that not only is acquiring the law, and in particular the ability to negotiate disputes (Reece 2019), a crucial means of making one's self, but also that self-making is a fundamentally relational, and ethical, endeavour. *Patlo* creates joint opportunities for self-making, on the part of the couple, their kin, those giving them the law and attending the event alike – opportunities shared as well as differentiated between genders, and across generations. More than a question of political maneuvering (*pace* Comaroff and Roberts 1981), self-making on this reading is a matter of ethical training and experience, the cultivation of judgement, enabling the extension of one's own relationships and the relationships of others.

The flexibility of *molao* in *patlo* echoes its dynamism and adaptability in the *kgotla* (Comaroff and Roberts 1977; Schapera 1970), but under radically different conditions. Where the *kgotla* relies on transparency, on debate and active consensus-building, and on the leadership and innovation of the *kgosi* (chief), *patlo* relies on secrecy, on assertion and the performance of an apparently pre-achieved consensus, led by married elders and maternal kin. While the *molao* at stake is roughly common to both, then, it also enacts a clear distinction between the family and the *kgotla*, and between the modes of negotiation that are appropriate to each.

Of course, *molao* is not confined to either kin or *kgotla*. In the next section, I turn to investigate how it is deployed by NGOs and the state in mass weddings, and with what effects.

A mass wedding: states, NGOs and *molao*

'*Ga leitse melao ya lelwapa!*' the speaker asserted to the couples, families and guests gathered under the vast white tent: you don't know the laws of the family (or home). 'Let's learn about them, so you can govern yourselves. We will teach you about customary law, we will teach you about English law, civil law, we will teach you about the law of the church, and the Bible. We will teach you what marriage means.'

The speaker stood behind a long table draped in white, flanked by the village *kgosi* (chief), the District Administrator and the Minister of Local Government – an exceptionally influential head table for a wedding. Annah Morwaakgole[7] was the founder of an NGO dedicated to facilitating the marriage of cohabiting couples, called Re a Nyalana (We Are Marrying). Seated at the round tables that filled the tent, dressed in shiny grey suits and elaborate white dresses, were eight such couples, mostly elderly, who had come with their family and friends to be wed at the village *kgotla*. They brought the count for couples married by the NGO in the village to 53 since 2016; and they joined well over two thousand other couples married nationally under Re a Nyalana's auspices since its inception in 2011.

While I half-expected her to launch into a disquisition on the laws of the family on the spot, Annah confined herself to referencing the Administration of Estates Act, Chapter 31:01 – a designation that made it sound uncannily like a Bible verse – before moving on to describe astronomical rates of divorce in the country, and linking them to the fact that couples simply hadn't been taught the law properly. In families where the parents had lived and built together but weren't married, and therefore didn't know or enjoy the protection of the law, she explained, potential disasters abounded: partners and children could be disinherited if the couple split or one partner died; children might be mistreated, their rights to care and maintenance left unprotected; the risk of domestic violence went up; fathers could not claim bridewealth on behalf of their marrying daughters; and so on. Re a Nyalana's pre-marital workshops, she noted – which all of the marrying couples had attended, and which covered the full range of legal systems, as well as emotional intelligence and communication, self-awareness and tips on building sustainable incomes – were a key means of ensuring people were married properly, educated in and brought under the protection of the law.

The *kgotla* was packed with the extended families, friends and neighbours of the marrying couples, though most of them stayed outside the tent, the tables of which were peopled with influential political figures and businessmen from the area. Botswana Television (BTV) was recording the whole proceedings so that memorable clips could be included on the evening news. Re a Nyalana enjoyed support from the Ministries of Local Government and of Gender, and most prominently from Botswana's new first lady, as well as reliable, positive coverage from the government news media; but not, as Annah often noted with chagrin, the financial support it needed. Botswana's highest-profile NGOs – especially orphan care centres – tended to be heavily funded by foreign donors, bound up in the networks of (and occasionally managed by) expatriates. While she was well networked herself, Annah's project struggled to draw the same interest and investment. Re a Nyalana offered a distinctly Setswana answer to a problem conceived in distinctly Setswana terms, based on a distinctly Setswana logic of social change; but it was institutionalised awkwardly in the transnational genre of the NGO, with its alternative logics, means and methods.

Every speaker at the event – from the *kgosi*, or village chief, to the Minister – took a tack similar to Annah's welcoming speech. Each stressed the growing prevalence of moral and legal *dikgang* – conflicts, problems or issues – with which contemporary Tswana families were beset (see Reece 2019, and Reece in press on *dikgang*). They described *dikgang* arising at funerals, where the deceased's partner might be dismissed as simply a friend without rights. The Minister spoke of the *dikgang* afflicting *masiela*, orphaned children, who were especially prone to abuse and disinheritance if their parents were not married. Special disapprobation was reserved for those '*go rata boswa jo ba sa bo itirelang*', who like to take inheritances from others that they have not made for themselves. '*Re na le melao*', the Minister stressed – we have laws – naming the Children's Act, Marriage Act and Married Persons' Property Act as examples. But for couples who were unmarried, all of the speakers asserted, the *dikgang* that arise were more than these acts in the civil law, or than the *kgosi* administering customary law, could address. Marriage was both the best way to avoid these issues, and the only way to access the laws that would help address them. Law, in the speakers' collective description, was necessary to sustaining marriage; and marriage also sustains the law. *Molao* and marriage, in other words, give each other meaning.

Much as *patlo* was a key event for transmitting *molao*, so too was Re a Nyalana's mass wedding. The NGO's approach was not so different from the civil marriage ceremonies I had seen conducted in District Administrators' (DA) offices, and the presence of the DA as officiant underscored the extent to which Re a Nyalana sought to adapt and facilitate government practice: DAs also conduct mass civil weddings, preceded by several meetings with marrying couples to advise them on relevant civil laws. And to some extent, the *molao* described at these mass weddings is reminiscent of that given the bride at *patlo*. The *molao* of *patlo* also sought to help the bride anticipate and avoid disputes, and offered clues as to how disputes would be handled if they could not be avoided. Her marriage allowed the *molao* to be passed on, and in time would enable her to practise and adapt it in negotiating the disputes of others as well. But beyond this shared orientation around the relational management of disputes among kin, the law being given at the mass wedding took a very different shape. The NGO founder listed all the kinds of law to which Batswana find themselves subject – customary, civil (or common) and church – but the mass wedding simultaneously introduced a rigidity to their interpretation, and a stratification among them, while foreclosing the means by which Batswana might expect to practise, contest, interpret and innovate with those laws themselves.

Perhaps the most striking undertone of these speeches was the suggestion that the *kgosi*, as the most senior authority in customary law to whom many family or marital conflicts would be taken, could not adequately address those conflicts unless people were married. As we have seen, there is a long-standing precedent of chiefly intervention and innovation in Tswana law (Gulbrandsen 1996; Schapera 1970; Werbner 2014) – particularly around marriage and pregnancy (Comaroff and Roberts 1977; Griffiths 1997), given their historically processual and indeterminate character, and their resultant tendency to generate novel dilemmas in times of significant socio-political change. While marriage and *molao* have long taken their meaning from each other, then, the suggestion that *molao* was inflexible, non-negotiable or set in stone sat at odds with the historical exercise of *molao* in customary courts – and, I suspect, with the experience most of the wedding guests would have had of *molao* themselves. Like *patlo*, a civil marriage ceremony may mark a key site for the transmission of law; but the law it is preoccupied with transmitting, and ensuring the ascendancy of in a legally plural context, is civil or common law. And the common law is oriented less towards innovation than to straightforward reproduction of social order; less towards collective interpretation, ethical reflexivity and the managing of relationships over time than towards identifying and resolving issues conclusively.

As was the case at *patlo*, *molao* in this context is a matter of expertise and authority exclusively restricted to the law-holders and law-makers. But in this case, those figures are civil institutions – the government, the courts and the NGO. Therefore, the distinctions marked by *molao* at the mass wedding are not simply distinctions of gender, generation or marital status; they are distinctions and hierarchies among political institutions, and between those institutions and families as well.

The top of this hierarchy, represented at the mass wedding by the Minister, the District Administrator and his attendant clerks, was the government – which promulgated, enacted and adjudicated all of the Acts cited by the speakers above. While the *kgosi* and customary court took part in this authority, the suggestion that the *kgosi* could not satisfactorily resolve marital and familial disputes independently of these Acts explicitly downplayed the *kgotla*'s autonomy, and rendered customary law both separate from and implicitly subject to civil law. This positioning echoed the *kgosi*'s somewhat awkward role in government structures as well; the *kgotla* formally falls under the jurisdiction of the Ministry of Local Government, though it takes guidance in interpreting customary law from the House of Chiefs, a national body convened separately from (and nominally on a par with) Botswana's Parliament. Positioning itself as a broker and mediator, the NGO situated itself as an implementing partner of the government, subject to but also participating in its authority – deploying *molao* in ways that explicitly and literally legitimated it as a political actor.

The *molao* put to these ends is not, notably, the sort of thing that can be acquired, practised and interpreted by married people in their own right, to address their own issues or those faced by their married and unmarried relatives. Indeed, the *molao* of *patlo*, on these terms, is not properly *molao* at all. Neither *patlo* nor *bogadi* (bridewealth) featured in the NGO's mass weddings, explicitly left to families' discretion.[8] In the documents used for Re a Nyalana's pre-marital workshops, *patlo* was listed as a mechanism for 'illegal cohabitation' which could delay the proper legalisation of the marriage, leave children with their mother's surname and increase risks of disinheritance. Thus, though the speakers at the mass wedding posed marriage as a means of addressing ethico-legal issues that the *kgosi* and others could not otherwise solve, and attendant laws as means by which people might 'govern themselves', meaningful ways of addressing issues within the marriage itself were also stripped from couples and their kin. They were rendered subject to, rather than actors in, *molao*.

This disruption of the meanings and practice of *molao* was not without consequences. It also disrupted the meaning of the marriages the NGO facilitated. Many people I spoke to were sceptical about these mediated marriages, and had mixed feelings about what they might mean. While I was discussing the NGO wedding with Mmapula one day, she wondered pointedly, 'And who mediates for these people when they have problems later, the NGO?' Another friend questioned the families' priorities, when they could find money for wedding dresses, but not for *bogadi*; and she further questioned their inability to create alternative routes to marriage, including by mobilising participants for *patlo*, without the NGO's help. She underscored the carnivalesque aspect of these mass weddings by describing one conducted in her own village, at which young people from the community had laughed at the elderly couples, making derogatory comments about their appearance. '*Ga se molao*', she added, referring both to the youths' disrespectfulness and to the weddings themselves; it's not lawful, or it's not right. Her concern was not that the marriages facilitated by Re a Nyalana were not 'real'; far from it – she stressed the protection they offered from inheritance disputes as a necessary and positive outcome. Instead, her concerns were explicitly ethical: they cast doubt on both the couple's and their families' abilities to mobilise relationships, to make-for-themselves, and ultimately to contribute to the self-making of others in turn. Her concerns were similar to those emerging around new forms of 'fast *bogadi*' (Solway 2016), specifically their likelihood of ending in divorce. Casting doubt on these new modes of marriage may have been a means of drawing them into the familiar uncertainties and creative possibilities of the Tswana ethical world. Certainly it asserted these ethics as the primary standard against which the claims of NGOs, customary courts and the government alike to political legitimacy must be judged – all of which claims, in this case, fell short.

Conclusion

The Tswana use of *molao* draws our attention to the intricate relationships between customary and common law (Good 2015; Griffiths

1997, 208), the shared ethical concerns and projects that permeate and bind them (Werbner 2014) and the ways in which they are actively distinguished in practice – and work to distinguish genders, generations and the domains of family and politics in turn.

What counts here as 'law', I suggest, is less about what carries the threat of official sanction or punishment (*pace* Schapera 1938, 1983) and more about the skill and judgement that equips people effectively to negotiate conflict – familial conflict above all. I have described the ethics that underpin this undertaking in terms of enabling, facilitating and protecting the ability to self-make through relationships, especially with existing or potential kin. And I have noted that as much as the concept and practice of *molao* binds people, legal forms and institutions together, it also distinguishes and stratifies them. To the extent that these distinctions convey power – within, between and beyond families – the knowledge and practice of *molao* shapes power as well; but it is not simply a mechanism of domination, and remains prone to doubt, contestation and innovation, often in ways that cannot be anticipated or controlled. Indeed, practices like *patlo* insulate *molao* from co-optation into various forms of governance, providing 'avenues of escape and resistance' much like those deployed in the *kgotla* during the colonial era (Roberts 1985, 86; see also Gulbrandsen 1996). In this case, it enables families to exclude intervention by states, NGOs and transnational political projects, as chiefs and customary courts excluded colonial projects in the past (Roberts 1985, 86). The practice of *molao*, in other words, continuously preserves and extends the possibility of dispute, as well as offering a means of addressing it; and as such, is a crucial means of producing and reproducing kinship (Reece in press), as well as ethical sociality more broadly.

Marriage, specifically weddings, prove unexpectedly central to these processes – not just because they are subject to *molao*, but as key sites at which *molao* is produced, transmitted and potentially changed. But as we have seen above, the change that marriage stands to generate in and through the law is frequently unpredictable, and difficult to shape. Marriage may create the possibility of change, but it does so in ways that are largely insulated from instrumentalisation. While this intractability may frustrate government and NGO initiatives that seek to deploy marriage as a solution to complex social issues, it allows the possibility of highly dynamic, responsive and collective sorts of transformation to emerge among those who negotiate and undertake marriage, who give and receive the law. More than conservative institutions that simply reproduce the status quo, then, marriage and law emerge as interpersonal projects that open up spaces for unanticipated innovation – and for novel possibilities of social change.

Acknowledgements

I would like to thank Mmapula, the Legaes and other friends and colleagues in Botswana cited here for their limitless generosity, patience and engagement. Special thanks to Annah Morwaakgole for recounting her experiences with Re a Nyalana, and inviting me to a RaN wedding. This chapter has benefited significantly from the input of the AGATM team and advisory board; from Julia Pauli's extensive, incisive comments; and from Jackie Solway's experience and insight. Research was carried out with the permission and support of the Government of Botswana.

Notes

1   All names are pseudonyms, unless noted otherwise (for public figures).
2   See, for example, Klaits 2016, 417 on how critical doubt of kin sustains their collaboration; and Dahl 2009 on how concern with the 'failures of culture' helps to renew and reinvigorate Tswana 'cultural values'.
3   'Setswana' is the noun used to describe Tswana culture, as well as language; 'wearing Setswana' means wearing 'traditional' or culturally distinct clothes, especially to formal, public occasions. So-called 'German-print' material in fact originated in Manchester, and was a colonial-era introduction.
4   See Reece 2019 on marriage as a process of gradually acquiring recognition – in terms of making a conjugal relationship seen, heard and known.
5   Pnina Werbner describes a very similar practice at the end of Tswapong girls' initiations, in which elder women whisper instructions and advice to the neophyte – a process also known as laying down or giving the law (Werbner 2009, 450).
6   I use this emic phrase interchangeably with 'self-making', though not to connote Michel Foucault's techniques of the self (Foucault 1997). The Tswana notion bears a similarity to Foucault's 'subjectivation' – but not so much in terms of cultivating the relation of the self to the self, as in terms of cultivating relations between the self and others as an ethical project. The ethical question of how selves and relations should, could and do interact is central to all of the chapters in this volume, suggesting that marriage condenses and intensifies that puzzle, as well as offering a key site for engaging it.
7   Her real name.
8   Given that many (though not all) of the couples married under Re a Nyalana's auspices were elderly, and that Botswana is a largely gerontocratic society, their younger extended families were sometimes reluctant to hold *patlo* or negotiate the payment of bridewealth; but others insisted, in order to better enable their newly married parents to participate in future *patlo* or receive bridewealth from their children's marriages.

References

Alverson, Hoyt. 1978. *Mind in the Heart of Darkness: Value and self-identity among the Tswana of southern Africa*. London: Yale University Press.
Comaroff, John (ed.). 1982. *The Meaning of Marriage Payments*. London: Academic Press.

Comaroff, John, and Jean Comaroff. 1991. *Of Revelation and Revolution: Christianity, colonialism, and consciousness in South Africa*, vol. 1. Chicago: University of Chicago Press.

Comaroff, John, and Simon Roberts. 1977. 'Marriage and extra-marital sexuality: The dialectics of legal change among the Kgatla', *Journal of African Law* 21 (1): 97–123.

Comaroff, John, and Simon Roberts. 1981. *Rules and Processes: The cultural logic of dispute in an African context*. Chicago: University of Chicago Press.

Dahl, Bianca. 2009. 'The "failures of culture": Christianity, kinship, and moral discourses about orphans during Botswana's AIDS crisis', *Africa Today* 56 (1): 23–43.

Ellece, Sibonile Edith. 2011. '"Be a fool like me": Gender construction in the marriage advice ceremony in Botswana – a critical discourse analysis', *Agenda* 25 (1): 43–52.

Faubion, James D. 2010. 'From the ethical to the themitical (and back): Groundwork for an anthropology of ethics'. In *Ordinary Ethics: Anthropology, language, and action*, edited by Michael Lambek. New York: Fordham University Press.

Foucault, Michel. 1997. 'Technologies of the self'. In *Ethics: Subjectivity and truth*, edited by Paul Rabinow, 223–54. New York: New Press.

Gluckman, Max. 1955. *The Judicial Process among the Barotse of Northern Rhodesia (Zambia)*. Manchester: Manchester University Press for African Studies.

Good, Anthony. 2015. 'Folk models and the law', *Journal of Legal Pluralism and Unofficial Law* 47 (3): 423–37.

Griffiths, Anne. 1997. *In the Shadow of Marriage: Gender and justice in an African community*. Chicago: University of Chicago Press.

Gulbrandsen, Ørnulf. 1986. 'To marry – or not to marry: Marital strategies and sexual relations in a Tswana society', *Ethnos* 51 (1): 7–28.

Gulbrandsen, Ørnulf. 1996. 'Living their lives in courts: The counter-hegemonic force of the Tswana *kgotla*'. In *Inside and Outside the Law*, edited by Olivia Harris, 125–56. London: Routledge.

Klaits, Fred. 2016. 'Grasping, trust, and truth-on-balance', *Hau: Journal of Ethnographic Theory* 6 (3): 413–18.

Laidlaw, James. 2002. 'For an anthropology of ethics and freedom', *Journal of the Royal Anthropological Institute* 8: 311–32.

Lambek, Michael. 2010. 'Introduction'. In *Ordinary Ethics: Anthropology, language, and action*, edited by Michael Lambek, 1–36. New York: Fordham University Press.

Livingston, Julie. 2019. *Self-Devouring Growth: A planetary parable as told from southern Africa*. Durham, NC: Duke University Press.

Matumo, Z.I. 1993. *Setswana English Setswana Dictionary*. Gaborone: Macmillan.

McKinnon, Susan, and Fenella Cannell. 2013. 'The difference kinship makes'. In *Vital Relations: Modernity and the persistent life of kinship*, edited by Susan McKinnon and Fenella Cannell, 3–38. Santa Fe, NM: SAR Press.

Pauli, Julia, and Rijk van Dijk. 2016. 'Marriage as an end or the end of marriage? Change and continuity in southern African marriages', *Anthropology Southern Africa* 39 (4): 257–66.

Reece, Koreen M. 2019. '"We are seeing things": Recognition, risk, and reproducing kinship in Botswana's time of AIDS', *Africa* 89 (1): 40–60.

Reece, Koreen M. In press. *Pandemic Kinship: Families, intervention, and social change in Botswana's time of AIDS*. Cambridge: Cambridge University Press.

Roberts, Simon. 1979. *Order and Dispute: An introduction to legal anthropology*. Oxford: Martin Robertson.

Roberts, Simon. 1985. 'The Tswana polity and "Tswana law and custom" reconsidered', *Journal of Southern African Studies* 12 (1): 75–87.

Schapera, Isaac. 1938. *A Handbook of Tswana Law and Custom*. London: Oxford University Press.

Schapera, Isaac. 1940. *Married Life in an African Tribe*. London: Faber and Faber.

Schapera, Isaac. 1970. *Tribal Innovators: Tswana chiefs and social change, 1795–1940*. London: Athlone Press.

Schapera, Isaac. 1983. 'Tswana concepts of custom and law', *Journal of African Law* 27 (2): 141–9.

Solway, Jacqueline. 1990. 'Affines and spouses, friends and lovers: The passing of polygyny in Botswana', *Journal of Anthropological Research* 46 (1): 41–66.

Solway, Jacqueline. 2016. '"Slow marriage", "fast bogadi": Change and continuity in marriage in Botswana', *Anthropology Southern Africa* 39 (4): 309–22.

Solway, Jacqueline. 2019. 'Single in Botswana'. Paper given at the American Anthropological Association Annual Conference, November 2019 (cited by permission).

Strathern, Marilyn. 2005. *Kinship, Law and the Unexpected: Relatives are always a surprise.* Cambridge: Cambridge University Press.
van Dijk, Rijk. 2010. 'Marriage, commodification, and the romantic ethic in Botswana'. In *Markets of Well-Being: Navigating health and healing in Africa*, edited by Marleen Dekker and Rijk van Dijk. Leiden: Brill.
Werbner, Pnina. 2009. 'The hidden lion: Tswapong girls' puberty rituals and the problem of history', *American Ethnologist* 36 (3): 441–58.
Werbner, Pnina. 2014. '"The duty to act fairly": Ethics, legal anthropology, and labour justice in the Manual Workers Union of Botswana', *Comparative Studies in Society and History* 56 (2): 479–507.
Werbner, Richard. 2015. *Divination's Grasp: African encounters with the almost said.* Bloomington: Indiana University Press.
Werbner, Richard. 2016. 'The poetics of wisdom divination: Renewing the moral imagination', *Journal of the Royal Anthropological Institute* 23: 81–102.

2
'You can learn to do it right, or you can learn to do it wrong': marriage counselling, togetherness and creative conservatism in Lynchburg, Virginia

Siobhan Magee

It was early autumn 2017 and I was in Lynchburg, Virginia, discussing with Sean, a white pastor in his forties, what marriage is. *'Phoffff'*, he said, expelling air at the expansiveness of the topic.[1] In Sean's office, as in this religiously and politically diverse city that was nonetheless considered by inhabitants and outsiders alike as the nucleus of US Christian conservatism (Harding 2000), it was understood that 'everyday people' held the potential to excel at marriage. Marriage was not only a matter of personal pleasure, but something people 'believed in': a spiritual-cum-political conviction held by people who said they 'weren't political' (were not interested in electoral politics), the backbone of happy and 'healthy' communities and the source of 'secure and stable' children who would grow up to nurture their own covetable marriages and righteous communities. People recalled with misty eyes couples who stayed together until death, and who kept 'commitment', 'connection', 'grace', 'gratitude', 'laughter' and 'appreciation' in their lives half-centuries after being together had anything to do with becoming parents. These memorable couples worked at marriage in the wake of devastating losses: children taken from them by death or by dispute; debilitating accidents and chronic illness; addiction to alcohol, drugs, food, shopping, sex; infidelity; getting fired, rotten business deals and foreclosed homes; humiliations served by two-faced friends and gossipy church communities or workplaces; for Black and interracial couples, segregation and racism. Throughout all of this, I was told, 'successful' couples usually kept their clothes, houses and cars clean. They kept smiling while 'out in the community'. People got annoyed by their partners but said, 'It's not like I'm too perfect myself.' No-one wanted to go to bed on an argument. They *expected* to go through rough times.

Sean reflected on how one other notable thing about marriage is what a mess it can be. So many people mistook lust for love, he said. Pursuing fun rather than purpose and meaning, they chose the wrong spouse, or else they married 'someone special' but took them for granted when paid employment got either too tough (or too scarce) or too satisfying, or when going out socialising with single friends seemed appealing. Faith could not immunise a person from these difficulties. Sometimes God determined that a couple got engaged, but then the couple did not create a strong marriage. Sean worried that they hid from their problems and displayed 'emotional immaturity'. They did not think deeply about how to give to this chosen person. They did not think about how issues from their respective pasts might reproduce themselves in this new relationship. 'Marriage isn't a Band-Aid', Sean said. 'If anything, it's a magnifying glass that blows up your issues, your history. And a married person has the chance to confront that history, but it takes work. It's a process of humbling yourself.'

Through the lens of marriage counselling, in this chapter I discuss the 'kinship ideologies' (Weston 1991; Kowalski 2016) and the 'philosophy of kinship' (McKinley 2001) that surround marriage and individualism in a place where, I was told often, 'there's a lot of marriage, and a lot of divorce'. I focus on the idea that a happy and successful marriage requires a couple to work towards 'intimacy' (see Jamieson 1998; Mayblin 2014) and 'togetherness', while maintaining their respective individualities.

As an anthropological subject, marriage can make palpable features of life that are otherwise obscured. Marriage and the work it entails ('work' being a cherished US ideal but, of course, central to marriage in other places too; see Papadaki in this volume) add nuance to pictures of the various Christian conservative milieux with which many (but certainly not all) people in Lynchburg identified. Those who on paper might be considered 'individualistic' cherished community and often altruism, or *service* (see also Stafford 2018). In the era of 'Make America Great Again', conservativism capitalised on nostalgia, but also on the tenet that marriage can have 'positive impacts' on the futures of individuals, communities and nations. Dogma surrounded kinship and could make the expectations surrounding it oppressive, *and* this occurred together with infinitely creative ways of thinking about what marriage is – what I call 'creative conservatism'. Conservative discourses about 'stable family structures' and anxieties about divorce were accompanied for some by a fierce credence that a person must pursue 'selfless happiness' (which some said they saw as following God).

In US history, marriage has told a story about who is and who is not legally 'recognised' (Lewin 1998) as a full person: from free and enslaved people of colour (Hunter 2017; Cashin 2017) to women whose legal personhood was 'covered' by that of their husband (Cott 2000; Coontz 2005), to the long history of queer marriages denied a legal stamp of approval (Frank 2017; Cleves 2014). It has no doubt also reified race, gender and sexuality. Marriage reveals the conflicts and collusions between nation state, religion (especially Protestantism: see Cannell 2013), and both 'community-based' and formal legal systems (see Ginsburg 1989; Rapp 1999; Barnes 2016; Briggs 2017). In Lynchburg, conservative people's discussions of legally recognised same-sex marriage in the recent past often foregrounded how challenging being married can be and indexed 'rising divorce rates' as a lamentation not only about marriage but more broadly about how people are in the world, with God, with each other. 'Shame on us heterosexual folks if we've reached the point where gays and lesbians can see that we have in effect *insulted God* with the way we don't always appreciate marriage as a sacred covenant, you know?' said an engaged white evangelical marketing executive in his mid-twenties.

After spending some time in Lynchburg, I realised with surprise that I had begun to absorb some aspects of acquaintances' lamentations about 'the tragedy of divorce' – or perhaps it was 'the tragedy of marriage'? These anxieties revolved around the idea that getting married was a radical break in a person's biography but that most people were not equipped with practical or conceptual tools to make their marriage both happy and lasting. Watching couples being photographed in their wedding outfits next to war memorials on Monument Terrace, or seeing in the wooded area next to the James River red rose petals and burned-out tea lights evidencing a proposal the evening before, I found myself (on fieldwork with my husband and daughter) asking 'But how are they preparing for what's ahead?' Kendra, a hairstylist in her forties, an Italian-American married mother, told me that once you had heard lots of people's stories about their marriages, as was a feature of her job, 'you get a perspective where you see your faith community, or people at the gym, or people getting coffee and you think – when you know what they've been through with marriage – "these *everyday people* are *the walking wounded!*"'

'Yes!' I agreed.

David Schneider famously argued that it is the 'order of nature' that creates 'blood relatives' but it is the 'order of law' on which marriage is based (Schneider 1968). 'What distinguishes relatives by marriage', he wrote, 'is their relationship, their pattern for behaviour, the code for the conduct' (1968, 27). And yet, when one is married, aside from 'clear' infractions such as infidelity within monogamous relationships and physical abuse, what such a code of conduct entails can be up for grabs. In Lynchburg, what the new kinship studies often situate as the making of relatedness (Carsten 1995) – the 'everydayness' of living together, perhaps raising children, managing money, managing in-laws – was often the very stuff that, as one man put it, 'shattered the dream' of married life. The familiarity of marriage, its associations with 'tradition', conservativism even, and the likelihood that one knows people who are or who have been married, does not make it easier to do.

In Lynchburg, an upshot of this was widespread talk of marriage education, preparation, training and counselling that took place variously before and during marriages, and the naturalisation of marriage as a set of skills and a matter of advice (see Liberatore 2019) and expertise (Boyer 2008). Many said they believed strongly in small government and that God and most parents (or sometimes grandparents) rather than the state knew what was best for their children. However, a person's marriage was not only a 'private' relationship, but also a matter of their interactions with those from the wider community who had agreed to help 'guide' the relationship. Further, to work on one's marriage meant to work on one's own shortcomings, one's scars. This could be difficult because married life could cause a person, but perhaps particularly women, to 'forget who they are' (see Papadaki in this volume). Religious leaders, Christian charities, conservative think-tanks, YouTube videos, self-help books and lay people debating life's most consequential conundrums asked aloud: how can a person better themselves in order to become a better spouse? How can they stop themselves from being obscured by marriage?

Something that particularly intrigued me about marriage education was its use of visualisations, metaphors and similes. Isn't marriage *metaphysically* strange, this seemed to suggest. Those who received counselling and those who provided it did not take as a given what we might mean by 'the individual'. Sean, the pastor I mentioned at the beginning of this chapter, said that he wanted the couples he married to think about how marriage 'is not "oneness" because they're still two individuals'. Sean did not 'vet' couples who wanted him to marry them, but he did want to 'sit down' with them during their engagement. Everyone pointed out that 'a wedding and a marriage are very different things', but it was Sean's experience that discussing a couple's plans for their ceremony was a good time to provide counsel on their relationship after the wedding. Preferences for certain rituals revealed engaged people's conceptualisations of marriage, but also of the individual. Sean said:

> It's like the sand in the pillar [that some people use in a wedding ceremony], you can still see the two colours of sand. And it's a more interesting metaphor than the two tapers lighting the unity candle, which is another ritual people do. People ask for all kinds of little rituals – when they light the unity candle, then I frame that in language where your two personalities still burn yet you create something new together. Some people want to blow out their separate candles and I'm like, no, it's not about extinguishing yourself, it's about creating something more. And the sand, it's like you've created something new but you're still there. *Togetherness.*

The frequent visual and material metaphors in weddings and counselling sessions alike did not reduce or explain away kinship's 'ineffable' (Cannell 2013, 230) qualities. Instead, they made them even more expansive, facilitating a valued form of discursive communion where participants (a couple, a minister, wedding guests, etc.) found that in relationships there is more than there is in other 'realms' of life to be turned over and over in the mind. As therapist Christine Kerr writes,

> A primary goal of couples' therapy . . . is to disrupt conventional ways of thinking as well as to facilitate more open communication between each individual partner in a marriage (Kerr et al. 2008). To achieve this goal, visual imagery and verbal metaphor may be combined in a couple's treatment to help the couple identify and express their individual and interpersonal 'life metaphors'. (Kerr 2015, 7)

People I met in Lynchburg who were attached to a range of political and religious subjectivities emphasised how important it was that a married couple conceptualise themselves as being 'two rather than one'. This surprised me. In a city where people were remarkably invested in both 'family' and 'community', and said things like, 'Susan's been my dear friend since high school – we've lived in each other's pockets since 1965!', it seemed odd to downplay one's closeness to such a special companion as a spouse. I was familiar with the words from the Gospel of Matthew, 'So they are no longer two, but one flesh. Therefore what God has joined together, let no one separate' (19.6). And indeed, this had currency in Lynchburg. You could buy wall stickers ('vinyl decals') emblazoned with these words to stick behind a double bed, along with your and your spouse's names and wedding date. An engaged student and wedding photographer told me, 'It's about a couple putting their relationship first – including above the kids – but it's also a reminder to the rest of their community – *do not break them up!*' A church website showed the sentences that preceded 'one flesh': 'At the beginning of creation God made them male and female. For this reason a man will leave his father and mother and be united to his wife, and the two will become one flesh' (Genesis 2.24). Marriage, in this church's conceptualisation, was a process of self-actualisation that occurs when a person is joined with 'who they were missing all along' and for whom their family of origin primed them: the right, opposite-sex partner, with whom they could create, to use a common local phrase, 'a unit'.

In this essay I ask how marriage in the US might *make* two people. Could the answer explain why, as historian Jill Lepore (2010) puts it, 'Americans [are] among the marryingest people in the world'? I argue that the 'challenge' of marriage (see Chiu in this volume on the 'trial' of getting married), and the way it inevitably requires some degree of personal transformation, map meaningfully onto highly valued subjectivities in my field site: industriousness, finding joy and pride in relationships, ability to narrate one's life and share this with others, and the capacity and willingness to create oneself in line with certain gendered modes of presentation. Whether or not a person actually gets married, the option of marriage has shaped what it is to be enfranchised, giving it an association with freedom, individualism and independence and rendering it not 'only' a matter of gender, but one of race and class too (Cott 2000). The apparent tension and 'contradiction' (Quinn 1996) between US cultural emphases on both individualism and marriage has intrigued social scientists (Cherlin 2009; Bellah et al. 1985). But here I argue that it was the very state of being a discrete person that animated a desire for affinal 'togetherness'. Further, people drew on this enduring individualism to find the power to make their marriage work.

In what follows, I explore these questions in five main sections. The first situates marriage counselling as the subject of media fascination. The second describes what one life coach and self-help author described to me as 'the epidemic of marital loneliness'. The third section unpacks a social logic in which marriage is something one must 'learn how to do'. In the fourth section, I discuss visualisations and conceptualisations of the married person as an individual, and in the fifth and final section, I turn to marriage as a state ideally based not in oneness, but in intimacy between individuals. I begin, however, by discussing briefly some of the details that make Lynchburg distinctive.

Lynchburg

A woman in her early twenties working at a supermarket told me, 'When I go somewhere else out of town, I say I'm from Lynchburg and they say "where's that?" and I say "it's the place with the giant Christian college' and they say "oh, *that* place"'. John Lynch, a second-generation Irish Quaker, who owned a James River ferry service, founded Lynchburg near Monacan territory in 1786. However, at the time of my fieldwork, the influence of a second ideological and economic 'father' to the city was more immediately palpable: Jerry Falwell (1933–2007), the pastor and televangelist who founded the Thomas Road Baptist Church and Liberty University (Lynchburg's biggest employer at the time of my fieldwork). His activist organisation the Moral Majority turned evangelical Christianity into Republican votes, most notably during Ronald Reagan's presidential campaigns (see Harding 2000; Winters 2012).

A favoured topic of conversation at the Community Market (as per the fridge magnets sold there, 'local and proud since 1783'), at the public library, 2017's Solar Eclipse Viewing Party, and Friday night's live music and food truck event, Cheers to the Weekend, was 'what is Lynchburg *really* like?' A pastor told me, 'People have this perception of Lynchburg as "the Christian place" but it was a *brothel town* at a key point on a river and train track! Sailors! Military! Tradesmen!' This history, along with the detail that 'Lynchburg was once one of the wealthiest towns in America', added an extra dimension to descriptions of Lynchburg as 'a faith-centred community' and 'great for families'.

Some exegeses of 'the truth about Lynchburg' concerned kinship, marriage and 'how race becomes socially legible through ancestry' (Mariner 2019, 846). Several (white) interviewees brought up the possibilities for learning 'the truth about this place' or about 'the haves and the have-nots' that could come from the relatively new technology of DNA testing 'proving that [going back quite far into the past] powerful [white] folks had had relations with people of colour'. Sometimes this referred to enslavers' rape of Black women. Sometimes this was about consensual yet prohibited relationships – it was not until the 1967 Supreme Court case *Loving v. Virginia* that it became illegal to deny white people and people of colour the right to marriage (see Cashin 2017). This had

had concrete, material implications for people's lives, for inheritance. However, as I now turn to discuss, while changes in marriage laws give a headline-worthy example of marriage as a technology of 'social control' in Virginia (Holloway 2006), the history of marriage counselling in the US reveals a project that is only superficially less political.

The cultural imaginary of marriage counselling

> 'Just because marriage is natural, it does not mean that it comes naturally.' (Pamela, a divorced and remarried white baker in her sixties)

Around the time of my fieldwork in 2017 and 2018, the US mainstream media presented marriage counselling and marriage-focused self-help as simultaneously familiar and intriguing. While some of the people who helped me with my research talked in relation to other topics about 'what happens in New York but not in Lynchburg' or 'bicoastal elites' or 'what might be more of a matter for Charlottesville or Richmond', counselling did not 'belong' to these communities that were imagined as wealthier and more progressive. That it was often provided free or at very low rates by charities, through insurance or by religious leaders took away some of its exclusivity and made it intuitive that there would be as many kinds of relationship counselling as there are religious and political subjectivities, and degrees of privilege.

Gwyneth Paltrow, in the lead-up to her divorce in 2016, made famous the marriage and family therapist Katherine Woodward Thomas's concept-cum-strategy of 'conscious uncoupling', provoking discussions about how a former couple could stay civil. In 2015, the co-founders of the millennial tech start-up Genius (a song lyric annotation service), two heterosexual men in their twenties who had become friends at Yale, 'turned to couples therapy' (Holson 2015) to help them learn how to work through disagreements. The *New York Times* reported, '"Except for the sex, founders have the same interdependency as married couples," said Peter Pearson, a founder of the Couples Institute in Menlo Park, Calif., who holds that businesses and romantic relationships fail for similar reasons' (Holson 2015).

That these aspirational young men had chosen to go to counselling rather than being, as some of the gendered cultural baggage of counselling would have it, 'coerced' by wives or girlfriends, framed counselling as the choice of a generation of men who wanted to talk about relationships. But it was also a 'productive' step for a business.

The apogee of marriage counselling's positioning as simultaneously sought-after and sensible might have been the publication and promotion of Michelle Obama's autobiography *Becoming* (2018). For example, *Time* reported,

> In an interview with *Good Morning America*'s Robin Roberts, Obama shared that she and the former president have gotten marriage counseling in the past to help 'talk out our differences'. 'I know too many young couples who struggle and think somehow, there's something wrong with them,' Obama said. 'I want them to know that Michelle and Barack Obama – who have a phenomenal marriage and who love each other – we work on our marriage and we get help with our marriage when we need it.'
>
> Obama also shared how while it may seem that marriage is 'supposed to be easy', it is also an opportunity to learn not only about your partner, but yourself: '"What I learned was that my happiness was up to me and I started working out more, I started asking for help, not just from him but from other people," she said. "I stopped feeling guilty"'. (Lang 2018)

Obama frames marriage as a 'project' (Hirsch and Wardlow 2006, 4) that takes 'work'. 'Differences', as Obama terms them, between spouses are not necessarily a reason to split up; they are inherent to marriage and can be grounds on which to seek external help. Creating a lasting marriage happens both parallel to and as a result of shoring up each individual's self-confidence and independence.

One might attribute the appearances of marriage counselling in contemporary US culture to the 1970s, when there was both a boom in self-help literature and a moral panic around 'marital breakdown'. (Cautioning those eager to ascribe legal changes to marriage to one side of the political spectrum or the other, it was a divorced and remarried Governor of California who in 1969 passed the first state 'no-fault divorce' law: Ronald Reagan.) However, marriage counselling goes further back, and further to the right. Historian Molly Ladd-Taylor has explored US marriage counselling's roots in so-called 'positive eugenics'. Paul Popenoe (1888–1979) was known by mid- to late-twentieth-century Americans 'as '"Mr Marriage", the father of modern marriage counselling in the US, sponsor of the popular *Ladies' Home Journal* feature "Can This Marriage Be Saved?"' (Ladd-Taylor 2001, 298). However, his first career was as a eugenicist, 'whose enthusiastic studies of compulsory sterilisation in

California provided an "essential basis" for the 1933 Nazi sterilisation law' (Ladd-Taylor 2001, 298). Eugenics and marriage counselling have certainly never been 'the same thing'. Yet Popenoe's biography reveals some overlaps between eugenics and 'the pronatalist domestic culture of the postwar period' (Ladd-Taylor 2001, 299). For Popenoe, it would be bad for society if white, relatively privileged couples dissolved their unions before they had produced multiple white, relatively privileged children (Ladd-Taylor 2001, 300).[2]

In the second half of the twentieth century, marriage counselling was part of the US social policy that naturalised the idea that being married, 'being happy' and being middle-class were substantially the same thing. Rebecca L. Davis observes:

> Throughout the twentieth century marriage counselors claimed that improving marital relationships could enable more families to pull themselves into the middle class; rescuing troubled marriages appeared to offer a solution to poverty and thus to promise an additional reward for taxpayers . . . By the century's end, public officials, arguing that saving heterosexual marriage could save the nation, had launched national campaigns to make marital status the benchmark for determining social welfare benefits and economic citizenship. (Davis 2001, 9)

It matters here that, as these histories attest, marriage counselling is so familiar in the US. I have found that friends and colleagues in the UK and the Netherlands have often assumed marriage counselling to be the preserve of white middle-class people – perhaps as a result of what is shown in film and television. In Lynchburg, however, it was a matter for Black and white people, and for working-class people as well as those who were very affluent. The obvious inference here is that marriage counselling flourishes in places where Christianity holds a lot of influence.

Lonely together?

> In our marriage preparation workbook, which my husband's aunt gifted us, was this visual of a 'Venn diagram'. The husband and wife are two circles. If the circles don't touch, that's bad – you're distant. If the circles are on top of each other, that's also bad – you no longer have your own life! (Lisa, a Black, newlywed nurse who grew up in Charlottesville before moving to Lynchburg)

Conceptualising marriage, as I was often told, meant differentiating between human individuality as an invaluable animating force (a site of action and, optimistically, the source of self- and social improvement) and human individuality as almost tragic (a state that condemns people to loneliness, misunderstanding, selfishness and secrecy). Catherine Allerton asked 'what does it mean to be alone?' (2007) when analysing the situations of unmarried women in Indonesia. But in Lynchburg, this question was often asked of married people. It was not just that married life might entail distancing oneself from friends or relatives, or, for some women, leaving paid employment. One's spouse could make one feel lonely, especially if they were reluctant to talk about their problems. 'Shame', I was often told, scared people off 'reaching out' for help. For example, I was told by Walker, a lay counsellor, a white man who was married with four children:

> You're on your side of the bed and you're thinking, 'I'm not alone, there's a ring on my finger, there's another beating heart right here next to me. Plus, this is a marriage, not something 'for one night only' and empty. So why do I feel lonely? Mainstream culture focuses on the sensation of emptiness that comes with not having a significant other. But when couples come to me before marriage or when they're already married, I want them to know that they're not alone if they feel lonely *in* their marriage.

On secrecy, on shame: several people from evangelical circles moved quickly from talking about marriage to talking about 'the pressure to look like the perfect family' and 'the pressure to be happy all the time'.

Jean, a life coach in her thirties, a Black woman of Jamaican heritage who was married with two children, and who identified as liberal, explained:

> I tell my clients to close their eyes and think of a romantic French film. Its opening scene shows Paris at midnight. You get the silhouette of the buildings, you see the windows, and you can see the light is on in many of these beautiful homes. Imagine if each of those lights showed you a home with loneliness and dissatisfaction in a romantic relationship. These people in all of these apartments with the lights on are in the same situation, but they don't know it about each other. Their *neighbours* feel the same but they don't know it. They can't see the other apartments, only inside their own apartment. Imagine if I told you every one of these lights in the

window was a lonely person. Isn't that when you could reach out for help?

While Jean emphasised that help is nearby, ready and waiting – particularly when you stop fearing other people's judgement – Walker saw the problem of loneliness in marriage as emblematic of the devaluation of relationships in contemporary life. He perceived a clash between what 'Christian culture' should be and its reality:

> The soulmate concept is rampant in our culture. It's 'God picked out someone for *me,* someone who's perfect for *me,* someone who's going to complete *me.*' You see a pattern here? It's all about *me. The soulmate concept is self-centred.* It says 'This person is going to be everything I need, therefore I don't need to do anything. I don't need to change.' People say 'Well, no-one's perfect for me, and a couple of years down the road I'm going to decide my soulmate person isn't the person I married. I thought he was going to be this or she was going to be that but it ain't that way at all. This must not be my real soulmate; my real soulmate must be out there.'

Crucially, the person who was misled about what it is to be married was the person who said 'I don't need to change.' They must improve their situation, but seeking a new partner is not the answer. Another pastor, during counselling, asked clients to think about the battle between 'me', which, evoking a toddler's 'me me me', was a person's selfish and lustful side, and 'I', one's potential to refine relationships by 'taking responsibility' and reflecting on 'what you want your story to be'. On a day-to-day basis some people reflected that 'women feel things deeper than men – and get hurt more'. However, if marriage was a 'school of affection' as it had been in Revolutionary America (Cott 2000, 19), it was no longer a woman's job to make her husband a better citizen or friend; he, I was told, should think about how he could make himself a good husband. 'I'm not saying women don't need patience with this!' said a church secretary in her seventies.

But if a married person had the will to improve their relationship, how did they know what kinds of steps would be beneficial? I now turn to discuss the ways in which the 'knowledge', 'advice', 'learning' and 'wisdom' central to marriage indexed both frictions in relation to changes to legal marriage, and ideas about the incommensurability of marital experience between generations. Again, what comes to the fore is the tension between life as a couple and individualism.

On 'not knowing what to do'

> Whether men want to do marital counselling or not, they're bound to do it. That's very popular amongst Southern ministers – to minister to that couple whether you go to that church or not. If he's marrying you, you have to go. My niece is getting married not by her normal minister but by a family friend, and he wanted to sit with them a couple of times to find out, did they know what they were getting into, basically. It makes them stop and think. So I guess the guys, young men, are forced to discuss it in an involuntary way. It gives them a basis of thought. It makes those wheels turn a little bit. (Martha, a white, 'divorced and dating' events planner in her fifties)

Many people told me that 'things had started to fall apart with the family' in the 1960s and 1970s, which I came to see as a reference to greater numbers of women working outside the home and to feminist and gay rights movements. Some told me that the late 2010s were even further along a path of increasing 'confusion': people wanted to fulfil certain roles, certain duties, but what action these roles required was increasingly ill-defined. A man in his fifties told me he 'didn't understand gay marriage', because he 'didn't know how [in a couple without a man and a woman] you would know what it was your duty to do within the home, within the family'. I got the sense that this man was imagining being married to a same-sex partner. 'I just think it would be awkward', he said, '*the quotidian* aspect of the situation'.

A man told me in relation to the sometimes twinned issues of marriage equality (legally recognised same-sex marriage) and the removal of Confederate statues in the South,

> people think that by being invited to think about these things a little bit differently, that they're being told that they're [as people] just wrong in general, that their history is being laughed at, that their community is being criticised, and before long they don't know who God is.

Marriage evoked 'the past', and was a pillar of what many people considered to be correct; some people found questioning it ontologically destabilising and socially humiliating.

At the same time, a conservative perspective on marriage naturalised some disappointment or even conflict. 'The Bible's the world's first marriage manual – that's how long our species has needed to work at love!' one pastor told me. Two women at a Lynchburg Museum event chuckled as they reflected on how the secret to a third friend's remarkably long and happy marriage had been her husband's frequent absence due to his work as an international businessman. A divorced real estate agent in his fifties looked me straight in the eye and spoke quickly as he said – in an unexpected turn from our conversation about event spaces –

> My lady friend and me have fun together, we go on trips, we do restaurants and wineries together. She owns her place. I have my kids. Does she want to get married? Do I want to get married again? Are all marriages the same? Am I the same person I was when I was with my former wife? Can you ever build yourself back up again after a marriage? How do you stay in sync?

Walker suggested that people were often fatalistic about their marriages and that they gave up too easily:

> That's what I mean by [how people need] the practical [advice], not a whole bunch of spiritual things . . . I'm a strong believer that this is all instituted by God, but for the everyday couple who walks in here, they're not thinking on that level. They're thinking, 'How do I deal with this guy who leaves his undershorts on the floor?!'

This specific image of 'a man who leaves his undershorts on the floor' came up many times when people were telling me of the shock of 'actually living' with someone after a wedding. (Dishes in the sink, lights left on, drawers left open, hogging the television, having too many friends over to the house, and out-of-sync bedtime and morning routines were common points of irritation and upset.) 'You can learn to do it right, or you can learn to do it wrong', Walker continued, using a phrase that several people used to describe marriage to me.

People who were middle-aged and older both celebrated newly married couples and pitied them. 'When my niece got married last year', Celia, an African-American academic told me, 'I told her that if she ever needs a break from her home, a little distance, there's a spare bedroom at my house with her name on it. I don't want her to have to take me up on this. It's normal for people with more experience in relationships to worry, though.'

How did guidance received from religious leaders, counsellors or self-help resources square with advice one might receive from parents or other older relatives? Marriage counselling was a symptom of contemporary kinship, I was told, because lots of people who are 'of typical marriageable age' had divorced parents or parents who were never married to each other. As one Christian counsellor put it, 'These parents [of today's young adults] have their own issues!'

Conversely, some people did not want to visit pastors at their 'home church' about marital problems because the pastors were 'too close', 'too close to my community' or too close to parents. 'It's not that I don't trust him not to tell', said one young woman. 'I don't think I can be myself talking about intimate topics with someone who's known me since childhood, who did my parents' marriage.'

There seemed to be a dialectical relationship between a married person's relationship with their parents, their relationship with their in-laws and their relationship with their spouse. How should a married person 'leave and cleave', as it is put in Genesis (that is, leave one's parents and bond with a spouse)? I heard parents quietly 'blamed' for their adult children failing to bond with spouses. But responsibility was placed largely with the couple. A white man in his early thirties who I had begun chatting to on the street about marriage counselling (as could happen in Lynchburg) told me:

> There are things you could be doing and you don't even realise they're wrong. Like, early on my pastor asked me, 'What did you do the last time you had a tough day at work?' and I thought to myself for a minute and I said, 'I called my mom and talked it through and I felt better,' and my pastor said – he's a humorous guy – 'OK, keep that as a sweet memory because that's the last time you call your mom for help rather than your significant other – the exception is if you need help with grandkids.' I learned that putting my wife first, giving help to her but also receiving help from her, and showing love to my parents, but also my own independence from them, that's the healthful way.

Marriage here reconfigures all relationships within a couple's orbit. Some ties are pulled tighter, others must be loosened. This has consequences for a married couple's friends and family, but also for each spouse's respective individualism. As I now turn to discuss, the imperative to reflect on what an individual is, which is present in many aspects of life in the US, comes to the fore in marriage.

'We need to see the *people* in the relationship'

How do couples visualise their relationships? How can spouses retain their individuality even in long marriages? How do these two questions connect? It was often said in Lynchburg that a married couple must 'choose each other every day'. Attendant here was the idea that a relationship is an organism that can be nurtured. This relationship was the work of both people involved, but the relationship was not 'them'. John Borneman, prior to the US's marriage equality ruling, described how legal marriage makes 'a personal relationship into a social fact: external, coercive, and enduring' (2005, 32). Borneman's point reminds me of a local jeweller's exegesis of her design for an engagement ring (she did not have the upfront capital to make the ring, so needed to wait to have it commissioned): three diamonds that signify 'you, me and us'. 'The "us" diamond', she said, 'could be the family [children] you're hoping to be blessed with; but it could also be your memories as a couple, the love between you, and so on.'

Hauntingly, historian Tera Hunter coins the term 'third flesh' to describe the presence of enslavers in enslaved people's marriages and the persistent threat of half of an enslaved couple being sold out of state (Hunter 2017, 6). This was part of the historical context for the twentieth century's civil rights movement's framing of the legal right to choose one's family as synonymous with the right to have one's personhood recognised. The language used here harkened back to Revolutionary-era legal thought, which regarded 'consent' as the making both of marriage and its analogue, the United States:

> In the aptly named *Loving* case in 1967, the court rejected the century-old argument that bans on marriage across the color line imposed equally on both races, and called such laws an effort to maintain white supremacy, insupportable in view of the fourteenth amendment. Marital intimacy was not the deciding point, but the opinion reiterated clearly that marriage was a 'fundamental freedom'. (Cott 2000, 198)

When the precedent of *Loving v. Virginia* was called upon in the Supreme Court ruling on marriage equality in 2015, a similar principle was upheld: that the right to marry is not so much conferred on a relationship as on an individual; that, in local parlance, 'it's OK to be who you are'. What this means for the recognition of a person was expressed by Dustin Lance Black, the screenwriter of the Harvey Milk biopic *Milk*: 'How amazing is it that when a young gay or person has their first crush, no matter where they live in the country, they can imagine it all the way to marriage?' (Wenger 2017). One of PFLAG (formerly Parents and Friends of Lesbians and Gays) Lynchburg's leaders told a local newspaper of her daughter,

'Marriage isn't on the immediate horizon for her. But the opportunity is there now' (Petska and Mohrmann 2014).

The legal and ethical imperative in the US of situating the individual at the centre of kinship law also came to the fore during the 1971 Supreme Court court case *Eisenstadt v. Baird*, which

> struck down a Massachusetts law that prohibited the prescription or sale of contraceptives to unmarried people . . . The court's view of equal protection for married and single individuals rejected traditional marital unity with the comment 'The marital couple is not an independent entity with a mind and heart of its own, but an association of two individuals each with a separate intellectual and emotional makeup.' (Cott 2000, 198–9)

As people spoke of it in Lynchburg, the enduring individualism of married people was not necessarily tragic, but rather a metaphysical, political and emotional state that made affinity, despite its significant challenges, covetable: the promise of unparalleled closeness that comes from the lifelong happy surprise of being tied to someone in a manner that is as important as or even overrides one's ties to a family of origin. The challenge, as I now turn to explore, was to stop oneself and one's spouse from, in the words of one divorced woman, 'collapsing into one'.

In search of intimacy

'The thing about marriage', as Sean put it,

> is that you are creating something that transcends the individuals involved, and so you plan your future much differently than if you were an individual, or just had a roommate or whatever. There are things that we must do or that I must do as an individual, in my thinking, in the way I plan my life, to ensure the health of this relationship because yeah, I might want to do things that are more fun but some things that I think are fun are going to damage and undermine the integrity of this third thing, which is the covenant, which is the sacred promise, the togetherness.

Here, a married person experiences more constraints than an unmarried person, but these constraints are not framed as sacrifices because the benefits of married life so far outweigh the benefits of being unmarried.

Peter, who was involved with marriage mentoring, told me:

> When we get to Heaven, according to Corinthians 13, we will see Him as He is and we will know Him as He has been known, so when we get to that point we will have that true intimacy, so to me that's what heaven is, having that final true intimacy with God, it's a mutual thing. But in the meantime God has given us this gift of marriage to sort of try out this thing here on earth. I don't want people to know who the real Peter is because that would be terrible, so I will build this brick wall around me and paint this pretty picture and hang it on the wall and then people will think it's the real me. Marriage is a process of taking down that brick wall, brick by brick, and seeing the real person and sharing and being vulnerable. But you don't want to be vulnerable unless you feel safe. So God has designed this thing called marriage to let us have this thing where we can be safe to be vulnerable with one other person . . . So intimacy in marriage is that point where there are no secrets. And we're never going to reach that on earth, but that's the goal.

Here are more metaphors and analogies: the 'brick walls' that people unhappily use to keep themselves lonely, but that can be 'taken down' through marriage. The removal of these facades creates vulnerability. A person's marriage was not the same as their relationship with God (and people tended to say that their relationship with God was the most important relationship in their lives), but marriage and an individual's relationship to God were in some ways comparable. The work of marriage here was to keep pursuing a 'goal', as Peter put it, 'that we're never going to reach . . . on earth'. In mentioning the aim of forgoing secrecy, Peter spoke to the emphasis on 'communication' between spouses. A couple are two people, I was told, and talking and physical affection do not create one person, but rather precious bonds between two: intimacy.

Sex and matters of self-presentation such as 'staying in shape' through diet and exercise and choosing clothes 'not only for comfort but for style', no matter what your age, were often spoken of in terms of the 'attraction' that comes with novelty and, as was sometimes implied, youthfulness. People who had been married said that engaged people should expect life after a wedding to be strikingly 'less romantic' than it was before. This meant, as one female cafe-owner put it, 'You and your spouse should work hard to remember why you "chose" each other in the first place, like by not giving up on your appearance.' Some counsellors, in contrast, used the image of a 'marital gut' as a metaphor for how married people might 'let themselves go' *emotionally* after marrying, for example by not bothering to ask their spouse how their day was or by failing to organise activities together. 'Say I love you five times a day', advised one counsellor. A woman at the public library told me, 'A lot of the Christian advice these days is to schedule sex, so you don't stop doing it just because he's got a presentation tomorrow and you're preoccupied thinking about someone who peed you off at your job earlier that day.' One pastor emphasised to me that 'Women need to take gentle care of men', which was a reference to sex. 'Date nights' for married couples were a taken-for-granted feature of everyday talk and a popular marketing tool. As one secular officiant in her forties put it, 'You need time without children, where you only need to give yourself to your spouse.' It was a given in a broad set of social contexts that having children could overwhelm married people's idea of who their spouse was (see Barnes 2016). Marriages where this had been allowed to happen were often marriages that had been insufficiently 'worked at'.

As one minister stressed to me, a balance had to be struck between constructing a new identity as a family and remembering the distinctiveness of one's partner:

> You wouldn't ever really want to take away your husband or wife's individuality because that's what brought y'all together. There's something in her eyes, there was something about her personality, there was something that just struck the groom. And vice versa. When you met your husband, there was something about him that struck you and you don't want him to lose his uniqueness, he doesn't want you to use your uniqueness because then you lose yourself. It's no longer you. It's somebody else. And yet you're still that one unit because there are things that a couple has to make decisions about that affect both parties and the entire family unit. Especially if there's children involved.

An evangelical woman in her twenties, a teacher, told me of her father's excellent example of how to maintain closeness in a long marriage, centring his wife's motherhood rather than pretending it did not exist:

> My father would give me and my brothers money to buy gifts for our mother. She appreciated this because she knew we couldn't get that kind of money ourselves, so when we gave her the gifts it was a *communication* between my father and her. He was saying 'thank you' and also 'thank you for being *you*'.

Conclusion

Changes to legal marriage such as the introduction of marriage equality have shown marriage to be responsive to shifting social, political and economic contexts. As an institution, marriage can be intriguingly tempting to anthropomorphise, but the reality is that marriage has not 'transformed itself'. It has been transformed by generations of civil rights activists, law-makers, progressive religious leaders and couples themselves (Cashin 2017; Frank 2017), whose lives and loves have questioned both the ethics and the sense of restricting access along lines of race and gender to marriage as a 'public' (Cott 2000) acknowledgement of commitment. However, creative approaches to marriage, and the appreciation of marriage as something that must 'change with the times', are not only part of a progressive (inclusive) understanding of what marriage is but also, as we have seen, part of what we might call 'creative conservatism'. Indeed, many of the people whom I met said marriage needed to respond to 'new dangers in the world'.

Themes of 'togetherness' and 'intimacy' and both their tensions and generative overlaps with individualistic notions of the person have come to the fore in this chapter. For many, God was part of the explanation for these experiences, and yet God did not 'explain away' the puzzles that made up the stresses and pleasures of marriage. Many of these quandaries possessed a 'chicken or egg' quality: is it that a person on earth is condemned to being an individual, so they do what they can to fight loneliness by getting married and working on this marriage? Or is it that when a person marries, they truly realise that they are an individual – *still* an individual – and they usually experience this as a gift rather than a burden?

While from a more etic viewpoint marriage might be a site of 'cruel optimism' (Berlant 2011), for the people described here, to value marriage and to perceive marriage as a straightforward path to 'the good life' are certainly not the same thing. In US history, federal and state legislatures, religious groups and communities have valorised marriage to a greater extent than in most other places. But this work in the name of creating 'union' (or, '*the* union') has often either made apparent or enabled exclusion. In the Virginia in which I did my fieldwork, people with a range of political and religious views, and across race, sexuality and class, grappled with cultural pressures about 'ideal' or 'perfect' marriages. And yet conservative ideologies draw not only on the idea of the 'perfect marriage' or the 'perfect family', but also on the value of *not* expecting a marriage to be perfect – for this is what keeps marriages, as the local terminology had it, 'intact'. Here one *learns* to love, and planning, giving and receiving advice, testifying, scheduling are not antithetical to romance: they are intrinsic to (some sections of) Christianity, as they are to capitalism. Just as marriage shows us how work and pleasure are entangled, people who have experienced tragedy cling to hope, and shattered dreams have new aspirations layered upon those former dreams (see also Papadaki, this volume). Freedom and independence are here associated not with rootlessness but with the 'stability' that some claim is crucial not only for the self but for society.

Notes

1   This research received ethical approval from the University of Edinburgh, the European Research Council and the University of Virginia. Names and some biographical details have been changed in order to maintain anonymity.
2   Just outside Lynchburg, people living at the Virginia State Colony for Epileptics and Feebleminded were involuntarily sterilised.

References

Allerton, Catherine. 2007. 'What does it mean to be alone?' In *Questions of Anthropology*, edited by Rita Astuti, Jonathan Parry and Charles Stafford, 1–27. Oxford: Berg.
Barnes, Riché. 2016. *Raising the Race: Black career women redefine marriage, motherhood and community*. New Brunswick, NJ: Rutgers University Press.
Bellah, Robert N., Richard Madsen, William M. Sullivan, Ann Swidler and Steven M. Tipton. 1985. *Habits of the Heart: Individualism and commitment in American life*. Berkeley: University of California Press.
Berlant, Lauren. 2011. *Cruel Optimism*. Durham, NC: Duke University Press.
Borneman, John. 2005. 'Marriage today', *American Ethnologist* 32: 30–3.
Boyer, Dominic. 2008. 'Thinking through the anthropology of experts', *Anthropology in Action* 15: 38–46.
Briggs, Laura. 2017. *How All Politics Became Reproductive Politics: From welfare reform to foreclosure to Trump*. Berkeley: University of California Press.
Cannell, Fenella. 2013. 'The re-enchantment of kinship'. In *Vital Relations: Modernity and the persistent life of kinship*, edited by Susan McKinnon and Fenella Cannell, 39–62. Santa Fe, NM: SAR Press.
Carsten, Janet. 1995. 'The substance of kinship and the heat of the hearth', *American Ethnologist* 22: 223–41.
Cashin, Sheryll D. 2017. *Loving: Interracial intimacy in America and the threat to white supremacy*. Boston, MA: Beacon Press.
Cherlin, Andrew. 2009. *The Marriage-Go-Round: The state of marriage and family in America today*. New York: Random House.
Cleves, Rachel Hope. 2014. *Charity and Sylvia: A same-sex marriage in early America*. Oxford: Oxford University Press.
Coontz, Stephanie. 2005. *Marriage, A History: From obedience to intimacy, or how love conquered marriage*. New York: Viking Press.
Cott, Nancy F. 2000. *Public Vows: A history of marriage and the nation*. Cambridge, MA: Harvard University Press.
Davis, Rebecca L. 2001 *Perfect Unions: The American search for marital bliss*. Cambridge, MA: Harvard University Press.

Frank, Nathaniel. 2017. *Awakening: How gays and lesbians brought marriage equality to America.* Cambridge, MA: Harvard University Press.

Ginsburg, Faye. 1989. *Contested Lives: The abortion debate in an American community.* Berkeley: University of California Press.

Harding, Susan F. 2000. *The Book of Jerry Falwell: Language and fundamentalist politics.* Princeton, NJ: Princeton University Press.

Hirsch, Jennifer S., and Holly Wardlow (eds). 2006. *Modern Loves: The anthropology of romantic courtship and companionate marriage.* Ann Arbor: University of Michigan Press.

Holloway, Pippa. 2006. *Sexuality, Politics, and Social Control in Virginia, 1920-1945.* Chapel Hill: University of North Carolina Press.

Holson, Laura M. 2015. 'Anger management: Why the Genius founders turned to couples therapy', *New York Times*, April 19.

Hunter, Tera. 2017. *Bound in Wedlock: Slave and free Black marriage in the nineteenth century.* Princeton, NJ: Princeton University Press.

Jamieson, Lynn. 1998. *Intimacy: Personal relationships in modern societies.* Cambridge and Malden, MA: Polity.

Kerr, Christine. 2015. 'The use of verbal and visual metaphors in couples therapy'. In *Multicultural Family Art Therapy*, edited by Christine Kerr. New York and London: Routledge.

Kerr, Christine, Janice Hoshino, Judy Sutherland, Sharyl Thode Parashak and Linda Lea McCarley. 2008. *Family Art Therapy: Foundations of theory and practice.* New York and London: Routledge.

Kowalski, Julia. 2016. 'Ordering dependence: Care, disorder, and kinship ideology in antiviolence counseling in north India', *American Ethnologist* 43: 63–75.

Ladd-Taylor, Molly. 2001. 'Eugenics, sterilisation and modern marriage in the USA: The strange career of Paul Popenoe'. *Gender & History* 13: 298–327.

Lang, Cady. 2018. 'Michelle Obama says she and Barack sought marriage counseling when they needed it'. *Time.com*, 9 November.

Lepore, Jill. 2010. 'Fixed: The rise of marriage therapy and other dreams of self-improvement', *New Yorker*, 29 March.

Lewin, Ellen. 1998. *Recognizing Ourselves: Lesbian and gay ceremonies of commitment.* New York: Columbia University Press.

Liberatore, Giulia. 2019, 'Guidance as "women's work": A new generation of female Islamic authorities in Britain', *Religions* 10: 601.

Mariner, Kathryn A. 2019. 'White parents, Black care: Entanglements of race and kinship in American transracial adoption', *American Anthropologist* 121 (4): 845–56.

Mayblin, Maya. 2014. '"People like us": Intimacy, distance, and the androgyny of saints', *Current Anthropology* 55 (S10): 271–80.

McKinley, Robert. 2001. 'The philosophy of kinship: A reply to Schneider's *Critique of the Study of Kinship*'. In *The Cultural Analysis of Kinship: The legacy of David M. Schneider*, edited by Richard Feinberg and Martin Oppenheimer, 131–67. Urbana and Chicago: University of Illinois Press.

Petska, Alicia, and Barrett Mohrmann. 2014. 'First same-sex marriage license issued in Lynchburg', *News Advance*, 6 October.

Quinn, Naomi. 1996. 'Culture and contradiction: The case of Americans reasoning about marriage'. *Ethos* 24 (3): 391–425.

Rapp, Rayna. 1999. *Testing Women, Testing the Fetus: The social impact of amniocentesis in America.* New York and London: Routledge.

Schneider, David M. 1968. *American Kinship: A cultural account.* Englewood Cliffs, NJ: Prentice-Hall.

Stafford, Charles. 2018. 'Moral judgement close to home', *Social Anthropology* 26: 117–29.

Wenger, Daniel. 2017. 'Dustin Lance Black: The screenwriter behind *Milk* and *When We Rise*, on coming out as a gay activist', *New Yorker*, 2 March.

Weston, Kath. 1991. *Families We Choose: Lesbians, gays, kinship.* New York: Columbia University Press.

Winters, Michael Sean. 2012. *God's Right Hand: How Jerry Falwell made God a Republican and baptized the religious right.* New York: HarperCollins.

3
Marriage, time, affect and the politics of compromise in Athens

Eirini Papadaki

Marriage is a social realm in which intimacy, kinship, processes of gender subjectification, discourses of modernity and social transformation are all entangled. In Greece, while alternative discourses of making families have emerged, marriage remains the core institution of mutual lives with children (Kantsa 2014; Papataxiarchis 2013; Paxson 2004). When I asked people in Chalandri, a middle-class suburb of Athens, to talk about their long-term marital experiences with children, I was struck by the fact that we seldom ended up talking about the marriage per se: instead, we found ourselves discussing time and change, transformations of the self, pasts and futures. Our discussions were centred on how people have changed because of marriage, how they evaluate life before and after marriage, how they became someone different from who they previously were, or sometimes how they had lost parts of themselves; how they had changed from being individuals to members of a couple in order to have a family and children, and how they struggled to make relationships that work and endure. Often I would hear that, through marriage and the creation of a family with children, people would gradually change the limits of what they could 'bear' in a relationship, becoming more and more tolerant and agreeable. 'Haven't you changed since you got married?' a co-discussant of mine asked me. 'Aren't you a different person since you had kids?' I started thinking more and more about these changes, how they occurred and what we had to lose of ourselves or change from within in order to become this 'something else', in order to uphold our choice to be in a long-lasting relationship, working as a couple, in a mutual and common life with our partners and being responsible for bringing up our children.

In this chapter, based on two years' fieldwork in Athens from 2017 to 2019, I reflect on conversations I had with middle-class women about our marital lives, with the aim of highlighting processes of subjectification laden with emotion and affect. Discussing, recounting and evaluating our lives is an historical and social experience, which depends on our various personal biographies and historical circumstances. Looking at affective kinship among middle-class couples, we can better understand the inseparable connections of kinship, emotions and time.[1] I argue that making kinship is about cultivating feelings and emotions, and that kinship becomes affective through time. This affective process has a dramatic impact on the formations of selves. Kinship changes us, and marriage, as a uniquely potent form of affective kinship through different articulations of love and care, or their opposites, changes us. Love, in particular, affects and organises middle-class lives, promising futurity and happiness, but also requiring re-evaluation when those promises are not fulfilled, and when those expectations are not reached.

I frequently heard people explain the transformations they had undergone through marriage by saying that they felt they were losing parts of themselves. But at the same time, they were describing new, creative work in becoming something else: a mother, a wife, a father, a husband – a recognisable social category of person. At other times, their transformative self was prescribed, pragmatically, through the language of responsibility and adulthood. People made efforts to explain how, by losing parts of themselves, what was actually being left aside was immaturity, and through this transformation they were becoming responsible adults and more fully fledged persons.[2]

These changes, and their explanations, are inextricably linked to time. Time, Veena Das (2007, 80–95) argues, creates, re-creates and transforms our subjectivities, allowing the stories of our relationships to 'be interpreted, rewritten, sometimes overwritten' and repaired, while at the same time giving us the chance to be the authors of our lives. In the discussion I present here, I focus on how time changes us, how as our bodies grow old, we become either tougher or more forgiving, how we manage our losses and how we recognise what we have. I reflect upon how we count time that matters and, following a very popular Greek song that says, 'but time, real time, is our sons, the elder and the younger',[3] I suggest that time is counted through relations, through kinship. Through kinship time, we make compromises, choices, forays and retreats that require us to reconsider and (re)form our selves. Time makes (or unmakes) kinship, providing the opportunity of becoming 'members of one another' (Sahlins 2013, ix) by creating common lives and histories (see also the introduction to this volume).

In what follows, I unpack the mechanisms of time in the formation of kinship, affects and selves. I begin by looking at the history of marriage in Greece, and the significant social changes that have occurred in the last decades, with their effects on gender and kinship. Then, following the story of Elena,[4] I explore anthropologically the notion of *staying* in a marriage, the social recognition of being in a marriage and the politics of compromise. I then follow various conversations I had with women in Chalandri and their efforts to see and assess – often after years of marriage – what they and their relationships had become. *Seeing* works across time, giving people the opportunity to recognise the affective labour produced inside marriage, the resulting transformation of their selves, and the emergence of new ones. These women struggle to balance options and alternatives, defending and recognising themselves, in order to find meaningful existence in ordinary lives.

A short history of marriage in Greece

To understand the intimate worlds and strategies of middle-class families, we have to consider the ways in which changes in the recent politics and social history of Greece have influenced perceptions of gender, intimacy and family, and how women, in particular, create relationships. Marriage, especially in rural Greece and especially for women, had been 'the absolute condition for having children and raising a family' (Papataxiarchis 2013, 221; see also du Boulay 1974; Dubisch 1986). Through extreme social crises after the Second World War and a civil war that ended in 1949, and during the rule of a military junta from 1967 to 1974, Greece confronted difficulties, pain and severe trauma in people's lives and in how families and intimate relations were created and established. Rapid social and demographic changes followed from the beginning of the 1950s. A massive movement from rural to large urban centres, for either study or work, established a new and expanding, upwardly mobile middle class. Urbanisation, women's increased participation in education and in the workforce, and the accession of Greece to the European Community in 1981 led to the transformation or questioning of existing perceptions of family and intimate life, and to an increased effort to modernise various aspects of it, including reproduction and the family (see Paxson 2004). Erotic and emotional fulfilment replaced previous 'expectations for marital relationships [that] were oriented towards economic collaboration, including the reproduction of heirs' (Paxson 2007, 122).

Before the major legal reform of family law that came with PASOK's rise to power in 1981,[5] the husband was the legal head of the family, and the acquisition of sons was always valued more highly than daughters. A daughter's dowry was a burden to the family; ideally, parents were obliged to offer either a house, or money or various kinds of goods in order for her to get married. This caused a great deal of frustration and strain, especially for poor families with many girls (Hirschon 1983; du Boulay 1983). Under the new family law in 1983, the legal concept of the husband's 'authority' was replaced by 'equality of spouses'; motherhood was equated with fatherhood; extra-marital children were legalised; common marital ownership of property was institutionalised; the institution of dowry was abolished; consensual divorce was introduced, together with the decriminalisation of adultery; and in 1986, abortions were legalised.

After a process of extensive urbanisation, nuclear households emerged as the basic middle-class family unit. Evthymios Papataxiarchis observes that nuclear marital households were the key metaphor of 'order, safety and happiness', and gave individuals 'the most viable cultural option according to which the self as a member of a corporate, conjugal group is entitled to a place in the wider community and to all the prerogatives that follow this recognition' (2013, 223). In the 1990s, making families – nuclear families – was still the basic desire and goal for adults in Athens, as Heather Paxson has noted (2004). Today, although other forms of relating and creating families are emerging and becoming visible, the statistical rates of alternative forms of kinship are extremely low compared to north European countries (Kantsa 2014, 827). Dimitris Papanikolaou has shown, through his study of recent queer Greek novels and films, the difficulty of recognition entailed in the newly emerging subjectivities (2018, 93), although a fruitful ground for radical expression has emerged, mainly among leftish parties and collectivities since the 1970s (2018, 238).

The resilience of more conservative forms of kinship, however, does not mean that men and women do not feel confined in marriage. While marriage and family relationships were researched extensively in early ethnographic work on rural households, the literature lacks ethnographic material on the construction of feeling and the affective dimension between spouses. People who do not choose the path of marriage are constantly asked, implicitly or explicitly, to situate themselves: to answer questions about marriage and children or to develop feelings about such issues, signifying the heavy ideological weight of marriage (Athanasiou 2006). This emerged clearly in my own research. For example, Evelina, a married woman with two children, demonstrated this tendency when she expressed her agony about her single, childless sister, already in her forties: 'She doesn't have much time; I am so anxious about what will happen if she doesn't find someone now to have children [with].'

As many of my informants indicated, starting a mutual life and expanding into a family with children is a moral project, a life purpose, 'to create good people in the future', 'to work with our children', 'to teach them to be good'. Perceiving parenthood and marriage as moral projects (Paxson 2004; see also Carsten in this volume on marriage as an ethical project of self-transformation), spouses go beyond their personal desires and their individuality in their search to create a mutual existence with their partners so as to fulfil the goal of parenthood (Chatjouli, Daskalaki and Kantsa 2015). But marriage is also a great risk. The decision to marry or about whom to marry is a great concern and worry, as it constitutes a decision for life and is seen as a permanent future. Moreover, it is a risk because change occurs inside marriage, too. People change, and these changes can be unexpected or negative, thus leading to divorce. My middle-class co-discussants were worried about alienation and 'routines that eat us'. They spoke too about the loss of love and care, that their spouse 'doesn't care' or 'is like a stranger to me'; about lacking desire for sexual contact; or about what has been lost or gone missing from the person they married. It sometimes seemed as though the spouse changed so much on their way to maturity that the other person in the relationship was left unsatisfied. Along the way to finding a balance between a previous and a new self, there are frictions and tensions. The articulation of those worries – affects that become words – as well as the efforts of spouses to think through time about their choices and to find answers about love and care, or 'why I am still here', were central concerns articulated in my middle-class encounters.

Staying: the politics of compromise

'My life is nothing special. I am a normal person with an ordinary life', Elena, a married woman in her early fifties, told me when I asked about her life story. Through her 'nothing special' life, I will try to unpack women's lives in long-term marriages with children, and the ambivalent feelings which they reveal when they recount their lives. After finishing high school, Elena worked as a secretary in a company for 20 years, and when she gave birth to her son, she left her job since she wanted to concentrate on bringing up her child. Her husband, Dimitris, is a lawyer, works long hours, returns home very late every night and spends time with his child only at weekends. 'I always had that dream, since I was a small child, to have a family with children, to have a nice home', Elena continued, 'and marriage was central in that dream.' Elena and Dimitris come from conservative families, with strict parents: 'Tidy houses and tidy lives', as she says. She first met her husband when they were both 19, soon after finishing high school, and they started dating and soon having sex, in secret from their parents. But after some years in this relationship, she realised that although he was a good man, she wanted to have a more social and open life, going out more, going to theatres and movies, having holidays and weekend excursions, things that Dimitris didn't like. 'I couldn't compromise with the idea that I would live such a boring life and I left him.' But after a year, in her early thirties, she came back.

> Suddenly, I felt I was growing old, my friends started having children, time was pushing me to take decisions, to think what kind of life I wanted, and I wanted a child, and an ordinary life, and I came back to him and got married. Did I compromise? I don't know. Aren't we all living with our small compromises? Aren't, maybe, our choices, compromises of something else?

'He is still the same person you know. Often, I feel trapped in here', she said to me with a sad expression. She stopped, looked at me and said quietly, 'There are many nights when I can't sleep and I wonder why I am still here, in this house, in this marriage.' She stopped again, and then with relief in her expression and voice said, 'But I couldn't be anywhere else, I belong here.' At other times, when we have coffee and chat with other women, you can hear Elena joking about her situation, about how unlikeable it is, but as she does so, she smiles. She has a very peculiar, sarcastic way of expressing and describing her life. Sometimes she consults with and advises other women about what to do so that they don't need to 'eat shit'. But in the beginning, I kept wondering: why does she stay? I was thinking that probably she was a quitter, giving up on life and on herself; that she chose to stay in a marriage with such an emotional vacuum because she feels weak and frightened. At other times, with other women, I heard similar descriptions of marriage, and I perceived these as stories of victimhood, sad stories with heroines who don't have the strength to divorce. But one day, after many months of knowing Elena, she told me,

Twenty-five years together, Eirini, one cannot throw away so many years. After twenty-five years, how is it possible not to love each other? Although love for me now is different from what I was dreaming of before I met Dimitris. I learned to love him after I accepted him as he is. Twenty-five years, twenty-five years of various feelings, contradictory feelings, but maybe, I don't know, all those feelings are love.

I started to understand Elena and other women's decisions to stay in marriages, which in their storytelling had sounded difficult. I started to realise how much life, emotion and labour goes into so many years of mutual living, and how careful we must be in explaining others' lives – especially lives that sound unfamiliar to us as researchers, who may have different affective and intellectual experiences. It was becoming more and more obvious to me that these women greatly valued the effort and the work needed, on the part of themselves and their spouses, to transform themselves from two individuals into a couple with a common life: a couple trying to create affective ties by testing their feelings through time, by creating and counting their affection through marriage, through their kinship. At the same time, marriage gives them the space to have a recognised sociality. Elena, for example, is very popular among the mothers who have children at the same school. Although she does not have a paid job, she is always busy, helping with celebrations and excursions at her child's school, taking care of her elderly mother and mother-in-law, visiting and helping relatives.

Living together with these women, I realised how a responsible Greek mother constantly weighs up her options. As the story of Elena shows, although she describes a boring marriage, this is exactly the place where she wants to be, a place that gives her (a kind of) companionship, the space and safety to be critical and sarcastic about it, yet at the same time to live as a recognised person in society. So, although compromise (*symvivasmos*) seems to involve defeat, at least as I perceived it in the beginning, after unpacking the lives of these women, I realised that maybe for some women marriage is a way of knowing something about the self, of cultivating both the affect and articulations of love, of flourishing in other areas of their social life. Of course, this does not mean that all women will act in the same way. Every woman has her own limits of compromise depending on her history, class and general place in social and economic hierarchies.[6] Making these compromises, the women, mothers and wives with whom I talked do not see themselves as victims of patriarchy. Precisely because of the patriarchy or the ideology of family life that still strongly organises the Greek social world, and the difficult and unequal position which women hold, a tactic of making compromises allows them to have a life, along with other types of initiatives. It is a strategy that could not be classified as an act of women's liberation, but one that allows them nevertheless to occupy a safe and dynamic place in the world, that will allow them to act and to realise their ethical and gendered selves.

Michael Herzfeld, referring to his research in the 1980s on Crete and Rhodes, two largely rural Greek islands, wrote about the poetics of womanhood, where women '*creatively deform* their submission' by performing 'their lack of performance . . . In doing so, they may also implicitly deflect the appearance of submission to their own ends' (Herzfeld 1991, 81, italics in original). Despite his limited access to the world of women, Herzfeld soon realised that women spoke little or not at all in public places, in contrast to men. Women in public performed silence and answered questions either monosyllabically or with a gesture or facial expression; privately, they used irony as a way of expressing their discomfort at men's actions. But women didn't only perform submission and silence, they also 'submitted to male control of material resources, decisions regarding their children's future, and the family's public image' (Herzfeld 1991, 94). Although the circumstances have changed and today women can have a public voice and participate in decisions regarding children, the tropes of accepting, enduring and compromising seem in many families to be the same. Women still do not speak up about many things that may bother them, and in similar ways they 'creatively deform' things that bother them in order to protect the stability of the family, to have a family as they wished, to be actively involved in children's lives and generally to have a life that gives them space to have a voice. Middle-class women in Athens today are not subjugated and do not submit in the same ways, but they fight for the same roles of mothers and wives, having nevertheless many more options, choices and alternatives. But the truth is that they do not easily choose these alternatives; they fight more to maintain those roles and they avoid using the alternatives by making those 'small compromises', avoiding action which might 'destroy' their family or 'blow everything into the air'.

Although in my very intimate discussions with women there were accusations against their husbands about specific attitudes, in their closing discussions most of the time they made general statements like 'You know all men are like this', implicitly meaning that all women have a collective problem to fight against and to live with this. Men's attitudes are seen as not 'deliberate': 'He learned to be like this', or 'His mother brought him up like this', they would say, even when these same women were also bringing up boys. Some of them talked about men's attitudes that may hurt them, such as men's indifference to them and their home, or their need to see men more actively involved in their home and their children's lives. Some others had different concerns, such as the need for a greater degree of companionship, their need to be felt for and to be listened to more by their husbands. Others definitely felt neglected. But despite these feelings, most of them perceived these interactions as normality, as how men are, and through these normalities, by accepting 'some things', families are built and exist. Some women are less bothered than others; some endure, some don't; some negotiate, and some give up; but most of them do their best in their efforts to make things work. They affectively work, in order to create the appropriate conditions to not lose their selves, and to make the promise of marriage stay alive 'for the sake of their family', as they often say.

Choosing to stay in a marriage that has problems can be perceived as a struggle, with its difficulties, pain and sacrifices. 'Keeping up the fight' is one of the performative actions, as Paxson (2004) has shown, which demonstrate that these women are good at being women, and specifically good Greek women. Similarly, Alexandra Halkias has stipulated that Greek women sometimes need to act *antrikia*, meaning 'in the way of a man' or in a 'manly' way. They 'should take their blows standing up, without "snivelling" . . . without any tears or display of pain at all. To register being hurt, [rather than] . . . angry or frustrated or disappointed, is to be "like a woman" and hence, in some contexts, not to be properly Greek' (Halkias 2004, 216). Being a mother in Greece, as Halkias has observed, means becoming a mother with someone else (a husband, a partner), not alone. Expanding this notion to marital life, considering also the moral stance of parenthood, and especially motherhood, means that being a parent involves being a parent with someone else, for which stoicism is often needed. This involves a commitment to make things work, without blowing everything up or giving up the fight, in order to succeed as a couple, to succeed at being a parent with someone else, to succeed in marriage, and as relational selves.

The story of Elena, which she thinks is nothing special, reveals both the work she has done on her marriage, and the work marriage has done on her. She has learned affection that sometimes mobilises her, sometimes gives her space to act and sometimes imprisons her. To understand why women choose to stay in marriages, or why they struggle to make them work, or why they leave, we need to look carefully at the processes of affective labour produced in intimate relations, and the creativity that surfaces in everyday life. Elena's *special* narration of her ordinary story as *her* life reminds us of Veena Das's thoughts on understanding the everyday as a space where people are involved 'in finding ways of containing . . . disappointments and not allowing them to be converted into a curse on the world' (Das 2018, 541). When we live lives together with others, she continues, following Jackson (1998), there are a 'myriad of minor moments of shared happiness and sympathetic sorrow, of affection and disaffection, of coming together and moving apart, so that what emerges is far from a synthesis to which one can assign a name or pin down as something one can know' (Das 2018, 541). And through all those processes and the moments of everyday lives, we can see beyond subordination or a lack of willingness to be flexible, to creativity and potentiality in intimate relations (Das 2018, 538).

Kinship time and kinship compromise

There are others, unlike Elena, who are much more concerned about, and struggle to balance, old and new elements of their transforming selves. They work hard to articulate and find new meanings in their married life, including new connections with the past. One day, I was talking with Sophia, a schoolteacher in her early forties and mother of two small children, about her life and her marriage, when she reminded me of some lines from a popular song in Greece:

> Don't go to work one day . . .
> To see if we love each other, don't go
> This house if we will tolerate it in the morning . . .
> Dad did the same I remember
> but this legacy has scared me
> Who knows, with your love for me
> what other dream of life you have written off
> Don't go, to see if we love each other, to see.

She told me, 'Often I feel like that, many times I think of all of that.' Lina Nikolakopoulou, the writer of the song, has long held a place in popular music in Greece as a woman describing the everyday battles and agonies of ordinary life. In this song, the woman is worrying about the couple's relationship, their love and their existential dead ends in the routine of their mutual life. 'Don't go to work one day . . . to see if we love each other' – in other words, if they will tolerate each other, says the song. Sophia wants to see what the routine did to them and how much they have changed in living their daily lives.

The song also depicts worries that I have heard expressed by women, especially in my own research: 'Am I becoming like my mum?' When I asked her more about the song, which I also like, Sophia told me:

> When I was young, I had this feeling that I didn't want to grow old and become like my parents. The routine of the house has always scared me. Their life, although they were a nice couple, scared me. The everyday routine scared me. They were teachers like me, with routines and a well-organised life, necessary, of course, for having our house in order. To cook, to clean the house, to get our homework done. But somehow, I didn't want to live this life. And all those things that were happening, the silences, the sorrows, even the happy moments caused me a sadness. And now, I know I am becoming like her and I start realising that, finally, this life is not so bad; and this is what causes my sadness, this change in me. I feel my mum now, after I made a family and had children. I really feel her.

Living this ordinary life, Sophia now understands and appreciates its precious moments; but somehow, at the same time, she wants to see that something of this ordinary life has changed since her mother lived it. She is like her mother, but not exactly. What Sophia and the song indicate is that she is confronted with a daily life that in the past scared her, but now does not. And the song reminds her that she is growing old, and that daily, family life reproduces itself.

One phrase in the song – 'Dad did the same, I remember' – depicts a past in which husbands worked long hours and usually wives looked after the daily housework and the life of the house. Sophia is now confronting her mother's past, creating a new narration of her mother's life. She is finding the words to tell a woman's life, in the past through her mother, and in the present through herself. She understands now that, after getting married and having children, kinship time unfolds and is counted differently, and requires us to acknowledge and realise different qualities of the ordinary, while changing the ways we narrate and recount past kinship. Through time, we create our marital and kin relations, and at the same time, we repair other meaningful kinship relations in our lives, the mutual existences we share with other people, such as the relationship with our parents, and with the previous generation.

Besides the timelessness through which the song bears its power – precisely because it touches various generations in the same way, if with different connotations – there is a much more time-bound, historically specific way it speaks to Sophia's generation. Her own parents were the 'generation of the Polytechnic', people who resisted the military junta, named after the mass uprising of the Polytechnic University in Athens in 1973. The Polytechnic days 'serve as an era that haunts in both a creative and an uncanny way all the following generations' (Karakatsanis and Papadogiannis 2017, 9), especially since participants in the events took such contradictory and conflicted roads. The junta fell a year later, and many of the protagonists in the uprising rallied around the dominant political parties – especially PASOK, the newly fledged party led by Andreas Papandreou. When PASOK was elected in 1981, many of the Polytechnic generation became parliamentarians and ministers, and a critical discourse emerged from the 'uncompromised left' against them and their reconciliation with the dominant political parties. The radical visions that many had developed were lost, and 'the Polytechnic generation' came to symbolise compromise of the worst sort – involving not just a negotiated meeting of minds, but the loss of principle. This compromise was widely depicted in novels, popular songs and literature following various aspects of the lives of the Polytechnic generation, not only in the political domain but also in regard to personal and private life.

Following Dimitrios Theodossopoulos's (2020) account of his own theoretical dilemmas around solidarity in times of austerity in Greece, we begin to understand both the changes involved in compromise, and their gendered dimensions. In trying to understand how people choose to act and by what means, both he and his co-discussants acknowledge conflicting perceptions about compromising either one's political beliefs or one's actions in order to be useful to people in need.[7] When his female informant, Georgia, tells him that a little bit of compromise on your political beliefs is necessary to help precarious people, she is also convinced that this is a step towards long-term resistance (Theodossopoulos 2020, 150). Theodossopoulos observed, as did I, that women were more preoccupied than men with giving pragmatic help to others, a long tradition in the Greek context depicted by previous generations of anthropologists (Theodossopoulos 2020, 149).[8] Compromise involves the pragmatism of making the everyday work, and its burden weighs more on women than men. Similar trends are observable in kinship relations, especially in marriage. But different actors and social contexts bring different evaluations into the mix over time. As Caroline Osella argues, 'Kinship has many things together: sacrifice, compromise, a little touch of pragmatic adjustment and realism, a love enmeshed in the everyday messiness of domestic duties and hidden bargainings' (2012, 242–3), things that are also quite obvious in the lives of Greek middle-class women.

'To see if we love each other', says the song – an open invitation to articulate the affective roads the couple walks, an important moment for understanding what brings us together or keeps us apart, what we have and what it is worth. 'Seeing' in this way is a technology of positioning affect and people in relation to oneself, as Halkias notes in her study of abortions in Greece, where women try through their unexpected pregnancy to ascertain whether their partner is the right one. Abortion is a topos where women test the limits of their relationships and prescribe their futures (Halkias 2004, 207–33). In marriage, too, many women want to see what affects and emotions the couple has cultivated through time and where they stand. It is as if they are searching for a balance in their transforming selves, becoming spouses and parents without losing the initial, basic elements of their previous individual selves, and without writing off other dreams of becoming. As the song asks, 'Who knows, with your love for me what other dream of life you have written off?' – a question that I came across in discussion, when people would admit to wondering about their own choices, and specifically about choosing to be in wedlock while relinquishing other dreams.

I often met people who thought hard regarding their feelings, trying to find names and descriptions for what they feel after many years in a marriage with their spouse. The main question was what this feeling is, the sentiment that holds them together besides the fact that they have to, and want to, bring up their children. 'Where are the feelings that brought us together in the first place?' and 'What is left of those feelings?' are questions I heard. Many couples expressed this agony about what they now have, and tried to define a whole range of emotions. The important thing about such couples is that they were recalling a return to the past, to those first feelings and their old qualities of their selves when they first met. 'I loved you for being like this and I don't want to lose that.' They made an effort to balance the initial feelings of the beginning with what they were becoming, with the demand that something had to stay the same from the very beginning for the relationship to survive. From assumptions such as 'You were my friend, we used to discuss everything together', to questions such as 'Where has our mystery gone?', or the important reflection that 'We don't have sexual desire for each other any more', the feelings of these couples emerged in contrast to the story of Elena, recounted above; they worked hard to articulate their situation and their feelings, and to repair what risked being lost.

Ariadne is a friend of mine in her forties who lives in Chalandri, married with two small children. I remember her years ago studying fine art in Athens, a beautiful, dynamic woman, joining feminist and radical-left groups. I remember her participating in international biennales with distinguished works; a well-known artist had written of her that she was a 'young artist of genius'. We all thought that she would have a successful career. Two years after graduation she met 'the love of her life', 'my other half', as she said, a young and talented architect. I remember them as a couple who were very much in love, affectionate with each other, with an increasing ability to articulate their feelings and discuss their ongoing situation with friends. Somehow, in my mind, I knew that those two would be together for many years and continue doing their amazing professional projects together. In their fourth year together, Ariadne found she was pregnant and without hesitation they both decided to keep the child and get married. Ariadne became an art teacher in a public elementary school, putting aside an international career, and her husband got a job in a construction company. For years, every time I visited them in their beautiful apartment, I got the feeling of a warm home, understanding and joy, but I always felt a certain sadness that they had both put their dreams and promising careers aside, especially Ariadne.

Making frequent visits to their home recently, I still got the sense of a warm atmosphere, although, as Ariadne confessed to me, there are some communication problems, but she believes that most of them are the result of tiredness and some financial problems they had been having lately. 'Many things have been lost somehow', she said to me, in a pragmatic way. And another night, as we were sitting on her veranda and conversing, she said to me:

> A lot of things I could have been, another life I could have had, a life of freedom; I could have been an artist in New York and talked all the time about art and made my living from art, but instead I am here in a marriage with two kids. That was my choice. Then I wanted to marry this man and wanted to have children. And I love my children. I am happy with them and with all the difficulties. But sometimes at night when they are all sleeping, I think about painting in my studio in New York . . . and having another life. I thought that I could manage it all, my career, my marriage, the kids, the passion with my husband, but finally I couldn't. No career, just kids. But again, I am choosing my children. We have created the most precious thing. We created people. We are writing our history

in this world through our children. If I could go back in time, I would do the same thing again.

Ariadne and other women I have met over the years often wonder about their choices, think and reflect on them. How would their lives be if they had chosen alternative lives and scenarios? How would they be without their marriages and life with children? Ariadne could be a single successful woman, outside Greece, a recognised artist; she could still not be alone, but be with a partner and live her life without children. Children delimit married life and force our daily life to enter into specific contexts.

When I recounted this in a recent workshop, most of the participants told me how sad it was, and asked why I chose to present such a sad story. Perhaps this was also due to the tone of my voice as I was reading it, and that I had missed out many details of her life. I was confused because I knew Ariadne and her husband really would not characterise their life as sad: quite the contrary. But on the other hand, I had had such thoughts myself at the beginning, and I started wondering about the moral and compulsory distinctions in our minds for evaluating our lives as happy or sad. Taking Ariadne's story as an example of a couple living an ordinary life, without violence or abuse, I want to indicate that I don't remember my informants situating their stories within a distinctive framework; their lives were presented as being lived (Das 2018). Ariadne seems in the first place to have exchanged the dream of a career for a life with her partner and her children, but I soon realised that this was not an exchange. It is her life as she lives it day by day, with the decisions and choices she has made, and 'happiness' is not her concept, it is other people's concept. Even if we want to think of her story in terms of happiness, then happiness is always a transforming concept, which changes its content through time. Ariadne lives and creates a kinship time different from before, creating mutual affection that can only be evaluated in her own time.

Conclusion: affective kinship

In this chapter, I have presented marital stories of women who, although they problematise aspects of their daily life, do not want to leave their relationships. They are staying put, and I have explored what this staying means in the Greek context. Although people ascribe different meanings to compromise, it seems that many people have to confront such meanings inside marriage. Marriage changes us. We come to this institution constructing our feelings and in efforts to realise promises that mobilise us to act, to compromise, to decide which paths to take. Through time, we evaluate our life decisions again, negotiating the losses of possible dreams while recognising what we have, our social status through marriage. We count time differently, in another way, after being married and having children; we acknowledge kinship time that entangles us in the politics of compromises, retreats or choices, reforming ourselves and assuring our middle-class positions.

Staying gives women the possibility of seeing: seeing the qualities of intimacy to test their feelings, to build emotions and subsequently to change them. But this change does not always mean that women have to lose something; rather, it allows them to acknowledge other new qualities of their selves. Although marriage is conventionally understood as conservative, we may also see that, in some cases, choosing and staying in a marriage is another way of performing affective intimacies in an un-affective world, through the most familiar, the most tried and tested method by which middle-class women get to know their selves.

Compromise means that we promise together to make something work; both sides lose something but gain a mutual co-existence. It is as if women make these compromises in order to make things work better, in order to have a future. Making compromises matters for women, dictating their actions, including the contradictions of creativity and risks in a marriage; marriage urges people to set or change the limits of what they can do in their mutual co-existence. Risk is part of this creative process, as people struggle to find their place somewhere between you and me, without losing their selves. Marriages start with dreams and expectations of togetherness, and the compromises in between help the couple to produce their common history, their own small social history, leaving traces of family through time (Papadaki et al. 2019). And if marriage, among other things, is a process of creating histories, being a self within a marriage means that sometimes we must navigate and reshape ourselves around a series of compromises, which depend on class, gender and personal histories (Holland and Lave 2001). In other words, we work constantly at repairing our endangered common lives with others (Das 2018, 544).

Compromises open up the possibility for relationships to last, and for networks of creation in other people, other, new kin narrations. They are necessary choices for making a marriage work, for making a relationship stronger, for a marriage to become a relationship that can create what is meaningful, a future, and perhaps, finally, a 'good' death. Such a death will leave behind a network of people who can recall and memorialise the dead person as a creative being. This, of course, is something one might say could happen to other people who have not married and do not have children, but who have left strong traces of their social, activist or intellectual lives. But what happens when people do not live such lives? Then marriage seems a well-recognised social place to fulfil the self. The limits of losing oneself and choosing to leave the marriage and get a divorce are different for every woman and man, and depend on their own biographies. When they start losing themselves, when the moment comes where they start realising that it is not worth losing themselves because of the preservation of the initial dream and the promise of marriage, that is the moment or the time where they will start considering divorce. But that is another story.

Acknowledgements

I would like to thank the women in Athens who shared their stories and thoughts about marriage with me. Janet Carsten, Aspa Chalkidou, Venetia Kantsa, Akis Papataxiarchis, Theo Rakopoulos and Koreen Reece helped me to think more about some of the ideas presented here. Maya Mayblin's and Susan McKinnon's extensive comments on previous drafts helped me to improve this chapter significantly.

Notes

1. On the failures of love in queer kinship and its affective dimensions, see Dahl 2014.
2. For marriage as a stage to maturity and adulthood, see Mayblin 2010 for the case of Brazil.
3. I am referring to the song 'What I've Played in Lavrio' (1979) by Dionysis Savvopoulos.
4. All names have been changed for reasons of confidentiality.
5. The Panhellenic Socialist Movement (PASOK) was founded in 1974 and constituted a new political force after the fall of the junta. PASOK, which symbolised a radical turn in the Greek political realm, campaigned for social justice and equality and was constructed by some of the resistance forces of the struggle against the junta, as well as other centre-left formations (Lyrintzis 1982).
6. On the interconnections of marriage, gender and social class, and for more on what has been called the 'global middle class', see Heiman, Freeman and Liechty 2012.
7. Papataxiarchis has also observed that, in the contemporary Greece of austerity, collective initiative 'puts pragmatic considerations over ideological concerns' in order to survive, to recover the social bond and to be able to imagine the future (2018, 245).
8. Theodossopoulos (2020, 149) cites the key works on this: du Boulay 1974; Hirschon 1989; Cowan 1990; Dubisch 1995; Paxson 2004.

References

Athanasiou, Athena. 2006. 'Bloodlines: Performing the body of the "demos", reckoning the time of the "ethnos"', *Journal of Modern Greek Studies* 24: 229–56.

Chatjouli, Aglaia, Ivi Daskalaki and Venetia Kantsa. 2015. *Out of Body, Out of Home: Assisted reproduction, gender and family in Greece*. Mytilene: (In)Fercit.

Cowan, Jane K. 1990. *Dance and the Body Politic in Northern Greece*. Princeton, NJ: Princeton University Press.

Dahl, Ulrika. 2014. 'Not gay as in happy, but queer as in fuck you', *Lambda Nordica* 19 (3–4): 143–68.

Das, Veena. 2007. *Life and Words: Violence and the descent into the ordinary*. Berkeley: University of California Press.

Das, Veena. 2018. 'Ethics, self-knowledge, and life taken as a whole', *HAU: Journal of Ethnographic Theory* 8: 537–49.

du Boulay, Juliet. 1974. *Portrait of a Greek Mountain Village*. Oxford: Clarendon Press.

du Boulay, Juliet. 1983. 'The meaning of dowry: Changing values in rural Greece', *Journal of Modern Greek Studies* 1 (1): 243–70.

Dubisch, Jill. 1986. 'Introduction'. In *Gender and Power in Rural Greece*, edited by Jill Dubisch, 3–41. Princeton, NJ: Princeton University Press.

Dubisch, Jill. 1995. *In a Different Place: Pilgrimage, gender, and politics of a Greek island shrine*. Princeton, NJ: Princeton University Press.

Halkias, Alexandra. 2004. *The Empty Cradle of Democracy: Sex, abortion and nationalism in modern Greece*. Durham, NC: Duke University Press.

Heiman, Rachel, Carla Freeman and Mark Liechty (eds). 2012. *The Global Middle Classes: Theorizing through ethnography*. Santa Fe, NM: SAR Press.

Herzfeld, Michael. 1991. 'Silence, submission, and subversion: Toward a poetics of womanhood'. In *Contested Identities: Gender and kinship in modern Greece*, edited by Peter Loizos and Evthymios Papataxiarchis, 79–97. Princeton, NJ: Princeton University Press.

Hirschon, Renée. 1983. 'Under one roof: Marriage, dowry, and family relations in Piraeus'. In *Urban Life in Mediterranean Europe: Anthropological perspectives*, edited by Michael Kenny and David I. Kertzer, 299–323. Urbana: University of Illinois Press.

Hirschon, Renée. 1989. *Heirs of the Greek Catastrophe: The social life of Asia Minor refugees in Piraeus*. Oxford: Clarendon Press.

Holland, Dorothy, and Jean Lave. *History in Person: Enduring struggles, contentious practice, intimate identities*. Santa Fe, NM: SAR Press, 2001.

Jackson, Michael. 1998. *Minima Ethnographica: Intersubjectivity and the anthropological project*. Chicago: University of Chicago Press.

Kantsa, Venetia. 2014. 'The price of marriage: Same-sex sexualities and citizenship in Greece', *Sexualities* 17 (7): 818–36.

Karakatsanis, Leonidas, and Nikos Papadogiannis. 2017. 'Introduction: Performing the left in Greece, Turkey and Cyprus'. In *The Politics of Culture in Turkey, Greece and Cyprus: Performing the left since the sixties*, edited by Leonidas Karakatsanis and Nikos Papadogiannis, 1–30. London: Routledge.

Lyrintzis, Christos. 1982. 'The rise of Pasok: The Greek election of 1981', *West European Politics* 5 (3): 308–13.

Mayblin, Maya. 2010. *Gender, Catholicism, and Morality in Brazil: Virtuous husbands, powerful wives*. New York: Palgrave Macmillan.

Osella, Caroline. 2012. 'Desires under reform: Contemporary reconfigurations of family, marriage, love and gendering in a transnational South Indian matrilineal Muslim community', *Culture and Religion* 13 (2). 241–64.

Papadaki, Eirini, Hsiao-Chiao Chiu, Janet Carsten, Koreen M. Reece and Siobhan Magee. 2019. 'Talking about kinship', *Anthropology of this Century* 25. http://aotcpress.com/articles/talking-kinship.

Papanikolaou, Dimitris. 2018. *Κάτι τρέχει με την οικογένεια: Έθνος, πόθος και συγγένεια την εποχή της κρίσης* [Something's Up with the Family: Nation, desire and kinship at a time of crisis]. Athens: Patakis.

Papataxiarchis, Evthymios. 2013. 'Shaping modern times in the Greek family: A comparative view of gender and kinship transformations after 1974'. In *State, Society and Economy*, edited by Ada Dialla and Niki Maroniti, 217–44. Athens: Metaichmio.

Papataxiarchis, Evthymios. 2018. 'Pragmatism against austerity: Greek society, politics and ethnography in times of trouble'. In *Critical Times in Greece: Anthropological engagements with the crisis*, edited by Dimitris Dalakoglou and Giorgos Agelopoulos, 227–75. London: Routledge.

Paxson, Heather. 2004. *Making Modern Mothers: Ethics and family planning in urban Greece*. Berkeley: University of California Press.

Paxson, Heather. 2007. 'A fluid mechanics of erotas and aghape: Family planning and maternal consumption in contemporary Greece'. In *Love and Globalization: Transformations of intimacy in the contemporary world*, edited by Mark B. Padilla, Jennifer S. Hirsch, Miguel Munoz-Laboy and Richard G. Parker, 120–38. Nashville, TN: Vanderbilt University Press.

Sahlins, Marshall. 2013. *What Kinship Is – And Is Not*. Chicago: University of Chicago Press.

Theodossopoulos, Dimitrios. 2020. 'Solidarity dilemmas in times of austerity: Auto-ethnographic interventions', *Cultural Anthropology* 35 (1): 134–66.

4
Getting married as a trial: deferring marriage in Jinmen, Taiwan

Hsiao-Chiao Chiu

The growing trends of later and less marriage in Taiwan since the beginning of this century have constituted critical issues for its government. The interconnected problems of an extremely low fertility rate and a rapidly ageing population are together feared to threaten the nation's survival (Chen 2012). These demographic shifts have encouraged researchers to compare Taiwan with Euro-American countries where similar changes occurred years earlier, and were summarised by sociologist Andrew Cherlin (2004) as the 'deinstitutionalisation of marriage'. Davis and Friedman (2014, 3) apply this term in their edited volume on marital changes in Hong Kong, Taiwan and urban China, but their attention is focused on how the changes came about and the new possibilities that will emerge regarding these societies' specific political and cultural contexts. This chapter contributes to this scholarship by exploring the phenomenon of deferring marriage in Jinmen island – a part of Taiwan where there has been notable resilience of patrilineal communities against the backdrop of wars and long-term military rule in the twentieth century (Szonyi 2008).

My focus, however, is less on why young people postpone their marriages than on how they reconfigure the ideas of marriage and their relations with their families in its prolonged deferral. As this chapter demonstrates, marriage appears to be an option that young people consider whether or not to include in their own lives, rather than a taken-for-granted goal as conventionally understood. Beck and Beck-Gernsheim (2001) identify an individual's pursuit of their own life as the leading characteristic of the phenomenon of 'individualisation' they see as occurring across the world, where people have in various ways become liberated from traditional roles and constraints. With his longitudinal research in a village in north-west China, anthropologist Yunxiang Yan (2003, 2009) unpacks how the process of individualisation played out in people's private lives following economic reforms. He argues that individualisation in China has differed from that in Euro-American societies because of the socialist state's crucial role in mediating this process. He also notes that the rising emphasis on individual interest and desires has eroded the traditional norms of children's respect for and obedience to parents, leading to a crisis of support for the elderly in China in general. This chapter takes Yan's insights forward by examining the correlation between individualisation and changing intergenerational relations through stories of delaying marriage – an under-explored aspect in Yan's works. Moreover, my Jinmen ethnography shows how the consequences of individualisation in Taiwan differ from those in China owing to their dissimilar political trajectories.

Jinmen is a group of islands off the coastline of south-eastern China, with a resident population of around fifty thousand (Liang 2018). The ancestors of the numerous patrilineal villages (a patrilineal group dominates a village's population and land) on the islands came from the Chinese mainland several centuries ago. Connections built on blood, marriage, adoption and various forms of relatedness among islanders have resulted in tight-knit social networks. Most patrilineal settlements survived the serious damage caused by military conflict between Taiwan and China in the context of the Cold War. In 1949, the Kuomintang (KMT, or the Nationalist Party) lost the war to the Chinese Communist Party (CCP) on the mainland and withdrew its government and army to Taiwan and Jinmen. Because of Jinmen's proximity to China and military significance, the KMT reshaped it into an anti-communist frontline and established a system of military rule there (which ended in 1992). As the KMT attempted to build a modern nation state grounded on Chinese traditions, in stark contrast to the CCP, Jinmen's civilians were able to continue a wide range of rituals and customs that manifested patrilineal values.

During my stay in a large patrilineal village for my doctoral research in 2013–14, I tried to involve myself in the community through participating in a village voluntary group mainly composed of women between the ages of 50 and 80. I also assisted in various rituals and customs, such as ancestral worship at home and in the grand ancestral halls, and distributing edible gifts for celebrating a marriage or the birth of a baby boy to all the households in the village. During my long-term participation in local family and social lives, I was impressed by these middle-aged and older villagers' strong feelings of moral duty to their ancestors and kin,

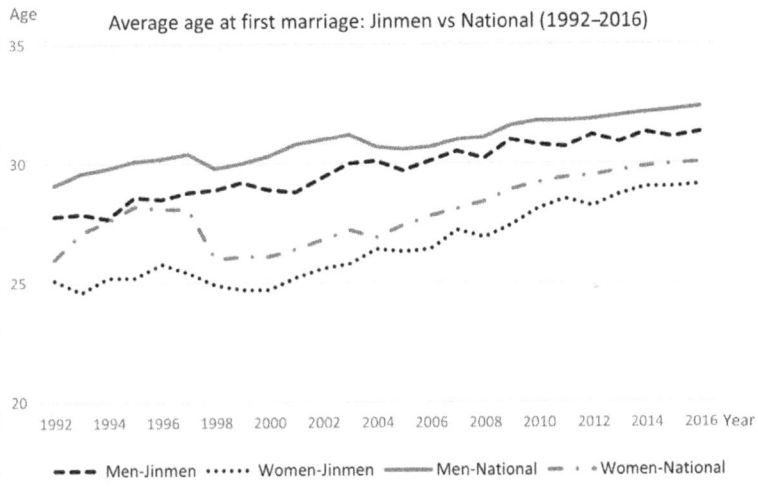

Figure 4.1 Steady rise in the age at first marriage for both sexes. Department of Household Registration, Ministry of the Interior, Taiwan (https://www.ris.gov.tw/app/portal/674).

and their eager expectation of extending the patriline. For them, marriage has significant social and moral value in upholding the cycles of patrilineage reproduction and sociality, and, in turn, a family-based social order. Nevertheless, marriage is not a universal experience for young people above the age of 30 today as it used to be. The official statistics indicate that Jinmen is in line with the national trends towards later and less marriage (see Figures 4.1 and 4.2).

During two periods of fieldwork in 2013–14 and in 2017–18, I heard many older people articulate their worries about the single status of their adult children or younger relatives who work in Jinmen, on the island of Taiwan or elsewhere. I myself, as a woman of marriageable age from Taiwan, frequently encountered queries about my marital status and my interest in marrying in Jinmen from older people – an experience that I seldom had in urban Taiwan. While some elderly female villagers wanted to introduce me to their sons or junior relatives, they expressed concerns about my doctoral degree, which was far beyond the level of education that most local men attained. My experiences suggest that finding a marital partner in Jinmen can be very difficult, but staying single is not easy either. These experiences are shared by my local informants, who were between their late twenties and early forties and still single when I interviewed them in 2017–18.

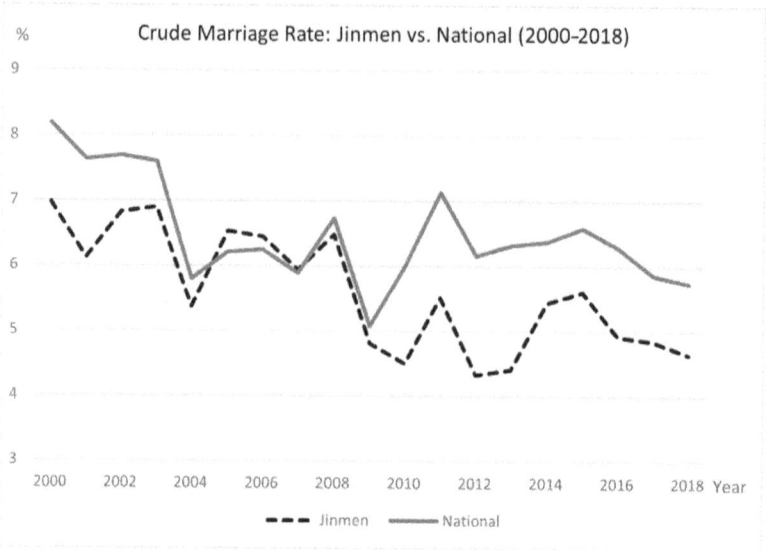

Figure 4.2 Declining marriage rates in Jinmen and throughout Taiwan. Department of Household Registration, Ministry of the Interior, Taiwan (https://www.ris.gov.tw/app/portal/674).

Informed by my interviews and interactions with young single people, supplemented by data derived from other groups of research participants, I suggest that getting married can be seen as a trial for young people in three senses: (1) they are constantly subject to the judgement of others about their social status and marriageability (and they themselves often judge potential marriage partners); (2) they struggle with vexatious people and circumstances pertaining to their private lives; (3) they go through a trial or 'testing process', during which their past experiences, present conditions and imaginings about the future have intertwined with each other and moulded their actions and ideas concerning marriage. I elaborate these three senses in the following sections, demonstrating how the intersections between personal trajectories, wider socio-economic changes and a resilient cultural repertoire make marrying difficult or unattractive for young people in various social positions. The fourth section examines how young single people interact with their families in a social atmosphere that emphasises the traditional values of marriage. With this ethnography detailing how they create their own life while valuing family ties and kinship morality, I argue that individualisation can be about reshaping, rather than undermining, the individual's relations with the family and perceptions about a socially recognised adulthood. Deferring marriage is not straightforwardly an expression of an individual's autonomy and freedom but a mixed outcome of his/her striving for a desired life against social constraints (cf. Lamb 2018 on being single in India).

Judgement about a person's marriageability

Jinmen's agricultural economy was significantly transformed during the period of military rule (1949–92) by the founding of a government-owned sorghum distillery (together with the replacement of the original subsistence crops by sorghum), increasing opportunities for women to earn money outside the home, and the growing reliance on remittances sent back by the islanders working in Taiwan. These new economic opportunities gradually improved local average living standards and the accessibility of higher education for both male and female teenagers (Chiu 2018). Education has served as an important means through which local youths of peasant or working-class backgrounds carved out different career paths and achieved a higher social status. Girls' attainment of schooling and even tertiary education, in particular, reflected a salient change in many parents' attitudes towards daughters: investment in a daughter's education was previously deemed wasteful because she was destined to marry out.

There are only two high schools in Jinmen; teenagers who perform well in their studies usually enter a normal high school preparing students for tertiary education in Taiwan, rather than the career-oriented vocational school. The only new kind of industry developed in Jinmen since the 1990s is tourism and tax-free shopping, targeting particularly tourists from China, together with the expansion of the sorghum distillery and the public facilities of an airport and ferry port. These have provided more job opportunities for local people but have had limited effects on attracting young natives with higher education and professional skills to return home. The first type of trial involves, in Jinmen's post-militarised economic circumstances, young people's experiences of being stratified into a hierarchy of social status according to the combination of their level of education, occupation and economic capacity and, following this hierarchy, how their marriageability is judged by potential partners and society more generally.

A large proportion of young people, who have university degrees or further training and live in Jinmen, work as civil servants or school teachers. These two careers are highly valued in local society not only because of the educational investment involved but also because of their stability and comparatively good salaries and welfare in the context of Taiwan's lingering economic recession. Local men and women who have passed the very competitive examinations to become civil servants or teachers earn a good reputation and gain credit in the marriage market. For example, a village woman told me that her nephew's family gave a large amount of bridewealth (*pinjin*) as requested by the bride's grandmother, who considered her granddaughter, a teacher in a local school, to have a higher social status than the groom, who was employed in a managerial position in a local private company.

Young people working in the sorghum distillery or at manual jobs, such as labourers in construction and logistics, were judged by locals to be in an inferior position on the local marriage market. When I had an unexpected talk with several older men about my research on marriage in 2018, one mentioned how a female schoolteacher in her early forties whom he knew remains single. He said that this woman had not been able to meet a suitable man in Jinmen and, as a teacher, it was not easy for her to accept a man with an inferior career. Another man added, 'It's impossible for a teacher to marry a *gongren* [labourer or workman]!' Based on my understanding that people now compete for a job in the sorghum distillery for its good salaries and generous company welfare, I asked, 'How about an employee in the distillery? Isn't that a well-paid job?' A third man replied that 'An employee in the distillery is still a *gongren*!' These older men did not comment on the female teacher's single status by using any pejorative terms, such as 'leftover women' (*shengnü*), used by the state media and general public in China to ridicule young women who have higher education and professional careers but remain single beyond their late twenties (Hong Fincher 2014; To 2015). They appeared to find it reasonable that a female teacher would not marry a *gongren* because of her occupation in a job with higher social status by local standards. This example also shows that a well-paid job in the distillery alone is not enough to elevate a person's social status and marriageability. Marriageability is evaluated by comparing the status of the potential groom and bride, which echoes a Chinese idiom, *mendang hudui* (marriage between spouses of equal standing), though a woman's hypergamy is very often expected objectively and subjectively (see Gaetaro 2014 and Obendiek 2016 on China; and Lamb 2018 on a similar phenomenon in India).

To a certain extent, the popularity of cross-border marriage between the men of Jinmen and women from other less wealthy countries, especially rural China, around the turn of this century was driven by the lower credit of male *gongren* on the local marriage market. Nevertheless, following rapid economic growth and expansion in south-eastern China in the last decade, the trend of cross-border marriage has significantly declined. When I began my second period of fieldwork in 2017, many locals quickly responded to my research on marriage by claiming that 'Chinese women no longer want to marry in Jinmen because China is so prosperous now!'

Intrusions on personal privacy

In an era of an expanding neoliberal economy and globalisation, young people from Jinmen appear to enjoy higher mobility and broader channels of developing romantic relationships than earlier generations. Several of my male and female acquaintances married citizens of China, whom they met during a tourist visit or during their study or work in China. It is not their lack of marriageability in the local marriage market but their mobility and autonomy that led them into a cross-border marriage. I also know some cases of marriage established through online dating. But for people who avoid using virtual platforms for matchmaking, mobility can be very restricted in day-to-day life. My younger interlocutors who are single and work in different sectors all said that 'Jinmen is too small' (*Jinmen taixiaole*), so they barely get to know new people during their everyday life on the islands. Living in Jinmen, where there is only a small proportion of younger residents of marriageable age, means limited opportunities to meet a suitable partner face to face. A female friend told me, 'When I decided to come back [for a long-term stay in Jinmen when she was approaching 30 years of age], I was indeed a bit anxious about the possibility that I would never be able to get married! I'm not joking!'

Research participants also told me that 'Jinmen is too small' when describing how the local kinship-based social networks have disturbed their daily work and private life – the second sense of trial that I refer to. For example, a friend of mine working in local government said that she would judge the situation in order to decide whether she would admit her identity as a Jinmen native or pretend to be a person from Taiwan. This was because, when she met local people in her workplace, most of them asked about her identity so as to see whether they had any connections with her, and whether they could gain any benefit by using this connection. Another male participant, Wade, described how personal privacy could be violated by the tight-knit social circles:

Wade: A problem that local young people face in developing a romantic relationship is that Jinmen is too small. I heard a very ridiculous remark, that a boy and a girl who went hiking on Mount Taiwu [the highest mountain in Jinmen] by themselves means that they are going to marry [laughed loudly]. Ridiculous!

Hsiao-Chiao: I heard similar remarks from many of my older interlocutors . . .

Wade: But I heard this from a person of my generation!

Hsiao-Chiao: Yeah, gossip [*xianyan xianyu*] . . . If your acquaintances spotted us having a meal here, they might gossip about our relationship.

Wade: That's it. The social relationships in Jinmen are too close-knit. One time, I and my ex-girlfriend strolled in the high street in Taiwan; the next day, in my workplace, I found that gossip about my date was circulating among my colleagues. I thought: 'Didn't I have the date in Taiwan? How come you got to know about it?' Frankly speaking, gossip won't do much harm to a man but this environment is stressful or unfair to women of marriageable age or who long for a romantic relationship. It is impossible for a woman to have a try [*shishikan*] with a man she feels OK with, and then break up with him if things don't go well. If a girl in Jinmen has the attitude of *shishikan* in searching for an ideal partner, she will soon be judged badly in local social circles.

Wade's words reveal that local tight-knit social circles not only make it hard to safeguard personal privacy but also put pressure on the development of intimate relations. Some gossip, like that of Wade's colleagues who talked about his date, is annoying to the person(s) involved but not harmful as long as it is based on what really happened. However, some gossip which is simply made up from partial understandings about a particular event – for example, a man and a woman doing something together by themselves – potentially causes problems for those involved, whose integrity may be unfairly judged by others. Wade's comments about a woman's avoidance of *shishikan* arose because it is almost impossible for her to hide her romantic history from local social circles, and a woman having several relationships before marriage – even if they were serious – may be judged as reckless and a bad marital partner. I myself was also cautious about this kind of moral judgement, so I avoided meeting any young married men alone during fieldwork. When I had an interview in a coffee shop with a man who was about to be married, I asked him if it was OK for him to meet me alone. He quickly grasped what I meant and said that he had already reported to his fiancée about our meeting and obtained her permission to share their stories with me.

Like my own experiences of encountering older villagers' recommendations of local men to me, my informants face these proposals and pressing questions about when they are going to marry in their kin communities and workplaces all the time. In the stories of my three informants in the next section, we will see how they tackled this kind of trial.

Deferring marriage as a testing process

In the preceding two sections I have discussed two kinds of trial faced by young people in their everyday lives, which pressure them to get married but also reinforce the stratification of social status that reduces some people's marital prospects. This section focuses on young single people's personal experiences that have placed them in a 'testing process' – my third sense of trial – of figuring out the meaning and place of marriage in their life. The testimonies of my three informants below illuminate that they were not simply justifying why they remained single past the age of 30 – the new threshold for when young Taiwanese people schedule their marriage plans today (Huang 2013). Instead, they were articulating what marriage means to them regarding their personal circumstances, and they do not foreclose the possibility of getting married in the future.

'Marriage is just a possible outcome of a relationship'

Wade (born in the early 1980s) gave up his plan of finding a job in Taiwan after completing his tertiary education there because he could not leave his divorced mother alone in Jinmen. He secured a contract-based job suited to his profession in local government, and he has been working there for several years. Though he dislikes many things about his workplace, his desire to change his career has been suppressed by his filial and financial duties. To fulfil his mother's dream of having a house of their own, Wade acquired a mortgage which, together with other expenditure, has prevented him from finding different work outside Jinmen. When speaking of the house, Wade asserted, 'I am not like most men in Jinmen. I don't treat buying a house as a definite goal in one's life, nor a marriage.' Rather than excluding marriage from his life, he emphasised that he still wants to have a partner but that 'marriage is just a possible outcome of a relationship'. I responded that many people of his generation have similar thoughts, but Wade countered, 'Not really. Many of my colleagues have made remarks like, "It seems the time to get married," which sounds like "It's lunchtime so let's eat something." This is how marriage is considered in Jinmen.'

Wade's remarks suggest deviation from his male coevals, who appeared to view marriage as a task that a man must complete in his life course, in line with the conventional understanding of marriage as a passage to socially recognised adulthood. Wade has therefore faced pressing questions about his marriage not only from his mother but also from people at his workplace, as shown in our conversation below.

> Wade: My mother tried to pressure me to get married, but as several years passed, she realised it's useless because I simply ignored her interrogation. My relatives also always asked about my marriage during the family reunion in the Chinese New Year holidays but I dismissed their questions.
>
> Hsiao-Chiao: How about your colleagues?
>
> Wade: The same, but they tended to ask about my marriage just as they had a gossip – 'You are not young any more. You should get married as early as possible!' or 'You are one of the only two people in our office who are still unmarried.' They used these words to hurry me into marriage. Some colleagues said they wanted to introduce someone to me but they were seldom serious. If they did find someone interested in meeting me, what we usually do in Jinmen is have a meal together and see if we both feel alright about exchanging our contact details. Even though we made the exchange, most of the time we didn't try to contact each other because we didn't find a reason to do so. What matters is whether or not we can *liaodelai* [have things to talk about with each other].
>
> Hsiao-Chiao: Haven't you met anyone you feel *liaodelai*?
>
> Wade: There was a woman with whom I hung out two or three times following our first meeting. She is a nice person, very good at studying, and we could talk about various things. It's enjoyable to talk with her. But perhaps I was not in the right mindset . . . I was very busy with my work after a date with that woman, and I didn't send her any message for one or two weeks. When I had time, I thought in my mind: 'It's tiring, do I have any reason to ask her out?'

As Wade seemed to run out of words, I changed the direction of my questions by asking him whether he had had any romance. He recalled how his relationship with a woman ended several years ago; this was not because he had lost his passion for the woman (as might have happened in the foregoing case) but because she thought that they 'did not share the same plan for the future'. Wade could not accept this explanation initially and had a very hard time getting over her. Because of this tough experience, Wade said that his mentality became stronger and he could now maintain a positive attitude towards developing a new romance, without trying to erase his memories of his ex-girlfriend and the women with whom a romance was impossible to establish.

Hovering between different prospects of life

Like Wade, Heidy (born in the mid-1980s) initially did not plan to return to Jinmen when studying at a university in Taiwan. But because of her lack of interest in working in the field that she had studied, she decided to become a civil servant, which her parents fully supported. After graduation, Heidy returned to Jinmen to prepare for the civil service examination. As she gradually became impatient and bored with studying for the examination, she found a job in a local university, where she has been working for some years on projects that she found very interesting. In answering my question of whether she still wanted to become a civil servant, Heidy admitted that this was a tough question for her.

> I like my current job very much but, you know, this is a contract job and unstable. We don't have the various welfare benefits that civil servants have and this is a big difference. I am therefore caught in a dilemma at the moment. To be honest, I paid money to participate in the civil service exam every year, but I never attended it. I am in a dilemma: one voice in my head says that I will enjoy a better salary, welfare and stability if I pass the exam; and the other voice says that I may not like what is involved in working as a civil servant. So, I don't really know... Moreover, if I plan to establish a family in the future, if I have children, public employment would be a better option. But for now, I tend to avoid making a decision because I am satisfied with my current job, including its flexibility, content and pay. Given that I am single at present, I am fine with my current state, but considering the long-term future, this job may not be good.

As Heidy's parents expected her to become a civil servant, I asked how they responded to her current conditions and single status. Heidy said that her parents are fine with her work but had started asking about her marriage after she passed the age of 30. 'But they are not like many other parents in Jinmen, who constantly pressure their children to get married', Heidy added. 'They just asked me occasionally.' Heidy also dismissed her relatives' enquiries and suggestions of marital candidates because she preferred finding a partner herself. But as illustrated by our conversation below, she did not make strong links between her ideal partner, marriage and childbirth.

> Heidy: I don't have concrete criteria for an ideal partner. What is important is the people-to-people interaction; what matters is whether we can *chudelai* [have good interaction with each other].
>
> Hsiao-Chiao: How about a man's economic capacity, house ownership, etc.?
>
> Heidy: I think I will see whether a man has a stable job, whether he is a diligent and reliable person. As for the house, if he has none, we can work together to buy one.
>
> Hsiao-Chiao: Do you think that marriage is something you must have in your life?
>
> Heidy: I think I should give birth to a child but marriage is not that necessary [laughs]. Do I sound too radical? [laughs] I don't dare to tell my mother about this!
>
> Hsiao-Chiao: It sounds OK to me.
>
> Heidy: I am saying so at this moment [as I haven't prepared for having a child]. If I really become a mother, from the child's perspective, it may be better to have a complete [*wanzhengde*] family.
>
> Hsiao-Chiao: Why do you want a child?
>
> Heidy: Because kids are so cute!
>
> Hsiao-Chiao: Would you mind adopting a child?
>
> Heidy: I think that is different . . . my thoughts are that only if a girl [*nühaizi*] becomes a mother [*muqin*] will her life become complete [*wanzheng*].
>
> Hsiao-Chiao: How about marriage?

> Heidy: As far as I have observed the people around me, I think that marriage and having a happy life are two different things... Though marriage is an element that constitutes a woman's complete life, it cannot guarantee a happy life. My life will still be complete if I have my own child without a marriage, though I may have some regrets about the absence of a marriage.

Though Heidy said that she might get married to fulfil her desire to give birth to a child, she has not made any plans to do so. Building a family is not something that she can think through for the time being for various reasons: she has not yet met a suitable partner; she is hesitating about changing her career; she has witnessed several unhappy marriages and divorces.

Expecting a partner for mutual care in old age

Unlike Heidy, Tina does not include childbirth in her considerations about marriage. Tina was born in Jinmen in the late 1970s, but grew up in Taipei. When she was about 30 years old, she came to Jinmen to recover her health after breaking up with a man. Her paternal uncle in Jinmen helped her find a short-term job in a government department. Tina originally thought that she would return to Taipei after one or two years of good rest, but her job contract was extended and soon she had been in Jinmen for several years. She bought a house as her own residence, which was also an investment because she can let it out if she decides to leave Jinmen some day. In reply to my question about her thoughts of marriage, Tina noted the difficulties of meeting a marital partner on the island:

> Tina: Frankly speaking, it became difficult for me to find a boyfriend when I came here. Many men around my age were either preparing to get married or were already married with two children. Moreover, everything was new to me here. I didn't have friends but relatives; I barely knew any local people at that time. Also, most of my colleagues are women...
>
> Hsiao-Chiao: Haven't your relatives tried to introduce any men to you?
>
> Tina: They did indeed, but I rejected them. Not because I didn't want to meet new people, but because they always pushed a man at me without trying to know what kind of a person that man is.

Hsiao-Chiao: But as far as I know, local elderly people always judge whether a man is a good match by looking at his education, work, economic capacity, etc.

Tina: Yes, they only looked at those things . . . but they never considered whether or not that man and I could *hedelai* [get along well or feel compatible with each other]. My aunt once phoned me about this kind of thing and I responded angrily [laughs]. I said, 'Never do this again! Don't create this kind of trouble for me! I will find a boyfriend myself!'

Though Tina has not been able to meet a suitable person in Jinmen, she prefers staying on the island because it is hard to find a new job in Taipei and easier to save money in Jinmen. She has used her savings to travel around the world and she developed romantic relationships with some Taiwanese men she met during her trips, though none of these relationships lasted.

Tina: One uncle of mine is a fortune-teller, who told me that all my ex-boyfriends treated me well and loved me; the problem was one Chinese character in my name, which was not good for my relationship to last, however good the relationship was. 'That's alright,' I thought. I decided to buy into my uncle's words and changed my first name. I also thought that I will still be picky [*tiao*] even though I am getting old. Some people said that I should not be picky now because I am getting old. I objected and said, 'Of course I should be picky, because I want to have a partner who will look after me in my old age and I will look after him too!'

Hsiao-Chiao: Do you think that marriage is something that you must have in your life?

Tina: Not really . . . what I think now is it would be good if I can find a man with whom I can get along well [*hedelai*].

Hsiao-Chiao: How about having a child?

Tina: Because I don't like children, I don't consider it at all. But I feel a bit sorry for my dad. [Tina is an only child.]

Hsiao-Chiao: Have you always thought like that?

Tina: This thought emerged in recent years because I found . . . perhaps I have been enjoying the freedom of being single; I can go anywhere whenever I feel like it. Having a child would occupy so much of my time . . . [She described the case of her female cousin.]

Hsiao-Chiao: But if your partner wants a child . . .

Tina: It's almost impossible because of my age. It will be very difficult for me to bear a child. I will therefore let a potential partner know this before going further. I am also fine with a divorced man and even a divorced man who has a child with him. What matters is whether I and that man can *hedelai* or not. It's OK for me to take care of his child . . . I think, in retrospect, my low expectations about marriage and establishing a family are linked to my family background. My parents did not get along well with each other and therefore, since my childhood, I have never had experiences of a harmonious family, such as parents playing happily with their children. Though this did not affect my developing a romantic relationship, sometimes, perhaps my temper and ideas about many things were influenced by my family background . . .

Despite her several unsuccessful romantic relationships, Tina appears to remain positive about finding a lifelong partner for mutual care in old age while excluding childbirth. Her freedom and financial ability to travel around the world have provided her with opportunities to meet a partner, instead of marking her rejection of marriage. She has been undergoing a testing process of identifying what factors (e.g. her previous first name and her parents' unhappy relationship) might have led to her failed romantic relationships, and in the meantime, making her single life enjoyable while waiting for the appearance of a suitable partner.

Individual configurations of marriage and temporality

In reply to my questions, my three informants moved between different temporal stages of their lives, reflecting on how their past experiences, present conditions and imaginings about the future have affected their actions and ideas about marriage. Their testimonies show that marriage for them is not about socially recognised adulthood and filial duty to parents and ancestors, nor simply an expression of love and freedom. In their prolonged deferral of marriage, personal and family trajectories, the kind of life they desire, and their observation of real stories of marriage and family around them, they weave together and constantly reshape their ideas. Temporality is salient in this ongoing process of figuring out the meaning and place of marriage in a person's life. For

Wade, a long recovery from a failed romantic relationship probably influenced his thoughts about marriage as just one possible outcome of a relationship. For Heidy, her current job to some degree prevents her from serious consideration of establishing a marriage and family. For Tina, thoughts of excluding procreation from her future marital life emerged after she reached a certain age and observed the effort involved in child-rearing.

The views of these three informants, as well as my other young interlocutors who have university degrees and experiences of the outside world, are not directly related to the social criteria of education, occupation and economic ability in their accounts of what would constitute a good mate for them. Though their descriptions of those whom they had affection for previously or whom they might find attractive suggest that their ideal partner would tend to have similar levels of cultural and economic capital as them, they emphasised the actual interaction with a potential partner. An ideal partner is a person with whom they feel compatible and have something in common – *liaodelai*, *chudelai* or *hedelai*. My interlocutors' portraits of an ideal partner echo many other scholars' findings across different contemporary Chinese societies, in which a transnational ideal of companionate marriage that is based on a couple's mutual affection and commonalities has been widely espoused by younger generations (Yan 2003; Nakano 2016).

Childbirth is traditionally closely connected to marriage not only through the idea of continuing the family line (*chuanzong jiedai*) but also in concern about care for the elderly. When speaking of their single sons and daughters, many of my older interlocutors were worried less about the breakdown of the family line than about the loneliness and lack of support that their children may face in old age. However, none of my young single respondents made any explicit links between their thoughts about having children and their concerns about support for the elderly. They reject the conventional idea of raising children to provide for one's old age (*yanger fanglao*), and many are considering how to support themselves in old age (for example, by buying a long-term care insurance policy). Among my younger interlocutors, women were more likely to mention childbirth in relation to marriage than their male counterparts because of the shared idea that it is harder for women to become pregnant after the age of 35. The case of Heidy suggests a paradoxical feeling that many other women may also have: while viewing childbirth as essential for fully realising womanhood, she was unsure about whether she wanted to have a child out of wedlock because she cared about her parents' feelings and thought that a complete family was better for a child (a similar paradox is also noted in Papadaki's chapter in this volume). Heidy's concerns were arguably related to the strong social prejudices against single-parent families (and the connection between low marriage rates and low fertility rates as noted at the beginning of this chapter). Given that Heidy currently has no plans for marriage and children, it is possible that she may change her ideas as time passes and as her conditions change.

By seeing young people's prolonged delay in marrying as an ongoing process of reflection and trial, I want to highlight a significant generational difference. Most of my older respondents, whether their marriages were arranged by parents or their own choice, tended to view marriage as an indispensable part of a person's life, and therefore a mingling of individual and social (and conservative) visions of life and the future. This view is also shared by many younger people, like Wade's colleagues, as noted earlier. But the growing trends of later and less marriage in Jinmen (including Jinmen natives residing elsewhere in Taiwan) imply that there are more and more young people, like my three informants, who may have different visions of life and the future that are inconsistent with the mainstream or traditional visions. This is similar to Carsten's discussion in her chapter in this volume of her two informants' life stories: rather than being the engine for self-transformation, marriage was enfolded within a story of moving beyond social and familial backgrounds. In the case of my informants, marriage is not considered as an approach to create the life a person desires, but as an option enfolded into the way a person works out the kind of life they want now and for the future.

Balancing personal desires and familial duties

Studies of family change in Taiwan and across East Asia usually focus on how young adults', especially women's, ability to be economically independent matters to their autonomy in their marital decisions, including the options of postponing marriage and non-marriage (see Chen and Chen 2014; Jones and Gubhaju 2009; Raymo et al. 2015; Yang and Yen 2011). But there has been insufficient attention paid to how young single people interact with their families and intimate social circles while deviating from the normative track of life – which is the focus of this section.

As demonstrated in these stories from my three informants, young single people dismissed or expressed resistance to any enquiries about their marriages and suggestions of marital candidates from their parents and wider social networks. Their responses were arguably related to their ability to be economically self-reliant, but notably, they do not detach themselves from their familial circles. Like most of their single or married cohorts in Jinmen, Wade and Heidy live with their parent(s) in the parental home partly to save money and partly out of filial sentiment. While Tina moved from her grandparents' house (where her uncle's family also resides) to her own house a few years ago, she keeps in touch with her relatives, from whom she had received considerable support in finding a job and settling down in Jinmen. In many other respects, my single interlocutors are also on the track of family-based morality. Wade, especially, suppressed his ambition to pursue a different job in another place out of concern for his divorced mother, who had worked hard to bring up her son by herself. He was also responsible for a mortgage and other regular expenditure of his family, including his mother's insurance. By being emotionally and financially supportive of his mother, Wade proved his maturity and could be assertive in dismissing his mother's and other relatives' questions about marriage.

For several of my unmarried informants who have two or more siblings and live with their parents and their married siblings' families in the parental home, their single status may be in certain respects beneficial to family members. They themselves may also receive emotional and other support from such co-residence. Cherry (in her early thirties), for example, is the youngest of her parents' four children. She now lives with her parents, a married brother and his family in her natal home. Before she returned to Jinmen in 2016, Cherry obtained a Master's degree in the UK and then had a well-paid job in Taipei. Though she preferred city life and liked her job, which she found interesting but also stressful, she decided to leave the job and return to Jinmen because she did not want to sacrifice her health and quality of life for work. Despite the clash between her lack of interest in marriage and social and family expectations for her to marry, Cherry said that she still wants to live in Jinmen, where her 'home' – the place providing her with a sense of belonging – is. She developed close ties with her two co-resident nephews and shared the parenting roles of her brother and sister-in-law by teaching her nephews English and supervising their schoolwork. She also followed her mother's and sister-in-law's advice to manage her money efficiently so as to ensure her financial security in old age. By being economically independent and nurturing emotional ties with her family members, Cherry has made her life in Jinmen enjoyable and her single status acceptable to her parents for the time being.

The story of Cherry resonates with the experiences of single women in Indonesia discussed by Catherine Allerton (2007) in terms of the fact that they are not really 'alone' despite their singlehood, because they stay with their natal families and keep close ties with their married siblings and their children. But as Allerton notes, being alone is a complexly gendered notion and understood differently in different socio-cultural contexts. For the group of people in Indonesia that Allerton studied, women who remain unmarried are never the subject of ridicule within the village and can inherit land from their fathers to sustain themselves financially. In contemporary Jinmen, Taiwan and China, though women are not necessarily excluded from inheritance of family property as they were previously, they tend to attain economic independence through paid employment outside the family. As mentioned earlier, single women with higher education and well-paid jobs are unjustly labelled 'leftover women' in China. Though Cherry and several of my single female informants enjoy their current lives, their parents are still worried about their daughters' potential 'loneliness' in their old age if they remain unmarried.

While I know some middle-aged never-married women who were commended by their families and neighbours for their thoughtful care of elderly parents, none of my younger interlocutors, female or male, mentioned such caring responsibilities as a factor contributing to their deferral of marriage. My older research participants who are pleased to have their single children's company still expect their children to get married in the near future. Though patrilocal co-residence (in which a married man's nuclear family resides with his parents) remains a dominant pattern in Jinmen, I observed that many married women have greater freedom and mobility to visit their natal home and provide care for their birth parents, whether or not the latter have support from married sons. I also heard of several cases of married sons who resigned from their jobs on the island of Taiwan and returned to Jinmen to look after their ill parents. In other words, a person's marital status does not much affect his or her care of parents because elderly support is not only a conventional filial duty but also linked to children's emotional ties with parents strengthened in the long-term processes of *yang* (care and nurturance) from parents (Stafford 2000).

What I have described above appears quite different from what Yan (2003, 2009) observed in post-reform China. As mentioned in this chapter's introduction, Yan found that the increasing emphasis on personal desires and interest among the younger generations has created a crisis of support for the elderly. He argues that young people in both rural and urban China experience a moral and ideological vacuum because the socialist morality that replaced traditional Confucian values in the Maoist era has collapsed along with rapidly expanding marketisation and consumerism. In contrast, in post-1949 Taiwan, the joint efforts to preserve traditional Chinese cultures by the government and ordinary people to some extent reinforced Confucian values. As I have argued elsewhere (Chiu 2017), the persistence of ancestral rituals in domestic contexts and across patrilineal communities in Jinmen has in some respects enhanced the structure and idea of generational hierarchy. Respect for a person's parents and seniors in wider social circles is widely regarded by my younger interlocutors as part of one's moral personhood. But respect does not mean total obedience and the suppression of one's own emotions and desires. Young single people express respect and care for their parents while rejecting unwelcome advice and intervention from parents regarding their life and future, including marriage. Despite worries about their single children's long-term wellbeing, parents try to accommodate their children's non-normative behaviour following numerous failed interventions and efforts at persuasion.

Conclusion

Drawing on material derived from young single people in Jinmen who have grown up in the context of Taiwan's democratisation and the expansion of the neoliberal economy since the late 1980s, this chapter has unravelled a paradox that these young people face: it is difficult both to find a partner and to stay single. Their deferral of marriage is entangled with wider social changes and a resilient cultural repertoire, which have generated different and gendered impacts on their marital prospects. A woman's higher education and reputable career may be emphasised to ask for a higher bridewealth from the groom, but may also reduce her chances to meet men who do not have similar levels of cultural and social capital. Men engaged in manual jobs and factory work are disadvantaged in the local marriage market even though they have a stable and decent income. The upholding of traditional values of marriage and the reproduction of the patrilineal family in this close-knit society also intrude on young people's private lives through incessant questioning about their prospective marriages and suggestions of marital candidates. Though young people tend to refuse these suggestions of marital partners, their restricted mobility in day-to-day experiences prevents them from getting to know new people.

These young single people are aware of the social constraints on their marital options, but they also challenge the conventional understanding of marriage in their ongoing 'testing' processes of figuring out the meaning and place of marriage in their life. In these testing processes, their past experiences, present conditions and imaginings about the future have intertwined with each other and shaped their thoughts about marriage, childbirth and family. Unlike the senior generations and married cohorts who view marriage as an indispensable part of a person's life, these single women and men constantly reconfigure their views in relation to their shifting, individual circumstances and visions of life and the future. As they usually have experiences of living in urban Taiwan from several years of advanced studies and work there, they tend to be more open to new discourses of gender and marriage equality that have sprung up rapidly following Taiwan's democratisation. Many of my young interlocutors (mostly cisgender) in Jinmen supported a set of referenda promoting the legalisation of same-sex marriage and LGBT-inclusive education in primary and junior high schools in 2018, in stark contrast to other opposing opinions within local society. There is potential for these single people to include new options, such as civil partnerships – whose legalisation is currently being promoted by an NGO in Taiwan – in their life plans, though their current imaginings about forms of intimate relations appear to be within the limits allowed by their familial networks.

The stories of my single informants also illustrate their efforts to balance personal desires and familial duties. They safeguard their autonomy in deciding their own lives and marriages not only through their economic independence but also through pursuing family-based morality. They keep harmonious ties with their families and intimate social circles while firmly rejecting any unwelcome intervention in their private lives. Despite worries about their single children's long-term wellbeing, parents have gradually learned to accept their children's visions of life and the future that are inconsistent with the normative visions that they themselves uphold. The growing trends of later and less marriage are thus not merely reflections of wider socio-economic changes but enfold possibilities of reconfiguring intergenerational relationships as well as exploring non-traditional forms of intimate relations.

Acknowledgements

I would like to thank my interlocutors in Jinmen cited here for generously sharing their life stories with me and for offering kind help throughout my fieldwork. This chapter has been benefited greatly from numerous encouraging and inspiring discussions with the AGATM team, from Charles Stafford's acute and thought-provoking comments, and from reviewers' useful feedback.

References

Allerton, Catherine. 2007. 'What does it mean to be alone?'. In *Questions of Anthropology*, edited by Rita Astuti, Jonathan Parry and Charles Stafford, 1–27. Oxford: Berg.

Beck, Ulrich, and Elisabeth Beck-Gernsheim. 2001. *Individualization: Institutionalized individualism and its social and political consequences*. London: Sage.

Chen, Yu-Hua. 2012. 'Trends in low fertility and policy responses in Taiwan', *Japanese Journal of Population* 10 (1): 78–88.

Chen, Yu-Hua, and Hsinmu Chen. 2014. 'Continuity and changes in the timing and formation of first marriage among postwar birth cohorts in Taiwan', *Journal of Family Issues* 35 (12): 1584–1604.

Cherlin, Andrew. 2004. 'The deinstitutionalization of American marriage', *Journal of Marriage and Family* 66: 848–61.

Chiu, Hsiao-Chiao. 2017. 'An Island of the Floating World: Kinship, rituals, and political-economic change in post-Cold War Jinmen'. Unpublished PhD thesis, London School of Economics and Political Science.

Chiu, Hsiao-Chiao. 2018. 'Women's labour, kinship, and economic changes in Jinmen in the era of authoritarian rule', *Journal of Current Chinese Affairs* 47 (2): 193–218.

Davis, Deborah S., and Sara L. Friedman. 2014. 'Deinstitutionalizing marriage and sexuality'. In *Wives, Husbands, and Lovers: Marriage and sexuality in Hong Kong, Taiwan, and urban China*, edited by Deborah S. Davis and Sara L. Friedman, 1–38. Stanford, CA: Stanford University Press.

Gaetano, Arianne. 2014. '"Leftover women": Postponing marriage and renegotiating womanhood in urban China', *Journal of Research in Gender Studies* 4 (2): 124–49.

Hong Fincher, Leta. 2014. *Leftover Women: The resurgence of gender inequality in China*. London and New York: Zed.

Huang, Lang-Wen Wendy. 2013. 'The transition tempo and life course orientation of young adults in Taiwan', *Annals of the American Academy of Political and Social Science* 646: 69–85.

Jones, Gavin W., and Bina Gubhaju. 2009. 'Factors influencing changes in mean age at first marriage and proportions never marrying in the low fertility countries of East and Southeast Asia', *Asian Population Studies* 5 (3): 237–65.

Lamb, Sarah. 2018. 'Being single in India: Gendered identities, class mobilities, and personhoods in flux', *Ethos* 46 (1): 49–69.

Liang, Huiling. 2018. 'Jinmenxian changzhu renkou tuigu zhi tantao [An estimation of the resident population in the county of Jinmen]', *Zhuji Yuekan* [*Accounting and Statistics Monthly*] 756: 38–44.

Nakano, Lynne. 2016. 'Single women and the transition to marriage in Hong Kong, Shanghai and Tokyo', *Asian Journal of Social Science* 44: 363–90.

Obendiek, Helena. 2016. 'Rural family backgrounds, higher education, and marriage negotiations in northwest China', *Modern Asian Studies* 50 (4): 1250–76.

Raymo, James M., Hyunjoon Park, Yu Xie and Wei-jun Jean Yeung. 2015. 'Marriage and family in East Asia: Continuity and change', *Annual Review of Sociology* 41: 471–92.

Stafford, Charles. 2000. 'Chinese patriliny and the cycles of Yang and Laiwang'. In *Cultures of Relatedness: New approaches to the study of kinship*, edited by Janet Carsten, 37–54. Cambridge: Cambridge University Press.

Szonyi, Michael. 2008. *Cold War Island: Quemoy on the front line*. Cambridge: Cambridge University Press.

To, Sandy. 2015. *China's Leftover Women: Late marriage among professional women and its consequences*. London and New York: Routledge.
Yan, Yunxiang. 2003. *Private Life under Socialism: Love, intimacy, and family change in a Chinese village, 1949–1999*. Stanford, CA: Stanford University Press.
Yan, Yunxiang. 2009. *The Individualization of Chinese Society*. Oxford: Berg.
Yang, Wen-Shan, and Pei-Chih Yen. 2011. 'A comparative study of marital dissolution in East Asian societies: Gender attitudes and social expectations towards marriage in Taiwan, Korea and Japan', *Asian Journal of Social Science* 39: 751–75.

5
(Un)certain futures: rhythms and assemblages of transnational Sri Lankan Tamil marriages[1]

Sidharthan Maunaguru

Three decades of war in Sri Lanka ended officially in 2009, but the prolonged violence had resulted in mass refugee migration of individuals and families escaping the conflict (Thiranagama 2011). Against the background of civil war, Sri Lankan Tamils resorted to a number of migration strategies to escape the violence: internal forced migration to safer parts of Sri Lanka; labour migration, usually to the Middle East; asylum seeking, initially in India and later in Europe and North America; marriage to Sri Lankan Tamils based in Europe and North America; and other forms of family reunion. Overall, half of all Sri Lankan Tamils have been displaced and nearly one in four lives outside the country (Sriskandarajah 2002). A large Sri Lankan diaspora has formed in the UK, Canada, the US, Norway and other Scandinavian countries, France, Germany, Switzerland and Australia. At present, the Sri Lankan Tamil diaspora consists mainly of refugees and former refugees bringing families and friends to the adoptive land through chain migration, which is seen as re-creating a 'homeland' in their host lands (Daniel and Thangaraj 1995; Cheran 2001; Maunaguru 2009, 2013). This continuous migration has also operated through marriage and the formation of communities in new homes (Fuglerud 1999). Major Tamil migration and marriage migration to Western countries took place from Jaffna, in the north of Sri Lanka (Maunaguru 2013, 2019, 2020).

Sri Lankan Tamil transnational marriages and war-related marriage migration have to be situated within the larger historical context of war rather than solely in relation to labour and economic factors.[2] During the time of war, before it ended in 2009, most wedding ceremonies within the Tamil diaspora took place in India because most Tamil refugees were not granted citizenship in their 'new home' country and the civil war discouraged them from returning to Sri Lanka even for a marriage. Married migrants then had to apply for a spousal visa to reunite, and to obtain it had to prove the genuineness of their marriage to the visa officer. Transnational marriages not only take place across borders but they need also to satisfy immigration officials' requirements to obtain a spousal visa. In this chapter, I focus on the transnational marriages of Tamils from Sri Lanka and Canada[3] as their marriage process takes place.

Sri Lankan Tamil marriage-related migration arose from the shifting socio-political landscape of Jaffna and of the Tamil diaspora during the war (Maunaguru and Van Hear 2012). The large Tamil diaspora and the links formed through marriage-related migration endure after the war, as a form of life for Jaffna and diaspora Tamils. Mobility within transnational marriages[4] also affects the temporality of the marriage process, for example, in how its duration is stretched out from the moment a marriage is arranged to the moment the married couple reunites in their adoptive country. Within the context of civil war in Sri Lanka, marriage migration became both an avenue through which people escaped from violence and a process bringing dispersed people together, transfiguring relatedness, rebuilding lives across borders and enabling the imagination of futures. This occurs through the ways marriage is associated with the futures of rebuilding life, procreating and living together, as well as the future desires, anxieties, fears and hopes that are attached to marriage. The practices, ceremonies and performances during the marriage process allow for an imagined future, one entangled with both past and present (Maunaguru 2020). The war-related marriage migration of Sri Lanka shifts the lens on transnational marriages from globalisation and labour migration to forced migration, experiences of war, dislocations of relatedness and questions of life and death. However, war-related marriage migration was not devoid of desire for future economic gain, dreams of living in a foreign country and hopes for a better life with the spouse in another country. The certainty and uncertainty of the transnational marriage process – from arranging the marriage to the reunion with the spouse across borders – endure, sometimes for years. I therefore foreground the *certainty and uncertainty* of the marriage process as a crucial element of how communities and relationships are made, unmade or remade through assemblages of things and humans in the time of war and migration by looking at the process of transnational marriage (Maunaguru 2019, 2020). The Tamil transnational marriage process brings out the uncertainty of the process, its temporal rhythms, imagination and anxiety over the future of the marriage.

Exploring Sri Lankan Tamil transnational marriages, I ask the following questions in this chapter. Within the context of a prolonged war and war-related migration, how does a community through the transnational marriage process not only re-create relatedness but also work out uncertain futures? How can we think about the ways in which people within the marriage migration process imagine, live and relive notions of future(s) and learn to live with the uncertainty and certainty of the transnational process? How do humans, spaces and documents (wedding photos, letters and court case files) come together during the marriage process as assemblages to make and unmake relatedness and make it possible to live with the uncertainty of the marriage process? In this chapter, I map out the certainty and uncertainty, aspiration and anxieties of futures that connect different ventures beyond the human. First, an image: the wedding photos that circulate between the bride and groom and their families to other spaces within transnational marriages; these are important evidence to prove that the marriage is genuine and for the Canadian immigration officer to grant a spousal visa. Second, an object and a place: a tree that gets planted during the marriage rituals, not in the adoptive or home country but in a transit place, India, during the transnational wedding process, and the temporary home that houses the guests and family attending the wedding in India. And finally, a figure: the waiting bride. After the wedding, the spouse from Canada has to wait for the partner to join him or her in their adoptive land pending the obtaining of the spousal visa to migrate to Canada. By looking at the assemblages of the image, object, place and human figure in the transnational marriage process, I map out how uncertainty and certainty are lived and imagined as things and humans associate within the migration and marriage process.

Transit places: houses and trees

First, let me turn to the temporary home of the wedding party and to the ritual tree that is part of wedding ceremonies, as they assemble with people in the marriage process. These bring out its certainty and uncertainty and point to different temporal rhythms. As I mentioned above, after the marriage was arranged, most of the Tamil transnational wedding ceremonies between the Sri Lankan Tamil diaspora and Sri Lankan Tamils during the civil war in Sri Lanka took place in India.

In other words, transnational Sri Lankan Tamil wedding ceremonies took place neither in their 'home country' nor in their 'new home country', but in a third place. Tamil Nadu in India functioned not only as a transit place for weddings, but also as a location in which large Sri Lankan Tamil communities live as refugees (Maunaguru 2019, 2020). The Sri Lankan Tamil community is made and remade here during the wedding season. Sri Lankan Tamils who live in Chennai often participate by providing the social texture (for example, food, wedding services and guesthouses), helping to create a 'Sri Lankan Tamil village' atmosphere during weddings. The Sri Lankan spouses who come from the UK, Canada or Europe to marry partners from Sri Lanka seek the services of Sri Lankan agents in India.

A transit or temporary place, in this context, is one where the spouses come to live for a few weeks before and after the wedding ceremony (their relatives, families and friends come there for the wedding and also stay for a few days afterwards). Normally, the bride and groom's family hire spacious guesthouses. Family members and friends of the spouses-to-be come from all parts of the world and stay in the guesthouse with them during the wedding ceremonies. The temporary house becomes festive as people gather, talk about the wedding, recall village stories and share news from their new life. All these conversations mingle the joy of homecoming with the sorrow of not being able to live together in one place, and of the loss of home. In the temporary house, the rhythm of the everyday is established for a short period. Everyone learns to pick up from where they left off when they dispersed or were separated. Daily routines, conversations, memories and life emerge within the space of this house. The parents would cook for their children. A familiar routine emerges for a short period, even though they all know that they will be departing soon and it is not a permanent togetherness. The temporary space turns into a home, and this home is made possible in the marriage process to remake and make relatedness, rebuild life and imagine and live possible futures together (Maunaguru 2020). Past, present and future are all entangled within the temporary home. This is thus not just a temporary home, but fully part of the homes the groom and bride plan eventually to live in. The assemblages (Deleuze 2001; Latour 2005) that take place within this home and between the home and people during the marriage process (re)make relatedness, continue relationships and allow the possibility to imagine a togetherness to carry back to their so-called homes in their respective countries. This creates a certainty in the face of the uncertainty brought by the war, dispersal and migration or even the marriage process. The uncertainty of the marriage is put aside within the temporary home. This allows people to imagine or live the possible futures of togetherness. After the wedding, most of the couples never return to Chennai, as they have no reason to do so. Homes, and the remaking of Sri Lankan community, thus take place even in temporary moments in a transit place (Maunaguru 2020). There is a form of certainty attached to home-making in any marriages. But here among the Sri Lankan transnational marriages it emerges within the assemblages of the temporary home and future homes during the marriage process, and thus makes possible to imagine some certainty within uncertainty.

Further, the temporary permanence of assemblages and possibilities of futures emerges also in ritual objects, such as the ritual tree during the wedding ceremonies in India. During my fieldwork, I had the opportunity to attend the wedding in India of Raja, who had emigrated as a refugee to the UK, to Rani from Sri Lanka. Raja's family had arranged the marriage. Some rituals are conducted before the wedding ceremony: one serves to make the *thali* (necklace with pendant) and another is called the *kannikal* ritual, where a *mulmuruku* (type of tree) is planted in front of the groom's house to announce the approaching date of the wedding to the village. The tree is then usually transplanted in the newlywed couple's garden, where its growth symbolises the couple's life together. In India, Nathan's place is one of the sites where these rituals are conducted. Nathan, a Sri Lankan, lives as a refugee in India where he has maintained his family practice of making *thalis*. I was surprised to hear he also conducted the *kannikal* ritual, given the temporary nature of India as a place for wedding ceremonies and the probable inability of the couple to take the tree back with them. So I asked Nathan what would happen to the trees. In response, he showed me his garden, where ritual trees were planted and, although they were a symbol of the couple's togetherness, were left behind in the transit place.

The tree thus never travels back with the couple or accompanies them on their journey. But by assembling with the couple during the wedding ceremonies, it helps create relatedness. Once the couple leave, the tree is left in the care of someone else. While in usual marriages, the tree's temporality would be closely associated with the couple's temporality, here those temporalities are disconnected. However, when the ritual is conducted, at the moment the tree is planted, it symbolises the couple's bond and the actualised and not-yet actualised future aspirations for the couple's married life (Maunaguru 2020). At the point of the ritual, the tree and people assemble to create certainty over uncertainty in the marriage process. This moment of assemblage, where all involved – priest, tree, goldsmith, the couple and their family – gather, opens up the possibility for multiple temporalities (Deleuze 2001) to come together and produce an entangled past, present and future (Maunaguru 2020). The tree ritual lends a possibility of certainty over the future while, at the same time, leaving behind the trees for someone else to care for brings back the uncertainty of futures. Even in a temporary place and time, by assembling through rituals with humans, the tree allows the families, friends and bride and groom to imagine a life together and a possible certainty of the marriage process. These moments of assemblage are crucial to make the uncertainty into certainty. Sri Lankan Tamil marriages which occurred before the war in the villages or place of origin now take in place in a third space, in temporary moments. Thus, here one could argue that such objects and temporary places bring about more uncertainty and lack of rootedness to the marriage, and family life in the new context. But by showing the story of the tree, I argue that temporary moments, transit places, non-humans and their assemblages are as important as permanent places/spaces and humans in making, remaking and unmaking relatedness and futures in marriage. Thus, marriage is constantly at work between the uncertainty and certainty of futures.

Wedding photographs

After the celebration of a transnational marriage in India, the spouse who needs to migrate to be reunited with his/her partner has to produce a number of documents to obtain a Canadian spousal visa. Wedding photos have become a crucial item of documentary evidence for Canadian state officials when granting visas to wives and husbands seeking reunion with their spouse. Such photographs, submitted as supporting documents for the Canadian immigration process, are assessed by authorities to determine whether the marriage is 'genuine' – specifically, whether the ceremony pictured in the photographs was carried out according to 'Tamil traditions' and shows a certain intimacy between the couple and their relatives participating in and performing the ritual duties (Maunaguru 2014, 2019). The immigration authorities request to see not only the civil marriage documents, but also other documents related to the relationship, along with the wedding photos, to prove that there is an ongoing relationship.

A vital feature of a transnational marriage is thus the necessity of proving to others that the marriage is legitimate. Couples trying to prove to the state that their marriage is genuine are anxious to produce documentation that will be accepted as authentic, and in this process photographs take a special precedence. For the immigration officer, visual documents such as photographs are assumed to prove that the event took place. Specifically, they document who has attended the marriages, what ceremonies have taken place, whether the ceremony pictured in the photographs was carried out according to certain 'Tamil traditions', the intimacy between the couple, etc. I have discussed elsewhere how Tamil traditions were also created and produced by the immigration officers in their scrutiny of wedding ceremonies in search of the genuineness of the marriage in order to grant a visa (Maunaguru 2019). Questions about how immigration officers are trained to look for cultural signs and ceremonies in arranged traditional marriages need further study to elucidate the figure of the immigration officer. At the same time, the Tamil community produces numerous documents and photos to prove the marriage is genuine. This production of documents and their circulation also creates and produces forms of ceremonies and traditions that become the 'norm' to define the 'traditional marriage ceremonies of Tamils'.

The photographs submitted as supporting documents hold the potential to come 'alive' as a witness in the immigration offices where they are reviewed. Such moments of association between the immigration officers and wedding photos re-enact intimacies, traditional ceremonies and relations between the couple and their family during the marriage migration process. The photographs as witness and as proof of genuine marriage hold the power for spouses to be reunited in Canada after the marriage process, and thus allow the spouses to imagine a certain future. At the same time, although certain family members are absent from the wedding ceremony, photos can create virtual families that hold memories of the past and imagine possible futures by capturing the wedding.

When I interviewed Ravi, a wedding photographer, he explained that, in the past, wedding photographers were worried primarily about the quality and outcome of the photos, 'but nowadays, we need to think about the frame, who has to be there, who is going to see it, which rituals have to be captured, and where to place relatives who did not come to the wedding in the wedding photos'. The new transnational wedding photos are captured not just to remember the past event, but also to answer future needs. The future-oriented photos of the marriage process hold the potential of both actualised and yet to be actualised moments (Deleuze 1994, 2001).

Ravi produces a certain kind of intimacy between the couple through the medium of photography, anticipating the visa officer's reading of such moments of romance. By asking the couple to look at the camera when they perform important rituals during their wedding, Ravi provides visual evidence of the faces to the visa officer, indicating that the people who are applying for the visa are the same people 'truly' marrying each other. By facing the camera, the spouses appear to be looking directly at the visa officer through the photographic lens. Through these photos, the photographer, the camera and the subjects come together to create a face-to-face relationship with the visa officer in their faraway office. This telescoping of time and space, by means of photographs, enables the visa officer to witness the event. The photographs come alive, staging a type of intimacy between the couple as they perform certain traditions, while also standing as the witness of the transnational marriage process. Through the future moments of association between photos and humans, the image carries its potential to be ambiguous, authentic, staged, certain and uncertain, and holding all of these together.

The wedding photographs from past decades do not include any written statements next to the photographs or imprinted within the photo frame. Ravi's wedding albums, on the other hand, include brief written statements such as 'Lovely memories, made for each other', 'Congratulations! Dreams never end' and 'With pleasant memories', which explicitly express particular notions of romance, stable marriages and enduring relationships. Printed alongside photos where the spouses are holding each other, hugging or standing in close proximity, the short statements usually share such sentiments as 'Made for each other' and 'Love your wife, live your life', inviting the viewer to read into the photos normative understandings of love and marriage. The viewer's observations are manipulated and drawn to a particular story of the marriage process (Maunaguru 2014, 2019).

The most contemporary wedding albums vividly bring out the performance of the rituals and enable the human eye to see the minute details of the ceremony. The camera eye's ability to capture such details and the photographer's role in enlarging and highlighting them in the wedding album bring a sense of staging and drama to wedding-album production (Abraham 2010; Adrian 2003). In other words, the modern wedding album brings out a more performance-oriented view of the marriage, and presents the rituals in more elaborate and dramatic forms. The modern wedding albums are characterised by certain dramatised and staged elements, as the photographers re-create what they consider to be important traditions of a Tamil marriage, knowing full well that these photos are going to circulate among Tamils as well as non-Tamils.

Even though photographers have the power to immobilise past events through the production of snapshots, a specific future is being projected in the wedding photos I encountered. The photograph should not end with the captured event; rather, it should have the power to come alive and re-create the intended effect (that is, emphasising traditions and intimacy) for the visa officers to convince them that this particular wedding is 'genuine'. This assemblage between the visa officer and the wedding photographs also creates anxiety and doubt (Navaro-Yashin 2007; Hull 2012), which certainly affects this government official's decision-making process. The photographs should show an actual intimacy between the couple, and also that the wedding was witnessed by relatives who accepted the union. Thus, we have seen that the wedding photos require a certain element of performance and staging. However, because a photograph functions not only as a 'witness' to the wedding but also as a medium to capture the presence of witnesses at the wedding, the 'stagey' element is mitigated. This, in turn, enables the visa officer to view the photo as an authentic record of an actual moment in time. The photographs have the potential of both being the witness and capturing the witnesses of the wedding. They hold the past and the future together as a medium of both actualised and yet-to-be-actualised memories and imagination.

The photographs in the visa offices come alive, breaking away from both the frozen time and the past (the assumption is that the event in the picture is over now); they become penetrable evidence. The production of the photographs, the perception of the viewer, the photographer, the eye of the camera and the performance of the subjects lead a photograph to be read in many ways. It has the potential of holding both certainty and uncertainty of its effect. Despite the photographer's intentions, however, the photographs do not always produce their intended effects on visa officers. The temporality surrounding the production of these photos and their circulation within the marriage process (from arranging the marriage to the reunion of spouses across borders) open the possibility that the images can be considered both genuine and not genuine, simultaneously, at every moment of their associations in the immigration office. It is possible that the question for us is not about how the photographs show that '*this thing has been there*' (Barthes 1981, 76, emphasis added), but about why and how this thing was made to be there to be read in the future (Maunaguru 2019). The photographs operate in the realm of potentiality (Deleuze 1994, 2001). The visa officer scrutinises the wedding photos for signs of stability, certainty and community participation to validate marriages within a community dispersed and dislocated due to war. While such stability and certainty are imagined in any marriage, they appear remote in reality for the Tamil community in the time of war and mass migration. However, the space of the photographs (visual space) creates such a possibility to imagine some forms of certainty and stability not only by bringing the family members within such spaces or convincing the visa officer of the genuineness of the marriage but also by efforts to create an 'ideal family'. The uncertainty created by war, displacement and loss is worked out not only in the physical space but also in the visual space and its assemblages with other humans and non-humans in different space.

These wedding photographs also become important documents that help dispersed Tamils to reconnect. The images circulate among the couple's relatives, who live in various far-flung locations. Moreover, through the medium of photography, photographers, priests and the spouses' relatives attempt to (re-)create a sense of a fragmented 'Jaffna Tamil marriage'. While working with Ravi, I learned that attempts were made to paste into the images pictures of relatives who were dead, disappeared or could not attend the wedding. In Tamil culture, the dead are respected but kept at a distance during the wedding ceremony out of consideration for what is auspicious for the couple's future. But in these moments of inclusion, the wedding photos literally become a record of the living relatives as well as the spectral presence of the dead.

These visual documents, where the living and dead relatives become part of one living family, open up conditions of possibility for making the dead relatives part of the important events of a living person's life. In the space and time of the marriage process, such photos are able to create space for the missing, the dead and living members of families to inhabit the same visual space. They make possible the re-creation of kinship and the imagination of futures with the living presence of the past. The wedding photos in this sense not only capture the transfiguration of relatedness between bride and groom during the marriage process, but also reimagine and transfigure the relatedness between dead and living persons. Thus, they open the possibility for the dead, absent and missing to reinhabit a space in a way that would otherwise be impossible. Such visual moments make the photographs 'living' documents, as they turn the dead into living participants in the marriage process. Photos act as a space where the Tamil community learns to live with death and the violent past.

One moment a photo is taken as proof and witness; at another moment it promotes the imagination of romance between the bride and groom; at yet another moment, it re-creates unions between the dead and the living and encourages the envisioning of different futures. In one context, it becomes 'authentic proof' of the event, and in another it fails to prove or stand as an authentic witness for the visa officer. The potential of photos to hold both certainty and uncertainty, actualised and yet-to-be-actualised futures, resides in moments of association. Temporalities of the image, temporalities of photographers, temporalities of the dead and the married couple assemble within the wedding photos and also at different places depending on the circulation of the wedding photos. At times, they create and connect temporalities, trajectories and mobilities but at another time, they also disconnect. For example, despite the evidence, the visa officer could reject the visa based on the absence of visible love between the couple in the photos. Here, the assemblage would result in a form of disconnected temporalities. The futures that wedding photos carry as proof and memory of the living and the dead are entangled with the future imagined by the photographer and couple of their smooth visa application, and with the visa officer's acceptance of their marriage and the couple's future intentionality of reuniting in Canada and becoming future Canadian citizens. They create a possible certainty of the future of the marriage. The certainty of the future created within the photographic space may also become pointless or unmade when the visa officer rejects the visa application based on the photos. The potential of the photos to hold both certainty and uncertainty resides in their moments of association. But they bring surprises, shifts, changes and different futures in their circulation within the marriage process. Every time photographs assemble they create as well as unmake relatedness within such moments. The certainty and uncertainty of marriages are constantly at play within and between these visual assemblages.

Processes, temporalities and assemblages

In the process of Sri Lankan transnational marriage, migrants, refugees, former refugees and non-migrants all come together. Marriage migration as a result of war and mass migration is a process which brought dispersed people together, transfigured relatedness, rebuilt lives across borders and enabled the imagination of futures. Practices, ceremonies and performances during the marriages hold an imagined future, entangled with past and present. As I argue in this chapter, those spaces, figures and documents are crucial in order to transfigure relatedness and constantly make and unmake relationships through their associations, as I have shown in the stories of the tree and the wedding photos. The multiple moments from arranging the marriage to the actual reunion of the couple hold elements of uncertainty and possibilities for the future. Those spaces (where marriages take place or are arranged or the visa is granted to reunite spouses, such as marriage brokers' and immigration offices), figures (such as photographers, priests, immigration officers and marriage brokers) and documents (such as visa application forms, bride and groom files and astrological charts) allow the imagining of futures through familiar practices, known categories and figures, without suspending everyday life, during the time of dispersal by war and migration (Maunaguru 2020).

The Sri Lankan Tamil transnational marriage process has become a site for people to rebuild their lives and imagine a certain future in the time of uncertainty and chaos; this rebuilding and remaking of life takes place within moments of association between figures, documents, state practices, wedding photos and temporary places in different temporalities. The uncertainty and certainty of a marriage are worked out, lived and imagined not only before or after the wedding but also during the prolonged marriage process. As Koreen Reece (this volume) points out for Botswana, relatedness emerges through uncertainty and kinship produces countless uncertainties, which are themselves productive and part of the mechanisms of kinship. Here, I look at transnational marriage, as it takes place, and at the different assemblages (Latour 2005; Deleuze 1994, 2001) between non-humans and humans in different spaces as they allow envisioning different futures and learning to live with uncertainty. The connection between things and humans can be perceived as 'assemblages as a collective' (Latour 2005); that is to say, both humans and materials come together as assemblages to produce sociality.

These figures/documents and places in transnational marriage appear as potential (Deleuze 2001) zones or times that allow the community to enter into the rhythm of life in a time characterised by the uncertainty of war and migration. Here the figures, documents, objects and places of the transnational marriage process can be seen as potential, where different kinds of transfiguration of life and relatedness take place and varieties of desires, futures and anxieties become possible (Maunaguru 2020). The transnational marriage process holds both certainty and uncertainty, but until it is actualised, we cannot know what it will be. Such actualisations also become part of its potential (Deleuze 1991, 1994, 2001; Povinelli 2011), which is endless (Maunaguru 2020). The potential is part of this process, and may be actualised differently at different times. This unknowability attached to the marriage process emerges through lived experiences of the entangled past, present and futures, as we have seen around the planting of the tree and the circulation and production of wedding photos. The marriage process can produce multiple futures, such as a couple reuniting across borders, or a refused visa, endless court battles to reunite with each other, a long period of waiting or a short period of arrival. This variable duration vividly brings out the uncertainty and certainty of relationships and marriages not only witnessed through the human involvement in the marriage migration but also through the non-human assemblages with it (house, ritual tree and wedding photos, from my examples). How humans and objects assemble and their associated temporalities are also explored in Carsten's discussion in this volume of objects and marriage, where objects allow the past to be brought into the present and future in Malaysian middle-class families (see also the introduction to this volume).

Finally, let me turn to Mythili's story to consider how the uncertainty of the marriage process and migration are worked out after the marriage until the bride and groom are reunited in what will be their joint home.

The waiting bride

Mythili came to Canada with her parents as a refugee and became a Canadian citizen. Her marriage was arranged by her parents with Sutha from Sri Lanka, who had been living in India as a Sri Lankan refugee. After the marriage in India, Mythili returned to Canada and her husband started the laborious process of applying for a Canadian spousal visa to reunite with his wife in Canada. The prolonged process of obtaining the visa and the uncertainty associated with the spousal visa process often place the newly married couples in a waiting period. Typically, after the transnational marriage, one partner would be in Sri Lanka and the other would be in Canada or another migration destination. Until the visa is granted, they communicate through emails, Skype and phone, waiting for the visa and trying to prove that the marriage is genuine, that the person seeking a visa is not associated with criminal or terrorist activities and that the husband or wife has the financial means to sponsor his or her spouse.[5] The prolonged waiting period for reuniting with each other places the couples in an uncertain relationship and an uncertain future. When I met Mythili, she had waited for two years after her marriage for her husband to join her in Canada. She said that this process of waiting is a common situation for the Tamil community in Canada. It was an uncertain moment for the couple, and she said it could have gone either way.

During the waiting period, they would speak over Skype or by phone almost every day, but it was difficult, since there was a 12-hour time difference between them. Mythili would be tired after work while Sutha would be fresh in the morning in India to talk to her. Sometimes this created small fights between them because each thought that the other was not interested in hearing their story. Mythili confided: 'Even though we were married officially, we were physically and mentally living in two different systems, routines, rhythms and worlds. So how could we learn to live and hold on to each other?' During her waiting time, she was studying and finishing her degree. She said that waiting for her husband and her studies became part of her daily routine and both became inseparable: Mythili had to finish her studies and find employment so that by the time her husband came to Canada she could support him initially. The prolonged two years of waiting was strongly connected to her other life routines in Canada. The marriage that may promise a future of stability and togetherness is put in question because of the visa regimes and transnational marriage process. The stretched process of the marriage does not necessarily place the couple in limbo or bring out the instability of the marriage; rather, I would say this allows them to learn to live with uncertainty. The uncertainty can be found not only within transnational marriages but within any marriage process. Thus, working with and living with uncertainty in the everyday of the marriage process make and remake or unmake the relatedness, imagining of stability and futures. The promise of future and stability in any marriage is always precarious but bears fruit through a constant work of learning to live with the uncertainty of marriage.

Mythili said that this experience helped her to learn about life. They were having fights, crying, loving each other over the phone and following their daily routine. These routines made this waiting period a part of their daily life, a way of establishing their relationship and bond through Skype and phone. In other words, the waiting time did not necessarily numb the life, freeze the time and place the couple in limbo, but the durability of waiting for a prolonged period also created a routine and mundane everyday activities within the waiting time, a temporal rhythm within the temporality of waiting. This period also led Mythili to learn about life and accumulating everyday experiences. Within this waiting time, the learning and relearning of life, of each other's aspirations, desires, hope and anger, took place across borders. This was not about some temporal slowness or speed but about living in connected and disconnected temporalities as an 'assemblage of futures' (future here is both actualised and yet-to-be-actualised living and imagining). Their rhythms become part of the assemblage of waiting time, bodies, images and new technologies. It meant turning the waiting time into a potential time through assemblages of the different temporalities. Here waiting also became an active and affective way of life (Kwon 2015). The connected temporalities of new technologies were part of the life rhythms of the bride and groom, while their times and rhythms differed given their two different locations, routines and experiences of everydayness.

This potentiality of the waiting time, then, entails a possible future, imagining a life together, creating intimacy but also bringing disappointments, uncertainty and moments of fear and despair. Both the uncertainty and certainty of the marriage migration unfold through connected and disconnected times which showcase the actualised and yet-to-be-actualised futures. It is not only the connections that build up the marriage migration process but also the disconnections of temporalities or rhythms of futures as part of the assemblages in the migration process. Leaning to live with waiting after the wedding but as part of the marriage process (until the spouses reunite in the new home) is how Mythili has learned to live with uncertainty by creating small certainties through daily routines. Learning to live with the uncertainty of the marriage process and turning it into creating futures through laborious work of the everyday (Das 2007) is what remakes and continues relatedness over the precariousness and distance of transnational marriages.

Marriage and uncertainty

In the extensive literature on marriage and kinship relationships in South Asia, the focus has been on marriage as grounded in kinship rules and obligations that reproduce caste, ensuring social reproduction and continuity (Kaur and Palriwala 2014; David 1973; Leach 1961). South Asian kinship studies have focused for a long time on cross-cousin marriage and arranged marriage patterns as a key issue rather than so-called 'love marriage' and scholars have extensively discussed how arranged and cross-cousin marriages reproduce social order, caste hierarchies and enduring relationships (Dumont 1961, 1966; Clark-Decès 2014; De Munck 1996). Thus, those earlier studies created a striking binary between love and arranged marriages in South Asia (see the introduction to this volume; Trawick 1992). These studies kept at bay notions of sexuality, pleasure, homosexuality, widowhood or death (Borneman 1996). Recent studies have focused on modernity, globalisation, urbanisation and social change as they have impacted on marriage in South Asia (Fuller and Narasimhan 2008; Parry 2001; Clark-Decès 2014). Most questions on contemporary marriage and kinship revolve around the transformation of marriage and its response to the 'newness' of the changing world (Kaur and Palriwala 2014; McKinnon and Cannell 2013). Further, the debates about love marriages versus arranged marriages and the tension, conflict, gender roles, pain and loss they create have been situated within the notion of modernity or social change due to modernity in South Asia (Parry 2001; Clark-Decès 2014). But the notions of love and arranged marriage may merit closer attention. In my study, transnational Sri Lankan Tamil marriages were mostly arranged by marriage brokers or relatives or friends. But the marriage process as it unfolds (with prolonged conversations between the couple, including intimate jokes that are established before the wedding) blurs the lines between the strict understanding of arranged and love marriages. I have argued elsewhere that marriage should be seen as a *process* (Carsten 2000) characterised by uncertainty and certainty (Maunaguru 2019, 2020). Looking through the process rather than social change related to marriage tells us something different about the marriage itself.

One could argue that the war and mass migration changed many practices of Sri Lankan Tamil marriage, including leading to a decline of cross-cousin marriage, because of the unavailability of a marriageable cross-cousin due to displacements and/or death caused by war. Further, war and mass migration changed the inheritance of property: marrying a bride or groom from a foreign country and monetary exchange became more important than property inheritance. Inter-caste marriage also became possible in post-war and wartime marriages (Paramsothy 2019). However, even earlier, in pre-war marriage, 'new members could be incorporated into bilateral kinship through marriage, to ensure political and economic gain, in a form of hypergamy' (Tambiah 1973; see Maunaguru 2019, 41). Even though endogamy prevails among Jaffna Tamil marriages, the possibility to incorporate new members (from the caste) into the marriage pool allows some flexibility in marriage arrangements (Banks 1960). Thus, rather than looking at the social changes in marriage and its patterns during and after the war, what I have proposed above through three ethnographic examples – a tree, wedding photos and a waiting bride – is to consider the process of transnational marriage as it takes place. This allows us to think about how the Tamil community live, rebuild and remake relationships across spaces through marriages in a time of violence and war. Further, it not only shines a light on the uncertainty and certainty of Sri Lankan Tamil transnational marriages in a context of violence but also highlights the uncertainty and certainty of marriage in general.

Even though it is not explicitly conceptualised, the idea of uncertainty in marriage has been captured in the work of numerous scholars who have studied transnational marriage migration or cross-border marriages in terms of instability in the marriages, divorce and domestic violence after the marriage (Brettell 2017; Constable 2003; Charsley 2012; Williams 2010) within the context of the South Asian marriage system (Palriwala and Uberoi 2008). In recent studies of modernity, social change and role of the marriage we can see the uncertain nature of marriage practices. Work on 'the right spouse' and preferential marriage in Tamil Nadu has traced a breakdown of the 'Dravidian kinship system' within the social transformation marked by modernity and urbanisation (Clark-Decès 2014, 21). This captures the idea that social changes create uncertainty in preferential marriage, and result in desires and anxieties concerning such a loss. A study of Chhattisgarh demonstrates the need to differentiate primary marriages from secondary marriages (Parry 2001). Secondary marriages appear to be free of some of the rules set for primary marriages. These secondary marriages create a condition of possibility for multiple relationships and movements between partners, along with resultant uncertainty. Only with the development of modern discourse and the emergence of a middle class does the idea of marriage stability enter this community (Parry 2001). Both of these studies – on Tamil Nadu and Chhattisgarh – indirectly point to the notion of uncertainty in relation to marriage. In the former, the uncertainty of marriage institutions and practices is vividly experienced as a result of historical and social changes. In the latter, the idea of uncertainty of relationships and their constant renegotiation in second marriages lessens with the modern development of middle-class ideologies (Maunaguru 2019).

The uncertainty of the marriage process and its aftermath provoke us to rethink what kind of futures can be imagined, desired, practised and feared for as marriages come into being. If marriage transforms two individuals into a couple and forges an alliance between families, then such a process works with certain ideas of imagined futures and current practices to bring some certainty to the uncertainty of marriage. Given the context of war and mass migration, transnational marriage processes have become moments in which another way of reinhabiting the world becomes possible for the Tamil community. In that sense, it is not just a strategy to escape the war, but also an effort to reinhabit the world, to make uncertainty into certainty and to imagine the future for the Tamil community. By focusing on objects, visual documents and temporary places, I shift the lenses on the uncertainty of (transnational) marriages and how they are worked out in the process of marriage with different assemblages at different times. Such a focus on the process, uncertainty and the making of futures associated with marriage indicates especially clearly how communities torn apart by war and migration remake their world through the marriage process, and illuminate marriage in the contemporary world more generally.

Conclusion

By looking at transnational marriages of Sri Lankan Tamils in this chapter, I have brought together four different examples: an image (a wedding photo); an object (a ritual tree); a place (a temporary home in the transit place); and the figure of the waiting bride in Canada. I argue that in the marriage migration process they all have the potential to create futures, remake and make relatedness and hold both uncertainty and certainty on their own or when they assemble. The photographic image holds the potential of the marriage to be seen as genuine when it associates with the visa officer. In other circumstances, the image was able to bring people who could not come for the wedding or relatives who have died or disappeared due to war and incorporate them into the marriage migration process. The image as a zone of potentiality is part of the marriage migration process, and its assemblages hold an entangled past, present and future. The futures held include both those actualised and those not actualised. Through this temporary dimension, their associations (dis)entangled within the marriage process produce both the uncertainty and certainty in which people learn to live with the uncertainty of marriage. The site of the ritual tree in a temporary place brings out a permanency within the marriage migration for the couple's imagined futures. But at the same time it substantiates the loss and disconnection of the tree from humans after the event, thus always bringing back the uncertainty of togetherness that lingers in the making of relatedness. Like the ritual tree, the temporary homes in a transit place such as India become part of the marriage process and are crucial in the making and remaking of relatedness. The objects and spaces and their assemblages with humans also allow remembrance of dead family members and make it possible to reimagine a certainty of the marriage and relationships even in the uncertain process of transnational marriages. The temporary house and the immobility of the trees in transit places are an important part of (re)making relatedness and are entwined with the future, lived and imagined. Finally, the waiting bride shows us the disconnected temporalities and rhythms of everydayness of the bride and groom, and also how such disconnections become part of the connected temporalities of the future that is imagined together and yet to be actualised. The actualised and yet-to-be-actualised temporalities, relatedness, imaginations and lived realities at different points of assemblages in the marriage process are moments where the certainty and uncertainty of the process are learned, lived and relived. These processes of learning, relearning, living, imagining and fearing are where the making and unmaking of relatedness emerge as a work in progress rather than a given.

Multiple futures are entangled in the marriage process and their assemblages, such as the wedding photographer's imagination of the married couple's lived futures, the Canadian state's imagination of its future citizen through the granting of spousal visa, and futures produced through documents and objects. Multiple futures and entangled temporalities are also part of marriage ceremonies and kinship production through uncertainty and unresolvable conflicts in Botswana, as shown by Reece (this volume), or can become a way to think about care, affection and individual expression during marriage counselling in the US as explored by Magee (this volume). These entangled futures display both the certainty and uncertainty of life. A spouse may end up in Canada or not; the marriage could be stretched over a prolonged period of waiting, or even after the long journey it may end in a separation. However, the potential of imagining the future, living with its uncertainty and certainty, constantly shifts and is expressed differently at different moments of the marriage process. This process as a potential zone/space/figure holds multiple futures that could be actualised in any form and will have multiple outcomes. The chapters by Magee, Chiu and Papadaki in this volume discuss the loss of personhood and the structural constraints of marriage as a site that produces innovative change. The innovation, creativity and possibilities of marriage can also be seen, as I have shown, through the interplay of uncertainty and certainty in making a marriage. Thinking through time, certainty and uncertainty, and process tells us a different story of contemporary marriages in general, one that illuminates the active work of making, unmaking and remaking relatedness.

Acknowledgements

I would like to thank all the participants in the workshop 'Marriage in Past, Present and Future Tense: Biography, Intimacy and Transformation', held at the University of Edinburgh, for their valuable comments that helped shape the arguments in the paper. I would especially like to thank Janet Carsten for all the feedback and encouragement that helped me to complete the chapter, Anojaa Karunananthan for all the edits and the two reviewers of the chapter. I thank University of Washington Press for granting the permission to reuse some sections from my book, *Marrying for a Future*, for this chapter. I acknowledge the Wenner-Gren Foundation Dissertation Fieldwork Grant in 2007 and National Science Foundation (USA) Dissertation Grant in 2006 that supported the research used in this article.

Notes

1 This chapter is based on sections of my book, Maunaguru 2019. I have also used an ethnographic example in this chapter from my recent article, Maunaguru 2020. The fieldwork this work is based on took place in 2006–8, before the civil war ended in Sri Lanka. Some forms of transnational marriage arrangements have changed with the end of the war in Sri Lanka in 2009. Further, the examples gathered about spousal marriage migration and Canadian spousal visa requirements are based on practices before 2009. There are a number of new changes regarding the spousal visa requirements and reunion of couples, which I have not addressed in the chapter since my fieldwork was conducted within a particular context and era and concerns the practices within that time.
2 A considerable share of marriage migration emerged for labour and economic reasons (Palriwala and Uberoi 2008; Brettell 2017), mainly due to 'global hypergamy' (Constable 2003).
3 The largest Sri Lankan Tamil refugee and migrant population lives in Canada, mostly originating from Jaffna. Because of these factors, a Jaffna atmosphere has been re-created in Toronto and its suburbs (Maunaguru 2013, 2014, 2019, 2020).
4 Even though mobility has increased in the lives of married couples in the contemporary world, earlier anthropological work on South Asian marriage also documented movements of goods, rights, gifts and people between households (Dumont 1983; Tambiah 1973; Banks 1960; Leach 1961).
5 The policies and rules of Canadian spousal immigration have changed since 2009. I have not looked into the new changes and how they affect or do not affect the transnational married couples' experiences. Since my work took place before 2009, it involves the experiences of married couples related to practices that were current at that time.

References

Abraham, Janaki, 2010, 'Wedding videos in north Kerala: Technologies, ritual, and ideas about love and conjugality', *Visual Anthropology Review* 26 (2): 116–27.

Adrian, Bonnie. 2003. *Framing the Bride: Globalizing beauty and romance in Taiwan's bridal industry*. Berkeley: University of California Press.

Banks, Michael. 1960. 'Caste in Jaffna'. In *Aspects of Caste in South India, Ceylon and North Pakistan*, edited by E.R. Leach, 61–78. Cambridge: Cambridge University Press.

Barthes, Roland. 1981. *Camera Lucida: Reflections on photography*, translated by Richard Howard. New York: Hill and Wang.

Borneman, John. 1996. 'Until death do us part: Marriage/death in anthropological discourse', *American Ethnologist* 23 (2): 215–38.

Brettell, Caroline B. 2017. 'Marriage and migration', *Annual Review of Anthropology* 46 (1): 81–97.
Carsten, Janet. 2000. 'Introduction: Cultures of relatedness'. In *Cultures of Relatedness: New approaches to the study of kinship*, edited by Janet Carsten, 1–36. Cambridge: Cambridge University Press.
Charsley, Katharine (ed.). 2012. *Transnational Marriage: New perspectives from Europe and beyond*. New York: Routledge.
Cheran, R. 2001. *The Six Genres: Memory, history and the Tamil diaspora imagination*. Colombo: Marga Institute.
Clark-Decès, Isabelle. 2014. *The Right Spouse: Preferential marriages in Tamil Nadu*. Stanford, CA: Stanford University Press.
Constable, Nicole (ed.). 2003. *Romance on a Global Stage: Pen pals, virtual ethnography, and 'mail-order' marriages*. Berkeley: University of California Press.
Daniel, Valentine E., and Yuvaraj Thangaraj. 1995. 'Forms, formations, and transformations of the Tamil refugee'. In *Mistrusting Refugees*, edited by E. Valentine Daniel and John Chr. Knudsen, 225–56. Berkeley: University of California Press.
Das, Veena. 2007. *Life and Words: Violence and the descent into the ordinary*. Berkeley: University of California Press.
David, Kenneth. 1973. 'Until marriage do us apart: A cultural account of Jaffna Tamil categories from kinsman', *Man* 8 (4): 521–35.
Deleuze, Gilles. 1991. *Bergsonism*, translated by Hugh Tomlinson and Barbara Habberjam. New York: Zone.
Deleuze, Gilles. 1994 [1968]. *Difference and Repetition*, translated by Paul Patton. New York: Columbia University Press.
Deleuze, Gilles. 2001. *Pure Immanence: Essays on a life*, translated by Anne Boyman. New York: Zone.
De Munck, Victor C. 1996. 'Love and marriage in a Sri Lankan Muslim community: Towards a re-evaluation of Dravidian marriage practices', *American Ethnologist* 23 (4): 698–716.
Dumont, Louis. 1961. 'Marriage in India: The present state of the question I: Marriage alliance in South-East Asia and Ceylon', *Contributions to Indian Sociology* 5: 75–95.
Dumont, Louis. 1966. 'Marriage in India: The present state of the question III: North India in relation to South India', *Contributions to Indian Sociology* 9: 90–114.
Dumont, Louis. 1983. *Affinity as a Value: Marriage alliance in South India, with comparative essays on Australia*. Chicago: University of Chicago Press.
Fuglerud, Øivind. 1999. *Life on the Outside: The Tamil diaspora and long-distance nationalism*. London: Pluto Press.
Fuller, Christopher J., and Haripriya Narasimhan. 2008. 'Companionate marriage in India: The changing marriage system in a middle-class Brahman subcaste', *Journal of the Royal Anthropological Institute* 14 (4): 736–54.
Hull, Matthew S. 2012. 'Documents and bureaucracy', *Annual Review of Anthropology* 41 (1): 251–67.
Kaur, Ravinder, and Rajni Palriwala (eds). 2014. *Marrying in South Asia: Shifting concepts, changing practices in a globalising world*. New Delhi: Orient Blackswan.
Kwon, June Hee. 2015. 'The work of waiting: Love and money in Korean Chinese transnational migration', *Cultural Anthropology* 30 (3): 477–500.
Latour, Bruno. 2005. *Reassembling the Social*. Oxford: Oxford University Press.
Leach, Edmund R. 1961. *Pul Eliya: A village in Ceylon*. Cambridge: Cambridge University Press.
Maunaguru, Sidharthan. 2009. 'Brides as bridges? Tamilness through movements, documents and anticipations'. In *Pathways of Dissent: Tamil nationalism in Sri Lanka*, edited by R. Cheran, 55–80. London: Sage.
Maunaguru, Sidharthan. 2013. 'Transnational Sri Lankan Tamil marriages'. In *Encyclopedia of Sri Lankan Diaspora*, edited by Peter Reeves, 61–2. Singapore: Editions Didier Millet in association with Institute of South Asian Studies, National University of Singapore.
Maunaguru, Sidharthan. 2014. 'Transnational marriages: Documents, wedding photos, photographers and Jaffna Tamil marriages'. In *Marrying in South Asia: Shifting concepts, changing practices in a globalising world*, edited by Ravinder Kaur and Rajni Palriwala. Delhi: Orient Blackswan.
Maunaguru, Sidharthan. 2019. *Marrying for a Future: Transitional Sri Lankan Tamil marriages in the shadow of war*. Seattle: University of Washington Press.
Maunaguru, Sidharthan. 2020. 'Thinking in time: Rethinking migration and diaspora through Sri Lankan Tamil transnational marriages', *American Behavioral Scientist* 64 (10): 1485–96.

Maunaguru, Sidharthan, and Nicholas Van Hear. 2012. 'Transnational marriages in conflict settings: War, dispersal, and Sri Lankan Tamil marriages'. In *Transnational Marriage: New perspectives from Europe and beyond*, edited by Katharine Charsley, 127–41. New York: Routledge.

McKinnon, Susan, and Fenella Cannell (eds). 2013. *Vital Relations: Modernity and the persistent life of kinship*. Santa Fe, NM: SAR Press.

Navaro-Yashin, Yael. 2007. 'Make-believe papers, legal forms and the counterfeit: Affective interactions between documents and people in Britain and Cyprus', *Anthropological Theory* 7 (1): 79–98.

Palriwala, Rajni, and Patricia Uberoi. 2008. 'Exploring the links: Gender issues in marriage and migration'. In *Marriage, Migration and Gender*, edited by Rajni Palriwala and Patricia Uberoi, 23–60. London: Sage.

Paramsothy, Thanges. 2019. 'Inter-caste marriage in conflict settings: War, displacement, and social conditions in cross-caste kinship formations in Jaffna, northern Sri Lanka', *Journal of South Asian Studies* 7: 39–49.

Parry, Jonathan. 2001. 'Ankalu's errant wife: Sex, marriage and industry in contemporary Chhattisgarh', *Modern Asian Studies* 35 (4): 783–820.

Povinelli, Elizabeth A. 2011. *Economies of Abandonment: Social belonging and endurance in late liberalism*. Durham, NC: Duke University Press.

Sriskandarajah, Dhananjayan. 2002. 'The migration–development nexus: Sri Lanka case study', *International Migration* 40 (5): 283–307.

Tambiah, Stanley J. 1973. 'Dowry and bridewealth, and the property rights of women in South Asia'. In *Bridewealth and Dowry*, edited by Jack Goody and Stanley J. Tambiah, 59–160. Cambridge: Cambridge University Press.

Thiranagama, Sharika. 2011. *In My Mother's House: Civil war in Sri Lanka*. Philadelphia: University of Pennsylvania Press.

Trawick, Margaret. 1992. *Notes on Love in a Tamil Family*. Berkeley: University of California Press.

Williams, Lucy. 2010. *Global Marriage: Cross-border marriage migration in global context*. New York: Palgrave Macmillan.

6
Marriage and self-fashioning in Penang, Malaysia: transformations of the intimate and the political

Janet Carsten

Two women, one in her sixties, the other in her thirties; both have married foreigners. One is a scientist, the other a businesswoman. One is a Malay Muslim, the other from a Sri Lankan and Keralan Catholic background. One reflects on a long and successful marriage; the other is in the immediate emotional aftermath of a marriage that has broken down. What could these women have in common? What can we discover about marriage as part of the life course from their stories?

The lives of Anna and Rashidah, the protagonists of this chapter, apparently have little that obviously connects them.[1] They were two women of different generations, backgrounds, ethnicities and religions, working in quite different sectors, whom I connected with in Penang through different pathways, and interviewed more than once in 2018–19. Both women struck me in initial interviews as exceptionally articulate and energetic; they seemed to have carved out unexpected lives largely through their own talents and efforts. Although the interviews concerned marriage, paradoxically, the role of marriage in these biographies was unclear. It was not obvious in either case that it had been as central as one might expect to the achievement of highly successful careers or life stories. What then was the significance of marriage in these trajectories? It is this puzzle that I address here to see if these two scenarios could illuminate how marriage may be a site of intimate, as well as more overtly political, transformation – and how this can be masked under a cloak of apparent conformity.

Marriage, as we emphasise in the introduction to this volume, links personal and intimate lives with the political, partly through its embeddedness in religious and state institutions, and its reliance on these for legitimation. Underlining how personal, intimate lives are framed by wider politics, the state has an all-too-clear interest in asserting its legitimising powers to secure and reproduce normative family forms. Yet the obviousness of the connections between the state and personal trajectories that coalesce around marriage may blind us to the minutiae of how they actually operate. In this chapter, I draw on the life stories of two apparently exceptional women in Penang, Malaysia. Both protagonists have apparently 'made themselves' in sharp distinction to any expectations that could be associated with the circumstances of their upbringing. What can these two marriage-and-life stories tell us about what marriage is and does, or the possibilities it offers for transformation of the self, of intimate worlds and of the wider public sphere – in Malaysia and elsewhere in the contemporary world?

Our two protagonists, Anna and Rashidah, who both live in urban Penang, were born in different eras – one in the early 1950s, the other in the mid-1980s. Anna is from a Keralan and Sri Lankan (Ceylonese) Catholic background; Rashidah is a Malay Muslim. Anna grew up on rubber plantations; Rashidah was born in Kuala Lumpur. By birth, ethnic affiliation and religion they could hardly be more different. And yet something has impelled me to place these two life stories side by side to see whether some wider understandings about the place of marriage in the life trajectories of upwardly mobile women might be gleaned from them. As adolescent girls, they were, in different ways, somewhat marginally situated, and both from relatively poor and uneducated families. And both of course are women, which might, from some points of view, constitute a unifying feature of their marginality.

Gender is a crucial feature of what makes these stories exceptional, and also emblematic of changes that have taken place in Malaysia over the last 40 to 50 years. Far from being straightforwardly unidirectional, one could map two quite different and rather contradictory trends in gender relations over this period. On the one hand, there has been a very marked rise in women's education and participation in the workforce, which is in line with trends in many other developed or developing nations (Jamilah 1994; Lee 2014; tan and Ng 2014). This has been accompanied by the co-opting of ideals of gender equality into public policy and governmental rhetoric – whatever the realities such rhetoric may obscure. Connected to this, the same period has seen a flourishing middle-class feminist movement and civil society activist groups emerge (see Ng, Maznah and tan 2006). On the other hand, and in apparent contradiction to these trends, as Maznah Mohamad (2010, 2013, 2020) has documented, the same period has seen the rise of a more conservative Islam in Malaysia, and its institutionalisation in legal and governmental procedures and policies. These changes have a direct impact on Muslim family law and on gender relations for Malays and other Muslims and, arguably, they also indirectly affect the sizeable non-Muslim, non-Malay population (even though these do not come under the same legal jurisdictions), and Malaysian society more generally.

It seems possible that the tensions between these two sharply distinct trends, with their sources in different roots of Malaysian society, might indirectly connect to the marked prominence of concerns about 'anomalous' or dysfunctional aspects of marriage and family life in public and academic discourse. This possibility is strengthened by the observation that, in Malay kinship, gender was not 'traditionally' a strong basis for hierarchy where (as elsewhere in the region) gender complementarity and a hierarchy based on age and generation were more significant principles of differentiation (Carsten 1997; Wazir 1992). So the push towards a more conservative Islam accompanied by a more hierarchical basis for gender relations might be expected to both produce new tensions *within* Malay kinship, and has ramifications for Malaysian society more generally.

Almost all of those whom I asked to consider intergenerational marital experiences in their own families spontaneously spoke about gender relations between wives and husbands. Probably the most marked and most commented-upon change over two or three generations is the increasing tendency of women to achieve tertiary education before marriage, and after marriage to continue to work outside the home. This reflects wider patterns in Malaysia; it is also perceived as fundamentally altering the dynamics of conjugal relations. Women whose mothers worked, or who themselves work – in contrast to their mothers or grandmothers – are described as more independent, more autonomous, and having more equal relations with their husbands. Although there are some variations, this is undoubtedly broadly the case across all ethnicities and religions.

The interviews about marriage that I have collected from middle-class people of different ages and ethnicities in Penang reflect some of these wider trends and patterns emerging over the last 50 years. Some of these social changes are evident in Anna and Rashidah's stories recounted below. Narrating a marriage – one's own or those of close family members – inevitably occurs in past, present and future tense. Such narratives involve reflecting on how things have changed, and they have an explicit or implicit temporality. They also imply and reveal ethical judgements – choices or stances taken in the past about an imagined future as well as retrospective assessments of actions taken long ago. These might be about small, seemingly 'everyday' matters or about larger issues, and they may be implicit in the way stories are arranged and told rather than made obvious in declamatory statements. Values and judgements, memories and sentimental attachment may be silently embodied, as I show towards the end of this chapter, in the material objects accrued in the course of a marriage. Objects may encapsulate in a quite implicit manner the emotional registers of childhood or marriage; or they may enable a recuperation or readjustment of difficult relations in the past without this being articulated. I want to convey here, following Veena Das (2018a), that the 'everyday' or 'ordinary' is elusive rather than obvious, that it does not reveal itself directly and that it cannot be taken for granted. For most people, kinship as it is lived and imagined is a realm of the everyday that is suffused with ethics. As Das puts it, 'the ethical is much more diffused into one's life lived as a whole, rather than in individual acts that can be separated and judged' (2018a, 547).

Marriage seems particularly rich in opportunities for ethical assessment and reassessment because it involves navigating and sometimes diverging from the past as well as imagining and planning a future. It can appear as a caesura in the life course, when actions with particular consequences are taken or not taken. Retrospectively too, it provides a point of entry for retelling a life, and for reflecting on the repercussions of earlier decisions and actions or their possible alternatives. Inevitably, the ethical judgements that pivot around marriage are also relational ones.

I have suggested that the stories that I focus on in this chapter trace exceptional trajectories rather than more common ones, and this prompts questions about the location of the exceptional. Marriage may encapsulate conformity or innovation – or aspects of both of these. It is not necessarily clear that exceptional lives, however they may reveal themselves, will be expressed in obviously exceptional or innovative marriages. On the contrary, as we suggest in the introduction, marriage might provide a conformist 'mask', or cover, for an unusual life. I take inspiration from another essay by Das (2018b), in which she critiques depictions of new forms of social engagement that privilege separation from previous relations by actors who, as a condition of such new engagements, emerge as autonomous individuals.[2] 'This cutting of relations', Das suggests, 'seems to constitute the condition for achieving agency' (2018b, 55). Rather than taking the everyday and its relations to be simply a realm of repetition and routine, Das seeks to show 'also how it contains possibilities of innovation and of moral striving by contrasting the actual everyday with the eventual everyday' (2018b, 58). What seems important here is how Das seeks 'ethnographically to see the potential of the everyday itself, to produce a different everyday' (Das 2018b, 58). Planning for and reflecting on marriage, I suggest, might instantiate occasions when this potential of the everyday to provide opportunities for innovation emerges especially clearly.

The idea that the emergence of new forms takes place in the flux of everyday life, and without necessarily rupturing previous ties, is highly pertinent to the two stories that I trace in this chapter. The narratives related here show how marriage can be simultaneously radical and conservative, and how the everyday permits a folding of new relations into pre-existing ones. Elsewhere in the South-east Asian region, Resto Cruz (2020, n.d.) has recently discussed the longer-term implications of social mobility for kinship over generations through the lens of cousinship (for urban Malays in an earlier era, see also Nagata 1976). This brings us back to the question of the place of marriage in the projects of self-fashioning that I describe here – a question I return to in the conclusion, together with a further consideration of the exceptionality of these biographies. Constrained by the past, but also offering openings to innovation, marriage here is not simply – as we might expect – a means to social or economic mobility. Rather than seeing marriage as the route to the successful attainment of unusual life projects, we see how it is instead enfolded *within* a larger ethical project of self-transformation.

A further question arises about the wider implications of these personal or familial life trajectories. I suggest here that what we deem to be matters of personal choice or familial matters do not simply *reflect* or echo wider social changes – such as those in gender relations discussed above. Partly through the way that they encompass ethical judgements and practices that are relational in nature, they impinge particularly on families. Actions and precepts that coalesce around marriages, apparently pertaining mainly to intimate personal lives, have a tendency to accumulate and amplify in a range of attitudes and stances taken by members of different generations of a family, and also to travel between families – partly through subsequent marriages. The ethics of gendered lives and relationships are also, simultaneously, contested in the contradictory public discourses and social trajectories mentioned above. Thus we might view the ethics of marriage as a particularly fraught zone of political, familial and personal concern, debate and transformation. Marriage, in life trajectories such as those described in this essay, is both subject to wider transformative processes and, I suggest, itself engenders ethical judgements that are at once intimate and political, and which have the capacity to effect both personal and political transformation.

In the sections that follow, I trace Anna and Rashidah's lives through their accounts of their parents' marriages and their own childhoods to adolescence and leaving their families, to making their careers and marrying, and finally to reflecting back on the marriages they have both made. Their own ethical assessments, as well as those of their relatives, are revealed through their narrations, and also in their accounts of the material stuff, the objects, accrued through the course of their marriages.

Parental marriages; childhood backgrounds; moving away

Anna described a difficult childhood. Her parents had been cousins, and theirs was an arranged marriage. 'It was a typical Kerala wedding – Catholic but it also had a Hindu slant', she said. Her father had come to Malaya as a child in the 1920s from Kerala; her mother's family had come from Ceylon. Her mother was 16 at the time of their marriage; her father was 28. Her mother died when Anna was a small child, and her father then lived together with her mother's older sister in an informal marriage. Her stepmother eventually came to favour her own two children over her sister's. Anna vividly described growing up on several British-owned rubber plantations in the 1950s and 1960s where her father was in charge of the plantation workers, and was also assistant at the plantation clinics. The family moved frequently, depending on where he was working. She described her father as 'very strict' and, as the oldest daughter, she had many domestic duties to perform, including making breakfast for the family at 5.30 before going to school, and cleaning. 'The boys didn't do anything. I used to get angry with them', she said. She also had a sometimes irascible father to placate who tried to keep her away from boys as she was growing up: 'My father said, "Don't stand at the windows." If you did, you were slapped. You were not supposed to look at boys.'

Anna recounted her vivid memory of humiliation as a young child at a Christmas party held in the estate manager's bungalow.

> The boss of the plantations was British. Christians were invited at Christmas. We got presents; there was a Christmas tree . . . We got invited. Dad said, especially, 'Be polite.' I called the lady 'aunty'. She got angry, shouted, 'I'm not your aunty.' After that, I kept quiet.

New pink dresses every year were another kind of ordeal. And in Anna's account of her childhood, one sensed the constraints of domestic labour, and a harshness to the tenor of familial relations. But it was also clear from these depictions that Anna was, from early on, something of a rebel at heart. She described listening to the Beatles, and putting up her hair to make it look short – 'My father gave me a tight [hard] slap.'

Rashidah was brought up in a different era – the 1980s and 1990s. The traces of the colonial past that are viscerally present in Anna's recollections of childhood are more attenuated in Rashidah's. Both her Malay parents came from large rural families with 12 or 13 siblings in each case. 'Their backgrounds were pretty much the same', she said. 'They came from the same village.' Neither was educated beyond primary school. They had an arranged marriage in the mid-1960s that was celebrated in their villages in a way that sounded familiar to me from my research in Langkawi in the early 1980s (Carsten 1997). 'They met for the first time one week before the marriage', she told me. Her mother was 15 and her father 25 when they married. The families were poor and there were no photographs from the wedding, and this too seemed familiar, as I was generally the photographer for the weddings I attended in Langkawi in the early 1980s. After their marriage, Rashidah's parents went to Singapore, and her father was in the British army for 10 years. Subsequently, they moved to Kuala Lumpur, and he worked as a lorry driver for a large state company while her mother made cakes for sale to supplement the low family income. This kind of mixed earning was also familiar to me from earlier rural research. Rashidah didn't describe her early childhood in great detail, but she conveyed that, although poor, it was an affectionate one: 'Theirs is a very harmonious marriage. I've never seen them in an argument.' Her mother was easygoing, she said, and her father had a kind of questioning attitude to life and a curiosity about the world that she thought might have influenced her. 'He was always reading newspapers, listening to news. Maybe I am more curious from him. My mother is more happy-go-lucky, I get that from her.' Rashidah did well at school, and at 13 was selected to be sent to a state boarding school until she was 15 – one typical way in which Malay children of perceived aptitude may find themselves on a path that diverges from that of their families.

Of an earlier generation, and non-Malay, Anna's career path was not forged through education, although one aspect of her paternal inheritance was to prove crucial: fluency in English. Her adolescent years were increasingly tied to servicing her father's domestic needs as he moved from job to job on the rubber estates while the rest of the family became less mobile. Irked by the sense of confinement and increasing drudgery, as well as an obvious need to supplement a meagre family income, at the age of 16, when she finished secondary school, she struck out. Seeing an advertisement in the newspaper for trainee blackjack croupiers in the newly establishing gambling industry, unbeknown to her father, she applied for a job. Once again, her description of how she made the move away from her father's control, beginning with a clandestine visit to Kuala Lumpur for a job interview, telling her stepmother it was for a position as a cashier, and under cover of visiting relatives, was dramatic and memorable. The relatives proved unwelcoming and severe floods considerably exacerbated the difficulties, but Anna was successful. The would-be employers were initially sceptical about her background: 'You're Indian. Are you sure your parents will allow it?' they asked. Somehow she convinced them. A combination of lively intelligence, talent, quickness and good looks might have played its part. After a period of initial hardship and very tough living conditions, gradually her earnings increased from 150 ringgit per month, while training, until after more then 10 years, she was earning 5,000 ringgit. During this time, although her relations with her father were rather distant, she regularly sent money home, and became the mainstay of the family income, renting and furnishing a house for them in Kuala Lumpur.

Rashidah spent less time than Anna in describing her childhood and adolescent years. For reasons that will become clear, she had other aspects of her story that she wanted to convey. By her own account, her parents, although religious, were not extremely strict, and her mother did not adopt a *tudung*, Muslim head covering, until the 1980s, when many Malay women who had not previously done so began to veil as a sign of more observant Islamic practice. In line with this movement, Rashidah described how, during her stay at religious school, she herself had conformed to a strict form of female Muslim dress with her wrists covered but, as an undergraduate in Australia, she had unveiled. At a certain point at boarding school, she became interested in science, and had gone on to a science college for a year from the age of 16 to 17, followed by a preparatory college, in different states of Malaysia. Achieving excellent results in science in her exams, she gained a scholarship to study for a first degree in Australia, and subsequently a PhD in the US.

These narrations enable us to get an initial sense of the geographic and social distance our protagonists began to travel from their families of origin. Neither of them followed pre-scripted paths. A combination of talents, aptitude, determination and hard work, as well as formal education in one case, enabled them to take their initial steps away from scenarios that might have been more predicted by their family backgrounds. Notably, they both initiated their careers without marrying.

In this respect, marriage seems to have been tangential to their self-fashioning.

Marriage and its sequels

After some years, the limitations of Anna's career as a successful croupier became constraining. Although she earned a good income, there was no sense of progression. Her father began insisting that, at the age of 28, it was time for her to marry. Her two younger sisters wanted to marry, and he told her that, as the eldest, she should marry first. In the early 1980s, she was head-hunted to work in a hotel chain in Kuala Lumpur, and from there once again selected to run a travel agency based in a hotel at Penang's popular beach resort. Spending time for her work in the lobby of the hotel, she noticed Michel, a Frenchman who had come to work for a large electrical company in Penang, who also frequented the hotel lobby and bars: 'I thought he looks quite cute.' Eventually, the two were introduced by the hotel chef. 'I thought it would be a casual thing', she said. Anna was at the time renting a suburban house, and her housemates included an Australian working at the nearby Royal Australian Air Force base in Butterworth. When the room was vacated, Michel moved in as housemate. In time, the two became partners. Michel, when I spoke to him, reflecting on this period, spoke of the attractions of Anna's great cooking.

The story of how their marriage came about had elements of romantic comedy. A visit from Anna's father to her rented home in Penang, accompanied by her brother as moral support for his sister, was recounted as farce – with Michel initially keeping to his bedroom. They lived together for a few years. In time, Anna found herself pregnant. Michel, before rushing into anything, announced that he needed to go to France to talk to his parents. On his return, he asked her to marry him. There was a reception at a hotel in Kuala Lumpur, and the matter of Michel's rather lapsed Catholicism to attend to. The local Catholic priest was sympathetic to Michel's initial reluctance to receive instruction, and the couple were duly married in church, Anna being several months pregnant. The couple had two daughters and, for a time, Anna gave up work to attend to the children and home-making. After some years, she established her own successful business, which combines her expertise in tourism, Penang heritage, cooking and an interest in antiques. One of many notable features in Anna's story is the successful and affectionate relationship she has forged with her father-in-law, partly through her aptitude for language learning and her interest in things European.

Rashidah's story also involves marriage to a foreigner, but the mood of this narrative is more sombre. The couple met and lived together while Rashidah was studying for her PhD in the US. Stephen accompanied her back to Malaysia, where she took up an academic post in Penang while he worked as a freelance media consultant. Her family meanwhile remained in Kuala Lumpur. Cohabiting in Malaysia was a different matter from doing so in the US, and illegal for Muslims. In order to continue the relationship, the couple were obliged to marry. Rashidah's mother counselled her to marry swiftly, and the couple duly did so after two weeks back in the country. At the time, she was 28 and Stephen was 30. Under Malaysian law, marriage to a Muslim required Stephen to convert to Islam – although, as she recounted, this did not extend to him changing his name or to following the precepts or observations of Islamic practice in daily life. Rashidah told me that she made all the arrangements for the wedding celebrations herself quite quickly and online: 'It took me two weeks to organise a wedding . . . There was the solemnisation and the meal straight after.' There was some discussion as to what to do about the customary marriage payments from the groom to the bride's parents (*belanja kahwin*). Stephen had been reluctant about this, she reported, 'because it sounds like the family is selling their daughter'. Eventually, as if to underline their ideological distance from the practice, a nominal sum was fixed on: 1234.56 ringgit, which she said she had given to her mother, 'out of my pocket money, not his'. This was much lower than the norm for a woman with her qualifications, and with a number pattern that made it seem somehow less serious. Meanwhile, her husband-to-be transferred a more substantial sum to her account.

Unfortunately, as Rashidah told me quite early on in a first interview, the marriage did not prosper. Already, when they were still in the US, she had discovered through emails on his computer that Stephen had been having an affair. 'There were arguments for and against staying. I gave him a chance. He promised he wouldn't do it any more. I was devastated. I gave him a chance', she said. Back in Malaysia, she was offered the opportunity of a one-year post-doctoral position abroad after their marriage. She suggested that Stephen accompany her, but he objected, citing the cold climate in Europe, and asking what he would do about their dog. Rashidah spent the year abroad on her own while Stephen stayed on in the house that she had bought in Penang. On her return, it became clear that he had engaged in a long-running affair using the house as a base while she was away. Rashidah's account of her discovery and the ensuing events was dramatic. She decided at once to turn him out of the house, and put her scientific training to the service of her anger by gathering forensic evidence of Stephen's adultery for laboratory analysis, and strategising on the best way to obtain a divorce through the Islamic court in Penang, which has jurisdiction on Muslim marriages. As she put it succinctly, 'Don't mess with a smart woman!' The application for a divorce had been speedily granted not long before I met her and, at the time, she was engaged in filing for compensation for the financial support she had given Stephen over the years of their marriage as well as return of property through the same courts. Meanwhile, she pursued her career with seriousness, went regularly to the gym and engaged in a social life that sometimes involved going out with groups of friends.

Although Anna's and Rashidah's marriages have turned out entirely differently, one could discern in both women's trajectories their purposeful and energetic attitudes, and a proactive approach to marriage, careers and the life course. The impetus to marry in both cases seemed to have come at least partly from the immediate circumstances – pregnancy for one, the impossibility of cohabiting for the other. But one could sense too the unspoken assumption of expectations to marry as part of the normative life course and its successful achievement.

The 'stuff' of marriage; registers of retrospection

I have been intrigued by the way that homes, furnishings and objects figured in both Anna's and Rashidah's accounts of their marriages, and could do so in either positive or negative registers. Anna spoke warmly and in some detail about the different houses she had made since she married. It seemed clear that home-making had been a source of pride and pleasure, and had been bound up with her marital status. She described the kitchens and gardens of different houses, and the household furniture acquired. A much-loved house in one neighbourhood eventually had to be left because of the persistent intrusion of snakes from the garden, which might have endangered the children. I interviewed her in the premises of her own small business in the tourist trade in Penang that she had established some 20 years after her marriage. There she had salvaged countless antique objects and old photographs (see Figure 6.1), about which she spoke movingly as somehow reconnecting her to her childhood homes on the plantations (see also Day 2018). This work of recuperation, I sensed, was also part of a process of patching over and reconciliation with the difficult relations of her childhood. Looking around her, towards the end of our interview, she said, 'On the estates, I had to clean. We had water filters, grinders for rice flour, pounders for

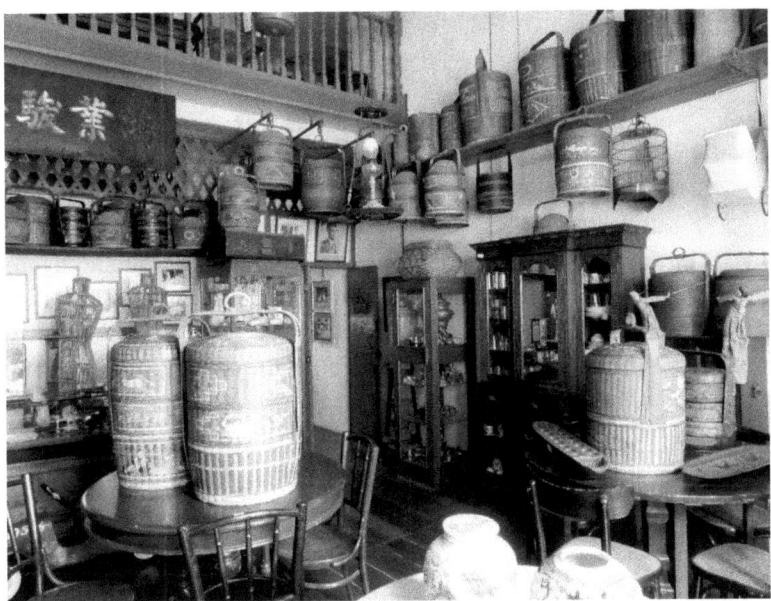

Figure 6.1 Some of the antique objects collected and stored by Anna at her business premises. © Janet Carsten.

coconut chutney. We used to use old gadgets.' Indicating the old railway lights hanging as ornamentation, she said, 'The lights at railway stations, I saw them and bought them.'

At first, it seemed that household objects had not really emerged as a theme in Rashidah's account of her marriage. But on reflection, my initial impression had ignored how the marital home and its property figured as the subject of harsh dispute rather than nostalgia. Although she did not speak of her house as entwined with her marital status in a positive register, it was her money that had paid for the house and furnishings, as Rashidah told me, and she was determined to keep them and to receive compensation for anything removed. Her account of the initial fight in Penang on the occasion when she had discovered Stephen's affair and thrown him out of the house featured furnishings, clothing and other household objects. There were the minutiae of domestic items taken to the forensic labs for analysis in her pursuit of evidence to use in her divorce case. And then there was the Harley-Davidson motorbike for which Rashidah had paid the instalments throughout the marriage. She had demanded the key of this when she 'kicked him out of the house', she said. 'I told him to give me the bike keys and get out. He said "no". I took his clothes and threw them out. He pushed me against the sofa. I called the police and filed a report.' With its resonances of status, value, masculine mobility and freedom, the bike seemed a peculiarly 'sticky' object whose attachment was difficult to sever. The focus of lengthy and complex paperwork in order to establish the case for its return, it cropped up in several of our conversations and updates on the divorce case, and considerably preoccupied her.

It is not accidental that in both Rashidah's and Anna's accounts of their marriage, houses, furnishings and marital property should figure largely. For both women, home-ownership had been directly linked to marriage and to the fulfilment of successful life trajectories in normative terms. The status afforded to women through the constellation of home, family and marriage was expressed even in the face of marital breakdown.[3] But the way that houses and household objects incrementally absorb and accrue positive and negative emotional value here is suggestive. Like other kinds of 'marital objects', such as wedding albums, trousseau items, wedding dresses or jewellery, houses and their furnishings encapsulate the emotional tenor and historicity of the marital relation itself. They have the capacity to embody and convey qualities of these relations over time (Carsten 2019; Trautmann, Mitani and Feeley-Harnik 2011). Such objects may overtly express the success of a marriage and the status of a husband and wife; they may be imbued with memories and become part of an inheritance down the generations. Here Anna's retrospective collection, and her recouping and ordering of a difficult past, suggest a complex temporal disposition that can travel both forwards and backwards in time. This echoes the insertion of images of deceased relatives in wedding photographs described by Maunaguru elsewhere in this volume. But we might take the location of these items – away from Anna's marital home – as equally suggestive. It recalls Rebecca Empson's (2007) discussion of contrastive modes of display and concealment in Mongolian homes of photographic montages of agnatic kin, women's embroideries and the hair clippings and umbilical cords of children secreted in household chests. These different kinds of object signify different kinds of relations and the separations they entail: 'Things kept inside the house become the site or body through which relations are maintained' (Empson 2007, 68).[4] Such objects, which convey attachment, are suffused with the loss of particular relationships.

What is highlighted by the juxtaposition of these two marital scenarios is that, although we may be disposed to emphasise sentimental attachments and the positive valency of objects as they accrue relational value, their negative capacities are equally potent. As in Mary Bouquet's discussion of family photographs, objects can have an 'associative' power that may be constitutive of kinship (Bouquet 2001, 86–7). A marriage undone necessitates fragmentation and dispersal of its property, and marital objects may absorb and convey the negative qualities of the dissolving relationship, but this does not diminish their emotional power. Here Lauren Berlant's rendering of 'the cluster of promises . . . embedded in a person, a thing, an institution' is pertinent (Berlant 2011, 23). The 'condition of maintaining an attachment to a significantly problematic object' is the essence of what Berlant calls 'cruel optimism' (2011, 24). Marital objects instantiate how emotional and ethical qualities may be silently incorporated and accrued in the intimate material world, bridging different temporalities, and transmissible over time and space. Their everydayness, like the everyday of a marital life, is elusive in Das's (2018a) sense, unarticulated, suffused with ethics, and also often fragile and temporary.

Not surprisingly, given the divergences between these two life courses and marriages, as well as the disparate ages and life stages of the protagonists, different aspects and elements emerged in their telling. Anna dwelt on the circumstances of her childhood; Rashidah was quite brief on this theme. Anna took pleasure in recounting the unusual path her career had taken as a young woman, and the early events of her relationship with Michel. Rashidah's account omitted to say much about any early romantic engagement, and concentrated heavily on her anger and sense of betrayal at the discovery of Stephen's infidelity and her ensuing actions. One interesting theme that emerged here was the ease and speed with which the Syariah court had granted Rashidah's application for divorce. This might not have been the case, she thought – and her lawyer had advised – if she had applied only on grounds of adultery, which she said 'is not a strong case in the Syariah court. But lack of support is.' The case was strengthened both by her former husband's lack of observance of Islam and because, far from financially supporting her, as required of husbands under Islamic marriage law, she had supported him.

Anna's two daughters are now in their thirties; both are living and working outside Malaysia. Neither has (yet) married, and it is unclear whether they will do so. 'They gave me an ultimatum', Anna related: 'Don't talk about marriage.' Anna and Michel's marriage seems a harmonious one. Both continue to work hard in their late sixties but, she told me, they always take one day off a week, and in the evening make sure to go to a favourite bar at one of Penang's beach hotels (perhaps reprising the early days of their romance), so that they have regular opportunities to talk with each other. On several occasions, Rashidah mused aloud about her parents' marriage and the mystery of how they had managed to achieve more than 50 years of harmonious cohabitation while, for herself and her siblings (one of whom was twice divorced and one still unmarried), this seemed so unattainable. Unsurprisingly, given her mother's early death, Anna's account of her parents' marriage was quite brief and schematic. She had more to say about how her stepmother (aunt) was treated by her father: They 'were very loving together in the beginning. Later he got irritated. I still remember when my [step]mother cooked curry, he would take it and throw it on her – hot. We would cry.'

Comparative assessments about the marriages in different generations of their families were woven through Rashidah's and Anna's retrospections almost imperceptibly and in the natural flow of their conversations. Inevitably, these carried ethical claims. One could sense that Anna felt her own marriage was a significant improvement on those of her father, while Rashidah strongly conveyed that she viewed her parents' marriage as a notable achievement – in marked contrast to her own. In this sense, although Rashidah may have viewed her own educational and career trajectory as a success story, her marriage had a more ambivalent import. At the time that it was contracted, one could assume it would have participated in, and at least partially expressed, her successful trajectory in normative terms – although this might have been tempered by the fact that she was marrying a foreigner and a non-Muslim. In asserting the positive values embodied in her parents' marriage in the aftermath of her own divorce, one could see a different kind of personal and familial ethical claim being made, against the devalued morals of her husband. But of course this is to take a snapshot at a particular moment. At the point of her wedding, Rashidah would presumably have articulated a different and more rosy view, and what may yet transpire in the future is unknowable.

Conclusion

What can we learn about contemporary marriage in Malaysia from the two stories recounted here? In some respects, they seem to make an unlikely, or non-obvious, pairing. I suggested in the introduction that this was partly due to the differences between the two main protagonists: their ages, the era in which they had gown up, their ethnic and religious backgrounds. We might add to these divergences the relative success or failures of their marriages. What draws the two stories together is that they both feature women who have somehow 'made themselves' in ways that have involved forging careers and marriages that are in sharp contrast to what might have been expected from their familial backgrounds. This might be the most obvious aspect of their exceptionality.

What of the place of marriage itself in these accounts of self-making? In both scenarios, marriage appeared as the sequel rather than the precursor to career-making – the latter already being well under way before either Anna or Rashidah married. In this sense, marriage does not seem to have been the engine for self-transformation in either case, but instead was encompassed *within* and affirmed a story of moving beyond social and familial backgrounds. Here the wider changing opportunities for women, and their movement into the labour force in Malaysia over the last 50 years that I mentioned in the introduction, are significant. We could view these stories simply as accounts of their protagonists' lives, reflecting a particular era and place rather than being 'about' marriage as such. But beyond the fact that both Anna and Rashidah initially responded to requests to be interviewed about marriage, I think this would also miss some more subtle intimations of what marriage is doing in these two scenarios.

Both women's marriages were part of already ongoing trajectories that were apparently removing them from the sphere of their natal families socially and geographically. In both cases, we might see marriage here as a kind of linchpin of conformity and transformation. In both accounts, marriage was required by the immediate circumstances – in one case, pregnancy, in the other, the illegality of cohabitation outside marriage for Muslims. The marriages were thus conformist in the obvious sense that they fulfilled and affirmed normative expectations of the life course in Malaysia. But they also substantiated and amplified the transformative trajectories that were already under way. Anna and Rashidah both married foreigners of different ethnicity from themselves. Notably, Anna's choice of partner did not cross any religious boundary, while Rashidah's required her husband's conversion – though by her own account it was not any difference in religious inclination or observance that undermined the marriage, and she described herself, rather frankly, as without religious leanings.

Marriage to foreigners and across ethnic or religious boundaries can be seen as 'transgressive' to varying degrees in the Malaysian landscape, and certainly it could have the capacity to challenge existing familial relations. But interestingly, both Anna and Rashidah maintained ties with their families. Anna mentioned at various points her brother's crucial supportive role in her tense relationship with her father, and spoke of her own continued remittances to her family. Rashidah was living on her own when I first interviewed her, but to my surprise, when I returned to Penang in 2019 after an absence of a few months, she related how her elderly parents and unmarried sister had moved to Penang from Kuala Lumpur to live with her on a long-term basis. This move did not seem to be predicated on any lifestyle changes on her own part, and it was clearly much welcomed as a gesture of support. Thus, Rashidah's independent marital home-making, after the failure of her marriage, eventually became a means to reabsorb herself in her natal family. Substantiating Das's (2018b) argument, which I referred to in the introduction, the achievement of new forms of social engagement for Anna and Rashidah, in terms of marriage, work and lifestyle, was not premised on the rupture of previous ties – although these may have undergone some temporary disruption.

We could see marriage here as having the capacity both to amplify transformative movement and simultaneously to restrict it. Non-conformist or 'transgressive' marriage may create or instantiate disturbances in lives and relationships – as, for example, described by Perveez Mody (2008) for love marriages in Delhi – but it may also mask these disruptions or allow them, like ripples on the social surface, to become gradually absorbed into familial relations and wider expectations, which may then adjust incrementally. These different destinations are arrived at through serial ethical judgements, which may be explicitly articulated or implicitly incorporated into whether and how, for example, decisions to marry outside normative bounds are accepted, or not, by parents or other relatives. Marriage may accentuate and enlarge, or alternatively reduce, social differences. We might say marriage allows departures from social norms precisely because of, and through, its normativity. Of course, what determines which, if any, relations may break in this process, or how disruptive marriages are likely to be, might partly depend on the direction of travel they allow in terms of social status as well as other factors. Both Anna and Rashidah's life courses have, thus far, been a tale of social and economic upward mobility. The selves being fashioned are socially successful ones. And this might have increased the likelihood of their families maintaining ties with them.

Comparison is one means through which we can observe the minutiae of how marriages are imagined, planned and accepted or rejected by spouses and their relatives. Both the stories that have been recounted here have incorporated comparisons and evaluative judgements within and between generations. Apart from those that I have relayed from the accounts of Rashidah and Anna, there will have been others too, of their relatives and friends. Such comparative work, involving the critical assessment of intimate relations and their viability, is both implicitly and explicitly also ethical work. It exemplifies Das's (2018a, 547) discussion of the way that ethical judgements are diffused through everyday life rather than necessarily being constituted in exceptional acts.

Through the accumulation of such judgements, we can see marriage as encapsulating and enabling elements of both conformity and transformation. It is important to recognise that while some of the evaluations made may be explicit, others may be unarticulated – resonant, for example, in the accumulation and safeguarding of objects that are suffused with the emotional qualities of marriage or other relations in the past. Over time, the gradual acceptance of new forms of marriage may adjust or expand the realms of what can be accepted into the everyday. We could thus expect a wider expansion of horizons in Anna's and Rashidah's families, particularly in the following generation, to ensue from their marriages. The non-marriage of Anna's daughters into their thirties and their residence outside Malaysia suggests just such an enlargement of possibilities. It thus becomes possible to understand how more radical social transformations – such as the gradual and ongoing acceptance of same-sex relations and marriage within kinship and legal regimes in Europe and North America – might have been made possible. A striking feature of the struggle for same-sex marriage, as Judith Butler (2002) and Tom Boellstorff (2007) have commented upon and as noted in our introduction to this volume, is the manner in which it appears as at once radical and conservative. Marriage is from some points of view inherently a conservative and conformist institution. And yet, examined more closely, it also holds within it the promise and possibility of change for individuals, families and wider societies. Rather than assuming that new family forms are necessarily brought about in response to wider politico-economic change or state policy initiatives, what is suggested here is that new forms of marriage and conjugality may become acceptable through an accumulation of the smaller ethical evaluations and adjustments that are part and parcel of everyday life.

The two stories related here, and their perhaps awkward juxtaposition, illuminate how marriage provides a window through which protagonists themselves assess and make sense of their lives both prospectively and retrospectively. It can be a way to tell a life, encompassing childhood, work and economic circumstances. And it can illuminate the turning points of a life – not having an illegitimate child or the discovery of a spouse's infidelity. Ethical judgements are implicitly and explicitly incorporated into how these accounts are rendered. Such judgements are conveyed too by the material objects that embody the marital relation, which provide an everyday register for their unarticulated expression. The way these stories have been recounted has been shaped also by particular anthropological conventions and concerns, adding further layers of interpretive complexity (see Reece in press). As part of intimate familial lives and, simultaneously, a state institution, marriage demands particular attention because it affords a privileged lens into how this connectivity operates, and its implications. The self-fashioning depicted here is personal and familial, but the possibilities and expectations it expresses at the boundaries of what is normative have the capacity over time to travel outwards, and gradually to become part of an expansion and transformation of wider political possibilities.

Acknowledgements

I am deeply grateful to the women portrayed in this chapter and to others in Penang for generously sharing their life stories and experiences of marriage with me. This chapter has benefited from the helpful comments of participants at a workshop on 'Marriage in Past, Present and Future Tense: Biography, Intimacy and Transformation' at the University of Edinburgh in September 2019, the audience at an anthropology seminar at UCL in October 2019, members of the AGATM team, two anonymous reviewers and Jonathan Spencer. Research was carried out with the permission of the Prime Minister's Department of the Malaysian Government.

Notes

1. All names and some details of biographies have been changed for reasons of confidentiality.
2. The essay (Das 2018b) is an extended engagement with Caroline Humphrey's discussion in 'Reasssembling individual subjects' (2018 [2008]), which, for reasons of space, I do not enlarge on here. I thank Resto Cruz (n.d.) for drawing this work to my attention, and for the generativity of his reflections on social mobility and kinship over time and across generations.
3. I am grateful for the suggestions of an anonymous reviewer on this point.
4. Thanks are due to Charles Stewart for making this connection and for emphasising the link to different kinds of relationships.

References

Berlant, Lauren. 2011. *Cruel Optimism*. Durham, NC: Duke University Press.
Boellstorff, Tom. 2007. 'When marriage falls: Queer coincidences in straight time', *GLQ: A Journal of Lesbian and Gay Studies* 13: 227–48.

Bouquet, Mary. 2001. 'Making kinship with an old reproductive technology'. In *Relative Values: Reconfiguring kinship studies*, edited by Sarah Franklin and Susan McKinnon, 85–115. Durham, NC: Duke University Press.
Butler, Judith. 2002. 'Is kinship always already heterosexual?', *Differences* 13 (1): 14–44.
Carsten, Janet. 1997. *The Heat of the Hearth: The process of kinship in a Malay fishing community*. Oxford: Clarendon Press.
Carsten Janet. 2019. 'The stuff of kinship'. In *The Cambridge Handbook for the Anthropology of Kinship*, edited by Sandra Bamford, 133–50. Cambridge: Cambridge University Press.
Cruz, Resto. 2020. 'Siblingship beyond siblings? Cousins and the shadows of social mobility in the central Philippines', *Journal of the Royal Anthropological Institute* (n.s.) 26: 321–42.
Cruz, Resto. n.d. 'How cousin Patrick did not become a seaman: Social mobility and the afterlife of the new'. Unpublished paper delivered at European Association for Southeast Asian Studies (EuroSEAS) Conference, Berlin, September 2019.
Das, Veena. 2018a. 'Ethics, self-knowledge, and life taken as a whole', *HAU: Journal of Ethnographic Theory* 8: 537–49.
Das, Veena. 2018b. 'On singularity and event: Further reflections on the ordinary'. In *Recovering the Human Subject: Freedom, creativity and decision*, edited by James Laidlaw, Barbara Bodenhorn and Martin Holbraad, 53–73. Cambridge: Cambridge University Press.
Day, Sophie. 2018. 'An experiment in story-telling: Reassembling the house in Ladakh', *Social Anthropology* 26 (1): 88–102.
Empson, Rebecca. 2007. 'Enlivened memories: Recalling absence and loss in Mongolia'. In *Ghosts of Memory: Essays on remembrance and relatedness*, edited by Janet Carsten, 58–82. Malden, MA and Oxford: Blackwell.
Humphrey, Caroline. 2018 [2008]. 'Reassembling individual subjects: Events and decisions in troubled times'. In *Recovering the Human Subject: Freedom, creativity and decision*, edited by James Laidlaw, Barbara Bodenhorn and Martin Holbraad, 24–49. Cambridge: Cambridge University Press.
Jamilah Ariffin. 1994. *Women and Development in Malaysia*, revised edition. Kelana Jaya: Pelanduk.
Lee, Molly N.N. 2014. 'Filling in the gaps: The pursuit of gender equality in Malaysia'. In *Routledge Handbook of Contemporary Malaysia*, edited by Meredith L. Weiss, 347–60. London and New York: Routledge.
Maznah Mohamad. 2010. 'The ascendance of bureaucratic Islam and the secularization of the sharia in Malaysia', *Pacific Affairs* 83: 505–24.
Maznah Mohamad. 2013. 'Legal-bureaucratic Islam in Malaysia: Homogenizing and ring-fencing the Muslim subject'. In *Encountering Islam: The politics of religious identities in Southeast Asia*, edited by Hui Yew-Foong, 103–32. Singapore: Institute of Southeast Asian Studies.
Maznah Mohamad. 2020. *The Divine Bureaucracy and Disenchantment of Social Life: A study of bureaucratic Islam in Malaysia*. Singapore: Palgrave Macmillan.
Mody, Perveez. 2008. *The Intimate State: Love marriage and the law in Delhi*. London and New York: Routledge.
Nagata, Judith A. 1976. 'Kinship and social mobility among the Malays', *Man* (n.s.) 11: 400–9.
Ng Cecilia, Maznah Mohamad and tan beng hui. 2006. *Feminism and the Women's Movement in Malaysia: An unsung (r)evolution*. Abingdon and New York: Routledge.
Reece, Koreen M. In press. 'Telling families, telling AIDS: Kinship and narratives of crisis in Botswana', *Ethnos*.
tan beng hui, and Cecilia Ng. 2014. 'Filling the gaps: The pursuit of gender equality in Malaysia' In *Routledge Handbook of Contemporary Malaysia*, edited by Meredith L. Weiss, 347–60. London and New York: Routledge.
Trautmann, Thomas, John Mitani and Gillian Feeley-Harnik. 2011. 'Deep kinship'. In *Deep History: The architecture of past and present*, edited by Andrew Shryock and Daniel Lord Smail, 160–88. Berkeley: University of California Press.
Wazir Jahan Karim. 1992. *Women and Culture: Between Malay adat and Islam*. London: Routledge.

Index

abortion 79, 88
adultery, decriminalisation of 79
adulthood, social recognition of 109
advice 13, 19, 21, 34–6, 38–42, 57, 65–7, 72–4, 112–14; *see also patlo*
affect 4–27, 70–91
affines *see* in-laws
age at first marriage 97
ageing population 95
Aids epidemics 13, 36–7
Allerton, Catherine 64, 113
ambiguous conjugal relations 26
anthropology 6–11, 26–8, 78, 87
   of marriage 8
arranged marriages 9, 12, 27, 120–4, 132–3, 145
autonomy 11, 48, 99, 101, 111, 115

Barnes, Riché J. Daniel 12
Bear, Laura 24
Beck, Ulrich 95
Beck-Gernsheim, Elisabeth 95
Berlant, Lauren 11, 26, 73, 153
betrothal 23–7, 99; *see also* ritual
Black, Dustin Lance 69
Blackwood, Evelyn 8
blood relatives 57
Boellstorff, Tom 25–6, 157
Bogadi 8, 35–8, 48–9; *see also* bridewealth
bonding with spouses 68
Borneman, John 8–9, 69
Botswana 5, 13–18, 21, 27, 34–51, 136
Bouquet, Mary 152–3
Bourdieu, Pierre 10–11
Brazil 7
bridewealth 17, 35–40, 46–8, 100, 112, 114; *see also* Bogadi
Butler, Judith 157

Camino, Daniel 1, 3
Canada 120, 128, 130, 136
Cannell, Fenella 4, 9, 16, 18, 48, 36, 56, 58, 133, 145
capitalism 74
careers 89–90
caring responsibilities 107–10, 113
Carsten, Janet ix, 14, 19, 22–3, 26, 111; author of Chapter 6, co-author of Introduction and co-editor
caste 9, 27, 132–3

certainty and uncertainty
   living with 119–23, 128–36
   and marriage 132–5
changes brought about by marriage 4–5, 13, 37, 76–8, 86
Cherlin, Andrew 95
Chhattisgarh 134
childbirth 110
children, attitudes to 108–9
China 17, 22
Chiu, Hsiao-Chiao ix, 13–17, 26, 136; author of Chapter 4, co-author of Introduction and co-editor
Christian culture 65
Christianisation 37
Christianity 63, 74
civil partnerships 115
civil rights movement 69
civil society 141
civil war 5, 17, 21–2, 128, 118–20; *see also* war
civil weddings and civil marriage 39, 47–8
civil servants and civil service examinations 99, 105–6
Clark-Decès, Isabelle 10
class 9–20, 27, 59, 63, 73, 76–9, 83, 88, 92; *see also* middle class
Cold War 22, 96
colonialism 5, 21
'companionate marriage' 11, 110
comparisons between types of marriage 5–6, 19, 28
compromise 13–17, 20, 77–91
   made by women 83, 91
   in marriage 16
concubinage 37
conformity 27–8, 140
Confucianism 114
conservative views 56
consumerism 114
consumption 3, 11, 17
contraception 70
Costa Rica 26
counselling 13, 15, 19, 24, 5–68, 136
couples therapy 58, 61
cousinship 144; *see also* cross-cousin marriages
Covid-19 pandemic 22
'creative conservatism' 55–6, 73
Crete 83

cross-cousin marriages 132–3
'cruel optimism' 11; *see also* Berlant, Lauren
Cruz, Resto 144
customary law 14, 18, 37–41, 50

Das, Veena 77, 85, 143–4, 153, 156–7
daughters, attitudes to 99
Dravidian kinship system 10, 133
Davis, Deborah S. 95
Davis, Rebecca L. 63
death 91–2
deferral of marriage 20, 95, 98–114
democratisation 114–15
Díaz, Alba 1
disputes, marital 38, 47
divorce 3, 6, 24–5, 37–8, 43–5, 49, 55–6,
    61–2, 66–70, 80–1, 92, 103, 109, 117,
    112, 134, 150–4
  'no-fault' 62
documents 20, 48, 120, 123–4, 127–9, 134,
    136
domaining 4–5, 16, 18
dowry 79

economic independence 111–13
education and educational level 97, 99,
    110–15, 141–2
Edwards, Sharni 2–3
Eisenstadt v. Baird case 70
elderly people
  care and support for 107–10
  respect for 114
emotion 2–5, 16, 18, 22–5, 46, 55, 70–2,
    77–8, 81–2, 88, 91, 112–14, 140, 143,
    152–3, 157
Empson, Rebecca 152
Engels, Friedrich 6
ethics 19–20, 27–8, 36, 41–2, 49–50, 73,
    143–4, 153
  of marriage 143
ethnicity 155
ethnography 8, 15, 27, 79
etic viewpoint 73
European Community, accession to 78

Falwell, Jerry 60
families
  choice of 69
  difference made by 72
  falling apart of 66
  marriage as the absolute condition for
    raising of 78
  relationships within 109–12
family reunification 9, 118, 130
'fantasy' of modern marriage 6
Feeley-Harnik, Gillian 23
feminist movement 66, 141
feminist scholarship 7, 15
fertility rates 95, 111
filial duties 103, 109, 112–15
Friedman, Sara L. 95
funerals 46
future-oriented needs 124, 126

gay rights movement 66
gender 7–21, 26

Genesis, Book of 59, 68
Genius (annotation service) 61
genuineness of marriages, proof of 123–4
globalisation 101
gongren status 100–1
gossip 20, 27, 54, 102, 104; *see also* rumour
Greece 13–17, 20–2, 76–8, 88–90

Halkias, Alexandra 84, 88
Herzfeld, Michael 83
hierarchy 14–20, 48, 99, 114, 142
history of marriage
  in Greece 78–80
  in the US 56, 73
HIV/Aids 5, 13, 36–7, 40, 42
Hong Kong 95
houses 23, 55, 81, 120–1, 150, 152
human rights 3
Hunter, Tera 69

'ideal families' 127
'ideal marriages' 73, 110
imagined futures 119
immigration 23, 55, 81, 120–1, 150, 152
independence of the individual 62
India 9, 18, 22, 121
individualisation 95–6
individualism 16, 59, 65, 70
individuality 64, 68, 73, 80
Indonesia 113
inequality 36
inheritance 45–9, 61, 113, 133, 146, 152
in-laws 39–41, 57, 68; *see also* affines
innovation 1, 3, 7–9, 14, 20–1, 25–7, 37,
    42–51, 136, 143–4
intermarriage 7, 69, 133
intimacy 6, 9–12, 18, 55, 60, 69, 73, 85, 115,
    124–6, 133
  searching for 70
Ireland, Republic of 1–3, 26

Jackson, Michael 85
Jinmen islands 95–6, 99, 101, 105–8,
    114
judgements 5–6, 19–20, 24–7, 142, 144,
    156–7

Karakatsanis, Leonidas 87
Kenny, Enda 2
Kerr, Christine 58
Khama, Seretse 21–2
kinship 4–10, 18, 23, 16–28, 36, 50, 55–60,
    67, 70, 76–9, 82, 85–7, 91, 98, 127, 129,
    132–6, 143, 153–4, 157
  innovative approaches to 7–8
  and marriage 132
  queer 25, 56, 79
  re-creation of 127
  social networks based on 101
  South Asian studies of 132
  see also relatedness
Kuomintang, the (KMT) 96

Ladd-Taylor, Molly 62–3
Lambek, Michael 18, 42
Lasch, Christopher 4

law 2, 6–9, 13–14, 18–21, 34–51, 57, 62–3, 70, 75, 82, 112, 142, 148–9, 153
 of marriage 37; *see also* customary law; Tswana people and their law
'leftover women' 100, 113
Lepore, Jill 59
'letting go' emotionally 71–2
Lévi-Strauss, Claude 7
LGBT groups 115
lived experience 8–9, 90
Livingston, Julie 43
loneliness 59, 64, 71, 73
Love Equality campaign 2
love marriages 9, 18, 133
Loving v. Virginia case (1967) 60, 69
Lynch, John 60
Lynchburg 54–63, 66–70

McKinnon, Suan 4, 7, 9, 16–19, 36, 133
Magee, Siobhan ix, 13–16, 19, 24, 26, 136; author of Chapter 2, co-author of Introduction and co-editor
Maine, Henry 6
Malaysia 5, 14, 22, 27, 130, 141–2, 154–5
male dominance 83
Maoist era 114
marital partners, difficulty in finding 97, 107–14
marketisation 114
marriage
 arranged 9, 12, 27, 120–4, 132–3, 145
 breakdown 3, 37–8, 49, 56, 80, 109
 by choice 9–10, 18, 133
 counselling 55–68, 136
 delayed 20, 95, 114
 innovation in 1–4, 12, 157
 planning 1–2, 5, 22, 24, 28, 74,7, 95, 111, 143–4, 157
 rates of 95, 111
 reform 1–4, 12, 95, 111, 157
 same-sex 1–2, 4–5, 9, 15, 19, 21, 56, 66, 115, 157
 transnational 9–10, 14, 118–25, 130–5
marriage market 100–1
marriage rates 3, 37, 98
'marriageability' 10, 99–102
marriages of convenience 9
mass weddings 47–9
materiality 5
Matthew's Gospel 58–9
Maunaguru, Sidharthan ix, 14, 18, 22–4, 27; author of Chapter 5 and co-editor
memory 23, 68, 128, 145
middle class 5, 11–12, 15, 17, 20, 63, 76–83, 88, 91, 134, 141
migrants 17, 119, 128; *see also* immigration
 marriage-related 118–19, 128, 130, 135
Mill, John Stuart 6
Mitani, John C. 23
Mmapula 35–6, 39–40, 49
mobile phones 34
mobility 101, 113
modern marriage 6, 9
modernity 4, 6, 9, 18, 20, 24, 27, 76, 132–4
Mody, Perveez 8–9, 18, 156
Mohamad, Maznah 141
Molao 14, 36, 40–50; *see also* law

money management 112
monuments 22
moral judgements 102
Moral Majority (organisation) 60
moral panic 62
morality 98, 112–15
Morgan, Lewis H. 6
Morwaakgole, Annah 45–6
motherhood 84, 86

Nambikwara people 7
nation 2–3, 8–11, 14, 18, 22, 25, 48, 63, 85–6, 95–7
naturalisation and denaturalisation 8
negotiation of conflict 50
neoliberalism 101, 114
'new kinship studies' 7–8
New York Times 61
non-governmental organisations (NGOs) 39, 45–9
normativity 8, 25, 156
Northern Ireland 2, 18, 26

Obama, Robin Roberts 62
Obama, Barack 62
Obama, Michelle 62
objects 2, 24, 122–3, 129–30, 134–6, 143, 145, 150–2, 157
online dating 101
'ordinary ethics' 19–20, 27–8, 36, 41
Osella, Caroline 87–8

Paltrow, Gwyneth 61
Papadaki, Eirini ix, 13–16, 21–6, 136; author of Chapter 3, co-author of Introduction and co-editor
Papadogiannis, Nikos 87
Papandreou, Andreas 87
Papanikolaou, Dimitrris 79
Papataxiarchis, Evthymios 78–9
parents 3, 5, 8, 12, 15, 20, 28, 30, 45, 54, 57, 67–9, 79–81, 84–8, 96, 99, 105–6, 109–15, 121, 130, 143–9, 154, 156
 accepting and accommodating to their children's behaviour 114–15
 adult children living with 112–13
 exerting pressure on children to marry 106
PASOK (party) 79, 87
patlo 14, 35 38–50; *see also* advice
patriarchy 15, 20, 43, 82–3
patrilineal values 96–7, 114
Paxson, Heather 78–9, 84
Pearson, Peter 61
Peoples, Robyn 2
performance and staging, elements of 126
personal desires and interests 113–14
PFLAG (Parents and Friends of Lesbians and Gays) 69
photographs 10, 18, 22–4, 56, 59, 123–9, 135–6, 146, 150, 152 *see also* wedding photographs
'political' aspects of marriage 2–13, 16–19, 25–6, 36–9, 43–50, 54, 58, 61–2, 70, 73, 78, 80, 87, 91, 95–6, 119, 133, 140–1, 144, 157–8

polygamy 37
Popence, Paul 62–3
positive eugenics 62–3
privacy 101–2, 115
public interest in marriage 3–4

queer marriages 56
queer time 25

race 56, 59–60, 69, 73
racism 65
Reagan, Ronald 60, 62
Re a Nyalana 45–9
Reece, Koreen M. x, 13–19, 24, 136; *author of Chapter 1, co-author of Introduction and co-editor*
refugees 118
Reilly, James 2
relatedness 20, 57, 96, 119–23, 127–32, 135–6
relations by marriage 57, 98
religion 9, 12, 18, 56, 140, 142
Republican Party 60
Rhodes 83
risk involved in marriage 80
ritual 2, 4, 8, 10, 18, 23–8, 38–9, 54, 8, 96, 114, 120, 122–5, 130, 135
rumour 27, 40; *see also* gossip
Rutherford, Danilyn 24

Sahlins, Marshall 77–8
same-sex relations 1–6, 9, 15, 19–21, 25–7, 56, 66, 115, 117
  referendum on (2015) 6, 26
Schneider, David 57
school teachers, status of 99
secrecy 40–1, 44
self-confidence 62
self-fashioning 11–14, 158
self-government 49
self-help literature 61–2
self-making 36, 41–5, 49
self-reliance 112
sex 40, 61, 71–2, 81
sexuality 8, 56, 72–3, 88, 132
single-parent families 111
single people 112, 115
social mobility and social engagement 17, 143–4
social status 103
socialism 96, 114
solo living 3
songs 87–8
sons, preference for 79
'soulmate' concept 65
Spain 1, 22
Sri Lanka 14, 18, 22, 118–37
Stalin, Joseph 24
standards 48–9
states 4–10, 16–18, 21, 25–7, 39, 45, 56–60, 64, 96, 123–5, 141, 157–8
  control and regulation of family matters by 4–5, 21, 141
  divergences and congruences between 5
  as drivers of change 27
  policies of and views on marriage 9–10
  political enterprise of 9

staying put in a marriage 82, 84, 90–1
stoicism 84
Storin-Chaikov, Nikolai 24

Taiwan 15–19, 26–7, 95, 100, 114–15
Tamil communities 118, 121, 134
Tamil diaspora 118–19
Tamil Nadu 10, 121, 134
temporality *see* time
temporary homes 135–6
Theodossopulos, Dimitrios 87
Thomas, Katherine Woodward 61
time 4–10, 16–18, 29, 43, 109, 119, 122, 126, 131, 142 *see* temporality
  time travel 24–5
Time magazine 62
togetherness 70, 73, 121–2, 135
traditional culture 12, 20, 114, 124-5
transformation 50, 77, 144, 157
  by marriage 4–6, 13–14, 21, 26–8
  of marriage 133
  of oneself 80, 82
transnational marriage 9–10, 14, 118–19, 123
  Tamil 119–25, 130–5
Trautmann, Thomas B. 23
tree-planting 23, 120–3, 129–30, 135
Tswana people and their law 14, 37–8, 47, 49

United States 15–16, 19–22, 26, 136
urbanisation 78–9

violence, domestic 45–6
visas 120, 123
visualisation of relationships 68

waiting periods for family reunification 130–2, 136
war 3, 9, 14, 18–19, 22, 35, 95, 118–23, 127–9, 133–5; *see also* Civil War
wedding albums 125
wedding photographs 123–8, 135
  images of the dead pasted into 127–8, 135
weddings 2–3, 10–11, 17–18, 22–3, 27, 36-9, 42–50, 58
  as distinct from marriages 58
  iconography of 23
  material culture of 10
  planning of 1–2, 22
welfare benefits 105
Werbner, Richard 41, 43
Williams, Ruth 21
women
  ambivalent feelings about marriage 80
  balancing feelings at the beginning of a relationship with those later on 88
  problems faced by 102
  role and status of 10–11, 16, 78, 83–4, 141
women's rights 6
work 5–15, 18, 23–8, 36, 41, 50, 54–63, 66–91, 97–108, 111–16, 120–3, 127–36, 140–2, 145, 153, 156
  of marriage 6–13, 55, 84–8
working-class people 63

Yan, Yunxian 96, 113
youthfulness 71

Lightning Source UK Ltd.
Milton Keynes UK
UKHW022215150821
388856UK00002B/8